THE AIR FORCE IN SOUTHEAST ASIA

TACTICS AND TECHNIQUES OF NIGHT OPERATIONS

1961-1970

by

Major Victor B. Anthony, USAF

OFFICE OF AIR FORCE HISTORY

March 1973

Published by Books Express Publishing
Copyright © Books Express, 2011
ISBN 978-1-78039-657-6

Books Express publications are available from all good retail and online booksellers. For publishing proposals and direct ordering please contact us at: info@books-express.com

FOREWORD

This historical report is the fifteenth of a series of studies dealing with Air Force plans and operations in Southeast Asia prepared by the Office of Air Force History. The author, a Master Navigator, was formerly a member of the Air Force Academy history faculty. He also served a tour of duty in the Directorate of Operations, Headquarters, 7/13 Air Force, at Udorn, Thailand, and is well qualified to tell the story of nearly a decade of Air Force night operations in Southeast Asia. During the course of his research, he interviewed over a dozen pilots and crewmen who flew night missions along the Ho Chi Minh Trail and in North Vietnam. They provided him invaluable information on the problems of operating at night and the tactics they devised against an elusive enemy in a hostile, jungle environment.

In his history, the author recalls the pioneering efforts of the Farm Gate detachment and the start of night flare operations. He describes the equipment available at the time, modifications that were subsequently made to improve effectiveness, and the successes and failures that were experienced. He discusses the introduction of new aircraft and avionics, examines the role of the slow as well as the fast movers, and also reviews the operations of the invaluable gunships. His final chapter covers night reconnaissance and Rolling Thunder operations.

BRIAN S. GUNDERSON
Brigadier General, USAF
Chief, Office of Air Force History

PREFACE

At the height of the Korean War the Fifth Air Force commander Lt. Gen. Earle Partridge noted: "...the paramount deficiency of the USAF today--certainly as regards air-ground operations--is our inability to seek out and destroy the enemy at night."*

General Partridge's 1951 comments strikingly paralleled the situation confronting the United States Air Force a decade later in Southeast Asia. The Air Force possessed a strategic and tactical nuclear capability, sizable airlift forces, and an elaborate computer-oriented technology. Nonetheless, with but minor exceptions, it could neither detect nor nullify the nighttime operations of a supposedly backward enemy. There were several reasons for this. Night operations are always difficult, more dangerous than day operations, and require trained, experienced aircrews and specialized aircraft. Moreover, the Air Force usually placed night operations low on the list of its funding priorities.

National strategy also accounted for the lack of an effective night strike capability within the Air Force. The 1950's saw the United States committing its air power and nuclear deterrent capability to the defense of the Free World. This required a nuclear force so overwhelming that the Communists would not dare attack. The force must be so superior and well-defended that it could survive a sneak attack and still destroy the Soviet state. Furthermore, this massive-retaliation strategy would apply not only to a general war but limited wars as well. During the Eisenhower years nuclear weapons and the means to deliver them received the highest funding priority. The Strategic Air Command's bomber force was expanded and dispersed and a powerful intercontinental ballistic missile (ICBM) program inaugurated. Seemingly, the single question stirring discussion was how "massive" must massive retaliation be, or how much nuclear deterrence was enough. †

Gen. Otto P. Weyland, Commander, Tactical Air Command (TAC), did not agree that the forces which deterred general wars

---

*Robert F. Futrell, The United States Air Force in Korea, 1950-1953 (New York, 1961), p 297.

†George F. Lemmer, A Brief Survey of Comparative Military Strategy (S) (Ofc/AF Hist, 1966), p 27.

could also deter limited wars. He frequently said the non-Communist nations faced a period of peripheral brush fire wars to be prevented or won only by superior tactical air forces. TAC would discourage limited wars as the Strategic Air Command (SAC) deterred general war. Towards this end General Weyland shaped TAC to resemble its big brother, SAC. Lower yield nuclear weapons became the mainstay of TAC strike units, a counterforce to Soviet (or Chinese Communist) manpower should deterrence fail. As a secondary mission, these weapons would roll back the enemy defenses prior to the penetration of SAC's heavy bombers. Conventional ordnance was considered "obsolete."[*]

Upon entering the Vietnam War in 1961, however, the United States saw that the use of tactical nuclear weapons was impractical. The low-key counterinsurgency conflict called for a fresh solution--one not found in general or limited war doctrine. In addition, the need to put available military funds into the nuclear deterrent during the 1950's left the Air Force ill-prepared for counterinsurgency warfare. Lacking an air power tactical doctrine for such warfare, the Air Force would now develop one from scratch using hard lessons learned in combat.

The Air Force discovered the "backward" enemy was rather ingenious and had learned his history well. Ten years before the North Korean and Chinese Communists had relied heavily on night operations to sustain the southward flow of men and materiel. Very early in the Vietnam War, the North Vietnamese and Viet Cong adopted similar tactics. The Air Force, therefore, faced an enemy who moved at night and hid by day. Lacking night-detection devices, the Air Force innovated and improvised until research and development could come up with the equipment to counter the enemy. How the men in the field did this is the core of this history.

Basically a hardware study, it goes far beyond how aircraft and equipment were used. Night air operations in Southeast Asia became a microcosm of the entire air war. Rules of engagement, weather, terrain, enemy capabilities and defenses--these reveal why the Air Force fought the way it did. Threaded through this

---

[*] Hist (C), Pacific Air Forces 1 Jan-30 Jun 58, I, Pt 2, p 68.

tale of men and machines is the constant theme of military history--the offense-defense pendulum or constant action and counteraction between the Air Force and the enemy. How each side reacted to changes impacted enormously on the entire conduct of the war. Clearly then, these underlying factors furnish this study's sinew and strength and thereby its value.

CONTENTS

FOREWORD	iii
PREFACE	iv
LIST OF FIGURES	ix
LIST OF MAPS AND ILLUSTRATIONS	xiii

I.	FARM GATE	1
	Tactics of C-47 Flareship Operations	6
	Problems of C-47 Night Flare Missions	10
	T-28 Operations	11
	B-26 Operations	14
	Problems of T-28/B-26 Strike Missions	15
	Farm Gate as an Experimental Laboratory	16
	The Tempo Increases	18
	Farm Gate's Contribution to Night Operations	21
II.	HAMLET-OUTPOST DEFENSE AND THE BEGINNING OF NIGHT INTERDICTION	24
	Mule Train and C-123 Flare Operations	24
	Early C-123 Flareship Operations	26
	The AC-47 Gunship	27
	C-130 Blindbat Operations	36
	Problems Associated with Blindbat Operations	44
	Summary	46
III.	NIGHT INTERDICTION	48
	The Ho Chi Minh Trail: Description and Geography	49
	The United States Begins Air Operations in Laos	52
	Aftermath of Tonkin Gulf: Upsurge in Force Deployments	58
	The Requirement for Effective Night Training	60
	Additional Sorties for Night Interdiction	64
	The Role of the Forward Air Controller	66
	O-1 SCAR/FAC Tactics--Preplanned Targets	67
	O-1 Tactics--Visual Reconnaissance	72
	O-1/T-28 Hunter/Killer Tactics	73
	The Search for a New FAC Aircraft	74

	O-2 Nail FAC's--Tactics and Techniques	75
	Ordnance	79
	C-123 Candlestick Operations	81
	C-123 Scope/Reconnaissance Techniques	83
	Marking and Ordnance Delivery Techniques	86
	F-100 Misty FAC	90
	OV-10 Bronco Operations	92
	Summary	96
IV.	THE SLOW MOVERS	97
	The Douglas A-26	97
	A-26 Characteristics Affecting Night Operations	100
	A-26 Night Visual Reconnaissance	102
	A-26 Trolling/Flak Suppression Operations	104
	T-28 Zorros	107
	The Douglas A-1 Skyraider	110
	A-1 Armed Reconnaissance	112
	A-1 Tropic Moon	115
	Tropic Moon Armed Reconnaissance--Steel Tiger	118
	TV Armed Reconnaissance in South Vietnam	121
V.	THE FAST MOVERS AND THE GUNSHIPS	123
	B-57 Tactics	125
	B-57 Tropic Moon II	127
	Tropic Moon III--The B-57G	129
	McDonnell-Douglas F-4 Phantom II	132
	C-130/F-4 Flare-Strike Tactics	134
	F-4 Armed Reconnaissance/Lightly Defended Area	135
	F-4 Armed Reconnaissance/Highly Defended Area	140
	F-4 Loran Bombing/Commando Bolt	144
	Pave Way	147
	AC-130 Development and Equipment	148
	AC-130 LOC Interdiction Tactics	153
	AC-130 Attack Procedures	157
	AC-130/F-4 Flak-Suppression Tactics	158
	The Surprise Package (Coronet Surprise)	164
	The AC-119G/K	166
	AC-119 Armed Reconnaissance	168
	AC-119/A-1 Escort Operations	169
	Commando Hunt V: The Gunship Shooting Gallery	171
	AC-123 Black Spot	172
	AC-123 Tactics	175

VI.	RECONNAISSANCE AND ROLLING THUNDER	177
	OV-1 Mohawk	180
	Problems Inherent in Night Reconnaissance	182
	The RF-4C Phantom	183
	RF-4C Out-Country Operations	184
	Rolling Thunder	189
	The Commando Nail F-105	192
	Commando Nail Operations in Route Packages V and VI	192
	Development of Iron Hand and Wild Weasel	195
	F-4 Operations in North Vietnam	199
	MSQ-77 Combat Skyspot	203
	F-111 Operations	206
CONCLUSIONS		208
NOTES		210
GLOSSARY OF TERMS AND ABBREVIATIONS		244

LIST OF FIGURES

Figure		Page
1	Farm Gate Flare Pattern	9
2	AC-47 Gunship Pattern	33
3	C-130 FAC/Flareship	37
4	FAC/Flareship Controlled Strike	42
5	Effect of Release Altitude and Resulting Variations of Slant Range at Release on Ordnance Impact	53
6	Effect of Dive Angle on Ordnance Impact	54
7	Effect of Airspeed on Ordnance Impact	55
8	Outside Holding Pattern	70
9	Overhead Holding Pattern	71
10	Bomb, Incendiary Cluster, M36	80
11	C-123 Orbit Pattern	87
12	155MM Howitzer Illumination for Air Strikes--Battery Located Parallel to Strike Run-in Heading	95
13	A-26 Flak Suppression	105
14	Wide-View Electronically Generated Video Presentations	116
15	Narrow-View Electronically Generated Video Presentations	117
16	Location of Tropic Moon I Operations	119
17	Typical Self-Contained Night Attack	120
18	B-57G Configuration	131
19	C-130/F-4 Flare-Strike Tactics	135
20	F-4 Two-Ship Cell	137
21	F-4 Two-Ship Attack Tactics	138
22	F-4 Parallel Flare Pattern	141
23	F-4 Short-Pass Flare Pattern	142
24	Commando Bolt Flasher	146
25	Blindbat Paveway Target Designation	149

Figure		Page
26	AC-130 Gunship Detection Devices	151
27	AC-130 Random Pattern	154
28	AC-130 Attack Orbit	155
29	AC-130 Parallel Search Pattern	156
30	AC-130 Spiral Search Pattern	157
31	The AC-130 Spectre Shuttle	159
32	F-4 Escort Tactics	160
33	Gunship Escort Position	161
34	F-4 Flak Suppression for AC-130	162
35	AC-130 Surprise Package: Sensor/Armament Configuration	164
36	Cutaway of AC-119	167
37	AC-119 Attack Procedure	169
38	A-1 Escort of AC-119	170
39	Cutaway of AC-123	173
40	BLU-3 and BLU-26 Bomblets	174
41	Typical Low Level Profile, RF-4C	188

LIST OF MAPS AND ILLUSTRATIONS

	Page
Map 1 Southeast Asia - Major Interdiction Areas	Frontispiece
A Farm Gate B-26 in South Vietnam, 1962	2
USAF Pilot and VNAF Airman Pose Before Their T-28	5
USAF/VNAF T-28 Crew Over South Vietnam, 1962	12
RB-26 at Tan Son Nhut AB, 1964	19
Flare Drop From a C-123	25
AC-47 Gunship	28
7.62-mm Miniguns on AC-47	29
Night Observation Device Mounted in Blindbat Aircraft	40
O-1E Bird Dog Over South Vietnam	68
Cessna O-2A Observation Aircraft	75
O-2 Crew Checks Their Ordnance and Aircraft	78
Cessna O-2 (left) and OV-10 Bronco Over Thailand	93
A-26 At Nakhon Phanom AB, Thailand	98
Phosphorus Bombing	109
A-1E Skyraider	112
B-57 Over Phan Rang AB, South Vietnam	124
B-57G Canberra	129
F-4E Phantom	133
AC-130 Gunship	150
RF-101C	177
RB-57	179
RF-4C	183
Map 2 Out-Country Operations	191
F-105F Thunderchief	197
Two F-4's Break Away from KC-135 Refueling Tanker	201

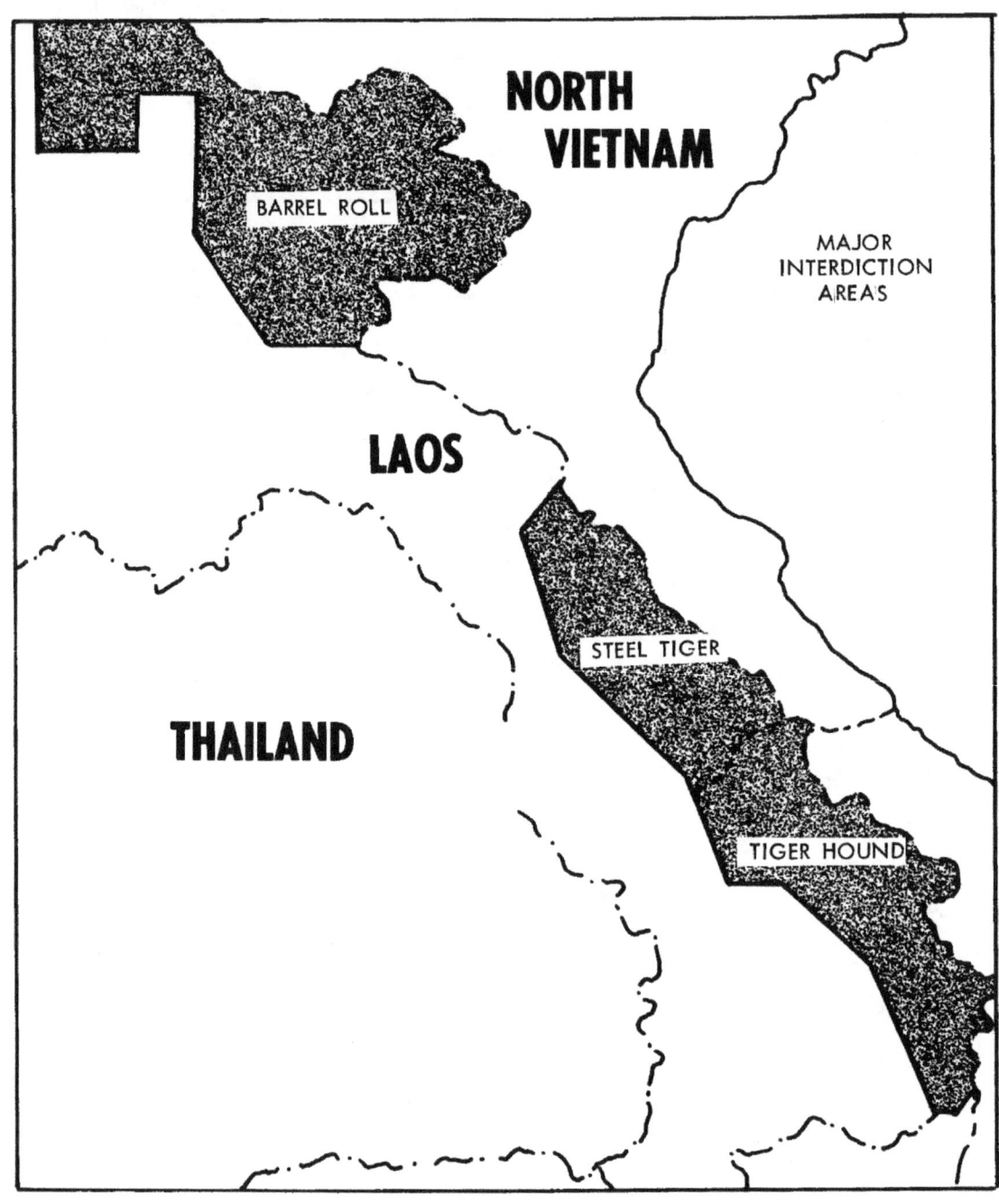

I. FARM GATE

On 11 October 1961, President John F. Kennedy decided to place an element of the 4400th Combat Crew Training Squadron on temporary duty with the Military Assistance Group-Vietnam (MAAG-V). The Tactical Air Command had activated this squadron in April 1961 under the code name, Jungle Jim, with the announced mission of training indigenous Air Force personnel to conduct counterinsurgency operations. In its development phase, the 4400th worked closely with the U.S. Army Special Warfare Center (the Green Berets) at Fort Bragg, N.C. On 14 November 1961, in line with the President's desires, the Joint Chiefs of Staff (JCS) ordered a detachment of the squadron to Bien Hoa AB, about 20 miles from Saigon. Later named Farm Gate, the relocated detachment included four SC-47 cargo/flareships, eight T-28's, and four RB-26's.* All these aircraft carried the orange and yellow star-and-bar insignia of the Vietnamese Air Force (VNAF). Moreover, since the Geneva accords prohibited the entry of tactical bombers in South Vietnam, the Air Force redesignated the B-26's as RB-26's to suggest reconnaissance aircraft rather than bombers.[1]

(U) None of the aircraft initially dispatched had been originally designed as counterinsurgency weapons. They were either modifications of tried and proved aircraft or the only ones available. The C-47 flareships, for example, still retained World War II, cargo-hauling capabilities, had an additional fuel capacity, a loudspeaker system for psychological warfare, and were JATO-equipped.+ The T-28 Trojan had been the Air Force's basic trainer in the 1950's. A new engine, a

---

*Further reference in this chapter to Farm Gate aircraft will be to the "T-28," "C-47" rather than "SC-47," and "B-26" instead of "RB-26."

In December 1961, to supply sufficient personnel for rotation to Southeast Asia, the Air Force augmented the 4400th Combat Crew Training Squadron with three similar squadrons. [See Counterinsurgency Ops Div, Dir/Ops, presentation to Lt Gen D.A. Burchinal, DCS/Plans and Prgms, subj: Air Force Role in Counterinsurgency, 1 Jun 62, pp 18-20.]

+JATO--jet-assisted takeoff.

stronger wing, and six ordnance stores stations converted it to a light tactical attack aircraft. The Trojan lacked suitable armorplate but could carry multiple ordnance including rockets, napalm, and fragmentary cluster bombs.

The B-26 Invader was used in World War II and Korea. Each of its eight nose-mounted, .50-caliber machine guns carried 350 rounds. The Invader could deliver a 4,000-lb bomb load plus additional ordnance hung on external racks under its wings. The latter included bombs, napalm, chemical tanks, rockets, or combinations of these. The B-26 was powered by reciprocating piston engines as were the C-47 and T-28. It was economical, comparatively slow, could operate from minimal tactical strips, and possessed a photo reconnaissance capability.*2

A Farm Gate B-26 in South Vietnam, 1962

---

*Although a time-consuming process, a solid-nose B-26 could be converted to a glass-nose reconnaissance version. Unconverted, the aircraft still had a photo capability since cameras were located in the fuselage's bottom and sides and the tail. [Intvw, author with Maj Charles W. Brown, Hq USAF, 14 Sep 70. Major Brown, then a 1st Lieutenant, served as a T-28/B-26 pilot in the Farm Gate detachment between May-November 1962.]

The B-26 was also a proven night attack bomber. Very early in the Korean War (August 1950) the Air Force began flying missions in which these aircraft bombed and strafed under flares dropped by high-flying B-29's. However, since 50 percent of the flares were duds, it was impossible to accurately assess the effects of these attacks on the enemy.[3] The situation improved in early 1951 with the introduction of C-47's carrying the U.S. Navy's Mk-8 pyrotechnic flare, dispensed through a homemade ramp installed in the rear cargo door. These Lightning Bug or Firefly aircraft offered Allied ground forces about 4 or 5 minutes of near-daylight illumination from flares dropped at approximately 5,000 feet. Tactics called for the B-26's to bomb and strafe the enemy as the ignited flares descended.[4]

The flareship/strike team in Korea was so successful that a curious psychological phenomenon developed. The Communists became conditioned to the tactic of flares followed by bombs and quickly broke off an attack the moment flares ignited. Eventually the flares alone deterred the North Koreans or Chinese from attacking.[5] This released many B-26 sorties for night armed reconnaissance missions. The Invaders roamed enemy lines and transportation arteries seeking out targets of opportunity, trying to deny the enemy the food, ammunition, and reinforcements he required for an all-out offensive. Throughout the Korean War, the B-26 flew 50 percent of all night sorties and over 70 percent of the night tactical strikes.[6] Reunited in Vietnam, the C-47 and B-26 (along with the T-28) served as an effective air counter to enemy night activity during the first two years of USAF involvement in the war.

As in Korea, U.S. air power operated under specific limitations or restraints known as rules of engagement. In a combat zone with no front lines, where friend and foe alike wore "black pajamas," where one side owned the territory by day and the other by night--these constantly changing rules were a necessity. The rules varied from one geographic area to another and restricted the Americans more than the South Vietnamese.[7] President Kennedy approved Farm Gate's rules of engagement on 6 December 1961. They authorized combat operations only if the VNAF lacked the necessary training and equipment to carry out the mission, the flight was confined to South Vietnam, and a combined USAF/VNAF crew was on board.[8]

These rules served in effect as a checklist and, when properly followed, allowed Farm Gate to operate as a tactical strike element. This was particularly true in regard to night operations. The only VNAF fighter squadron operational at the time of the Farm Gate deployment lacked night training and the aircraft had no landing lights.*9 These circumstances satisfied the requirement of the rules that the VNAF be unable to carry out the mission. When the additional requirement for a combined USAF/VNAF crew was fulfilled as set forth below, night strike operations became one of Farm Gate's main missions.10

So long as a VNAF crewman was aboard the USAF aircraft, "training through operations" could be conducted. Since few VNAF pilots were available, VNAF noncommissioned officers and airmen filled the crewmember role. That the crewmember was often nonrated, spoke no English, and rode in the jump seat didn't matter. What did matter was to have a Vietnamese in the aircraft to satisfy the rules of engagement and make the Farm Gate mission legitimate. These crewmembers were organized into a unit commanded by a VNAF Master Sergeant whose spoken English made him invaluable in translating instructions of Farm Gate pilots. The unit's high "no show" and desertion rate required Farm Gate crews to "guard" the airmen closely to have them on hand when the order to scramble was received. Col. John L. Piotrowski, a Farm Gate

---

*The consensus of former Farm Gate personnel interviewed by the author was that VNAF strike pilots, either due to lack of instrument training or disposition ("They hated to fly at night"), could not adequately conduct night operations. The Air Force, informed Secretary of Defense Robert S. McNamara of this fact at the Fourth Secretary of Defense Conference, held at Pacific Command headquarters in Hawaii on 21 March 1962. These VNAF shortcomings may have been the direct result of their training by the French. The latter were observed in 1954 to be well-qualified in day ordnance delivery but woefully lacking in instrument and night flying capability. A VNAF training program based on such inherent deficiencies may explain the South Vietnamese inability to conduct night operations. [See Trip Rprt (C), Dep for Intel, FEAF, 9 Mar 54, in Hist (S), FEAF Support of Indo-China Operations, 1954, II, p 17 (Sup Doc No. 47).]

T-28/B-26 pilot, recalled: "You had to remember that their only mission in life was to fly with Farm Gate and they knew sooner or later they would be in an aircraft that would be shot down." Colonel Piotrowski remembered only two instances where Farm Gate pilots took off without VNAF observers on board; the pilots were severely reprimanded.[11]

USAF Pilot and VNAF Airman Posed Before Their T-28

In light of the above, differing views on Farm Gate's actual mission are understandable. Much has been written about the mission describing it as twofold: "training through operations" of the VNAF, and development of proper Air Force organizational procedures for conducting sub-limited wars. To Farm Gate personnel, however, the mission had but one aim-- to conduct air operations in support of the Vietnamese government. As for the detachment's training mission, writers often construe it as a subterfuge to mask Farm Gate's true purpose for being in Vietnam from the International Control Commission (ICC). On the other hand, the T-28 Farm Gate pilots did accept a training function and developed a checkout program in their aircraft for the VNAF. No attempt was made to check out VNAF personnel in the B-26.[12]

Tactics of C-47 Flareship Operations

(U) In 1962, the tactics for Farm Gate operations were not as formalized as they would later become. No air power tactical doctrine for counterinsurgency existed. More important, the night operations tactics developed in Korea had not been retained. Hence, Farm Gate became a combat laboratory, to develop within the Air Force a "blue-suit capability" for conducting counterinsurgency operations. It had to hammer out the tactics by trial and error using the hard lessons of combat. The latest refinements in tactics were passed to each group of personnel rotating to the detachment for the 6-month duty tour.

When the air commandos[*] first arrived in South Vietnam, the urgent need was night flare drops tied in with close air support of hamlets and outposts under Viet Cong attack. Farm Gate, however, entered into the flareship mission very obliquely. An enterprising air commando obtained flares from a VNAF unit and determined exactly how they worked. Next a C-47 took off and, upon reaching altitude, the crewmembers threw the flares out the cargo door. This so impressed the crewmembers on the ground they quickly clambered aboard their T-28's and, while the Gooney Bird continued to manually dispense the flares, made drop passes over the field at Bien Hoa. Col. Benjamin King, the detachment commander, noted "That was the first time anybody in the outfit had ever worked flares. So the next day we went down and told them [the 2d Advanced Echelon] we had a capability to operate at night."[13]

Pursuing this pioneer effort the detachment, chiefly through trial and error, determined the proper flare-dispensing interval, necessary altitude separations, and flare/strike patterns. It sent the lessons learned to the Special Air Warfare Center, Eglin AFB, Fla., where they promptly appeared in the training

---

[*]"Air Commando"--An Air Force member engaged in counterinsurgency operations. Here it denotes personnel of the Farm Gate detachment.

syllabus. Consequently, the second 6-month group rotating to Farm Gate knew thoroughly flareship/strike techniques.*14

Farm Gate flareship/strike operations focused on supporting the defense of strategic hamlets and outposts under attack. The hamlet, the lowest rural population element, was the heart of the Saigon government's pacification program. Pacification sought to establish an effective government presence in the hamlet, and secure the countryside by isolating the rural population from Communist pressure. Each hamlet built defense works behind which the people (often supported by U.S. Special Forces teams) could fight off an attack until help arrived.15

Specific rules of engagement applied to the flareship/strike combination. Before summoning any attack to support troops in contact, the flareship had to (1) have reliable radio communication with the installation under attack; (2) identify the installation by sight; (3) positively identify the target either by radio using visual reference points, or fire arrows (a favorite device at night),† white phosphorous, or similar target-marking devices; (4) know the location of friendly forces in relation to visual reference points; and (5) have reliable radio contact with the strike aircraft. In addition, a forward air controller (FAC)‡ had to control night close air support missions aiding friendly

---

*Former Farm Gate air commandos believed cycling a new group of the 4400th squadron's Jungle Jim personnel to the detachment every 6 months was an excellent way to provide them all some type of combat counterinsurgency training and experience.

†Located within the defense area, a fire arrow could be made of many materials; metal gas cans filled with gasoline-soaked sand were often used. Ignited, it was easy to see at night. Hamlet defenders relayed to the flare or strike aircraft the enemy's position with reference to the fire arrow. [Intvw, author with Major Brown, Hq USAF, 14 Sep 70.]

‡Chapter III discusses the use of FAC's in support of night operations. For a definitive account of FAC operations in Southeast Asia, see Maj. Ralph A. Rowley, Forward Air Control in Southeast Asia, 1961-1964 (S) (Ofc/AF Hist, Jan 1972) and a follow-on volume by the same author to be published in 1973.

ground forces under attack in the field, as opposed to the defense of an installation. In early Farm Gate operations, the flareship often performed as FAC.[16]

Besides regularly preplanned or fragged[*] sorties, Farm Gate kept one fully loaded flareship on alert each night from dusk to dawn. (Later as Vietcong attacks on hamlets increased, flareships flew airborne alerts over specified geographical areas.) After receiving word from the joint operations center (JOC)[+] to take off, the flareship would fly to nearby Tan Son Nhut AB to pick up a VNAF navigator and a frequency modulation (FM) radio. Once the C-47 was back in the air, the Vietnamese crewmember contacted the hamlet under attack. If he spoke English his value doubled: he not only satisfied the requirement for a VNAF crewmember on all Farm Gate sorties, but helped surmount the language barrier between flareship and hamlet as well.[17]

When about 5 minutes from the hamlet, the copilot or VNAF navigator contacted the friendly ground forces by FM radio. Then the C-47 (navigation lights on) gave the strike aircraft (navigation lights off) its heading and altitude. The flareship selected the heading after evaluating target information, wind direction and velocity, weather conditions, international borders, and terrain features. In the early days, C-47 Farm Gate operations normally took place 2,500 feet above the terrain. Occasionally, flareships worked below that altitude, but 1,000 feet was the stated absolute minimum.[18]

---

[*]Frag--to issue a fragmentary field order covering details of a single mission, i.e., what is required, where, and when. A fragmentary order, usually issued on a day-to-day basis, is an abbreviated form of an operations order.

[+]In January 1963 the South Vietnamese renamed the joint operations center at Tan Son Nhut the joint air operations center (JAOC). This was to avoid confusing it with the Vietnamese Joint General Staff JOC established at the same time. Six months later, CINCPAC dropped JAOC in favor of air operations center (AOC). For clarity, however, the term JOC will be used in this discussion of Farm Gate. [For details on this matter and the tactical air control system (TACS) in South Vietnam, see Hist (S), 2d ADVON, 15 Nov 61-8 Oct 62, pp 81-85.]

The standard pattern flown by Farm Gate flareships (with or without strike aircraft) involved a right-hand orbit about 2,500 feet above ground level (AGL), consisting of 15-second legs and 1-minute turns. When Mk-6 flares were dropped, two were normally released upwind at 7-second intervals during each pass. The lower candlepower Mk-5 flares were released at 5-second intervals. The standard fuse setting delayed ignition until the flare was 300 feet below the aircraft. In a successful drop, the flares would drift over the target, bracket it at the midpoint of their descent, while furnishing maximum light and eliminating any shadow effects. Many flares, unfortunately, had been stored for several years so preignition or complete failure was quite common.[19]

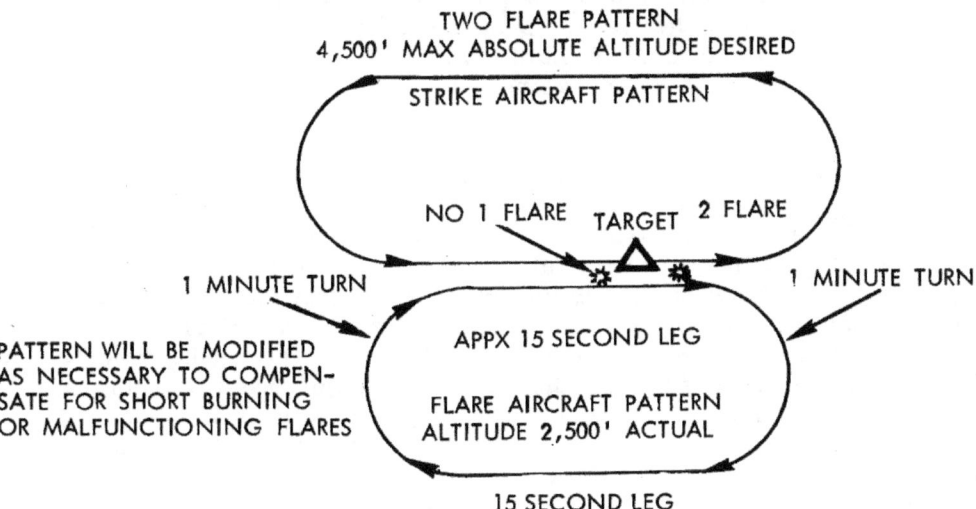

Figure 1 (U)

The loadmaster dispensed the flares, assisted at times by the flight mechanic or other crewmembers.* Wearing a safety harness, the loadmaster pushed out the flares while sitting on the floor or standing in the door. During late 1962 and early 1963 some aircraft were equipped with a jury-rigged chute dispenser. Made of wood and built into the door, it consisted of five parallel chutes. When the loadmaster moved a lever, the flares were dispensed and the ignition lanyard pulled.[20]

As in the Korean War, flareship crews soon discovered that, in the absence of strike aircraft, the dropping of flares alone deterred the enemy from attack or caused him to break off contact. This led to adoption of a standard tactic to scare the enemy off--the flareship dropped only one flare in lieu of the usual two or three. A minimum of 60 flares was carried on board to perform this increasingly frequent mission.[21]

Problems of C-47 Night Flare Missions

Communications became the most perplexing problem associated with flare activity, both between crewmembers within the aircraft and between the flareship and the ground. More often than not, the Vietnamese navigator spoke little or no English. Thus the mission began with a language barrier. Over the target, the problem compounded when the VNAF navigator tried to relay strike information to the flare crew who, as FAC's, had to pass it to the strike aircraft. In addition, the flareship radio equipment varied from one aircraft to the next, although it most always included an ultra high frequency (UHF) radio. The hamlets (or outposts) under attack, however, possessed only an FM radio. Hence, the fragile FM set, which the VNAF navigator brought on board at Tan Son Nhut, formed the tenuous link between flareship and hamlet. Frequently the FM transmissions grew so confused

---

*Often the crewmember who helped dispense the flares was one of the Civic Action Section's medical personnel. [Intvw, author with Maj. James D. Carson, 17 Sep 70.]

and garbled, that a USAF crewmember would use the radio and ask the hamlet to "put a GI on the horn." Furthermore, many flare missions aborted due to transmission difficulties between hamlet and aircraft or malfunction of the FM radio equipment.[22]

Two additional problems hampered night flare missions --slow communications and navigation. At times, slow communications added to the reaction time of strike aircraft. By the time the JOC cleared the B-26's or T-28's to the target area, the enemy had already withdrawn or overrun the hamlet. This pinpointed the need for strike aircraft to be near the flareship ready for an instant pass. As to navigation, Farm Gate found the available maps not completely current, particularly with regard to stated terrain elevations. Nonetheless, with the few radio navigation aids available, most navigators depended on mapreading or dead reckoning. The limited view from his table forced the navigator to scurry back and forth from his station to the jump seat between the pilots where, standing, he could observe a bit more of the terrain. Of necessity all C-47 cockpit crewmembers came to be proficient mapreaders.[23]

T-28 Operations

The Farm Gate detachment flew its first operational strike sortie in November 1961. Four T-28's performed night, visual, armed reconnaissance of the rail line linking Bien Hoa and Nha Trang. Two aircraft flew the lead with the other two 1 mile behind and 500 feet above. In the target area, the first pair flared* while the second pair attacked. The process continued with the cells changing positions.[24]

Regularly scheduled night sorties were rare. Normally, two T-28's stood alert with two more as backup. The latter became the standby aircraft once the first two T-28's had been scrambled.+ Before Farm Gate aircraft could take off in daylight, the Vietnamese director of the JOC had to indicate the

---

*Flared--To drop flares.

+Scramble--To take off as quickly as possible (usually followed by course and altitude instructions).

mission was beyond the VNAF's capability. The JOC could bypass this procedure for night missions, since the VNAF lacked a night capability. This resulted in speedier processing of night strike requests by the JOC.25

USAF/VNAF T-28 Crew Over South Vietnam, 1962

Farm Gate pilots also received word to scramble--but not approval to take off--from the Combined Studies Division (CSD).* While the aircraft were taxiing to the end of the runway, CSD requested strike approval from the 2d Advance Echelon (the USAF controlling agency, later to become 2d Air Division and then Seventh Air Force). Coordination being quite good, the clearance from 2d ADVON, relayed through the JOC, was usually waiting for the strike aircraft by the time they reached the active runway. After takeoff, the T-28's would proceed to the target

---

*The U. S. State Department operated the Combined Studies Division, which included U. S. Army Special Forces and Farm Gate personnel. Located in the basement of the Military Advisory Assistance Command-Vietnam (MAAC-V) building, the CSD could communicate directly with many of the strategic hamlets. Later, with improved communications and better defined command and control in South Vietnam, the 2d ADVON fragged all Farm Gate sorties through the JOC. [Intvw, author with Maj. Charles Brown, 14 Sep 70.]

area using low-frequency omni* and mapreading for navigation. Altitude would be compatible with the terrain and weather en route. It could vary from treetop level to 2,500 feet AGL, the upper limit of small arms fire. Upon rendezvousing with the flareship the two ship strike cell would contact it for the necessary strike information.[26]

Unlike many of the flareships the T-28's were equipped with an FM radio, either the U.S. Army PRC-10 or the USAF ARC-44. Both radios could be set to many frequencies, but their inaccessible location in the aircraft made it impossible to change or reset them in flight.+ The pilot, therefore, preset the hamlet's operating frequency before takeoff. If the hamlet could not be reached or for any reason changed frequency, contact was lost. Accordingly, the flareship became a vital communications bridge and eventually operated as a FAC for the strike aircraft.[27]

The flareship controlled the mission if it arrived on station before the strike aircraft. The T-28's established a slightly longer left-hand orbit, alternately descending below the flares during the strike phase and recovering in a left climbing turn to an orbit altitude of about 4,500 feet AGL (2,500 feet AGL for strafing). This sequence continued until the strike was completed. The format varied during a four-ship-cell attack to a box or touch-and-go pattern with the strike aircraft flying about 500 feet below the flareship. The lead aircraft turned in the direction of the flares, and the other aircraft peeled off in the same direction after a specified interval. This maneuver gave each aircraft in the cell proper spacing and interval and,

---

*Omnirange (omni)--Radio aid to air navigation which creates an infinite number of paths in space throughout 360 degrees azimuth.

+The PRC-10 was strapped to the front seat armor plating; the ARC-44 was attached with Dzus fasteners. The 9-foot whip antenna of the FM radio could not be mounted properly on strike aircraft, so reception came through the aircraft's automatic direction finder (ADF) antenna. On flareships, a crewmember thrust the FM antenna through an open cockpit window. [Intvws, author with Maj. James Carson, 17 Sep 70; Lt. Cols. John Pattee and Donald C. Hatch, 18 Sep 70; and Lt. Col. John Piotrowski, 21 Sep 70.]

above all, a view of the flareship. Each T-28 pilot knew the position of his cellmates through radio calls, for example, "Number one on base," "Number two turning downwind." This tactic proved invaluable, in view of the reduced visibility at night and each pilot's paramount desire to avoid midair collision with other strike aircraft or the flareship.[28]

Occasionally, two T-28's arrived on the scene before the flareship, contacted the hamlet over the FM radio for required strike information, and attacked under the light of their own flares. With lights off, the first T-28 attacked in a shallow dive, usually dropping napalm. During pullup the pilot reached down between his legs and switched the selector from ordnance to the outboard station carrying the flares.* He then dropped his flare, unignited and upwind, while the second T-28 attacked with lights off. After the second aircraft pulled up, the flares from the first ignited. As the flare drifted down and across the attack zone, the T-28's again attacked. When the lead aircraft's flares gave out, the aircraft switched positions.[29]

B-26 Operations

Essentially B-26 operations resembled those of other Farm Gate aircraft. Like the C-47 and T-28 crews, the Invader's pilot and navigator stood night alert after their regularly scheduled day activities. Generally only one B-26 was placed on alert, receiving its notice to scramble by way of the JOC. (Later in specified corps areas the order would come from the air support operations center (ASOC). Like the T-28 mission profile, enroute altitude depended on the weather and varied from treetop level to 2,500-4,000 feet AGL. The B-26 crew navigated en route by mapreading and low frequency radio (later, by ground radar). While the T-28 carried a USAF pilot in the front seat and a VNAF member in the rear, the B-26 had the pilot and navigator sitting side by side with the VNAF member occupying the jump seat behind the navigator. This enabled pilot and navigator to work as a team in solving the navigation problem. Moreover, after

---

*This was a tricky maneuver considering the attitude of the aircraft at that moment, the location of the selector switch with reference to the pilot, and the need for the latter to keep his eyes on the instruments.

the attack began the navigator set the bomb switches, armed the .50-caliber guns, and monitored the aircraft instruments.[30]

Problems of T-28/B-26 Strike Missions

Limited visibility at night was one of the most vexing problems that Farm Gate and other strike pilots faced. The inability to see the ground or other aircraft adequately, the fast closure/turn rate with no way to determine what that closure/turn rate was, had a sobering effect on most pilots. No aircraft commander wanted to fly into the rice paddies or collide midair with a flareship. In the 4-ship T-28 attack formation, designed to prevent such accidents, the pilot knew his position in relation to the flareship and his cellmates. Additionally, the attack dive angle was more shallow than in comparable day operations. Offsetting these pluses were inadequate (or excessive) cockpit illumination, reflected canopy glare, and inaccessible or poorly located switches--all contributing greatly to eye strain, pilot fatigue, and degraded flying safety.[31]

From a flying safety aspect, the B-26 with two USAF crewmembers was better suited for night strike missions than the T-28. During the attack phase, the navigator monitored the aircraft's position and altitude, relaying corrections to the pilot seated next to him. This allowed the aircraft commander to concentrate on acquiring the target, positioning the aircraft for attack, and visually tracking for ordnance delivery. As in Korean War operations, the B-26 pilot needed to know his exact position at all times when operating in rugged or mountainous terrain. He further had to recognize his own limitations as well as those of the aging Invader.*[32]

Despite its small advantage of crew composition, the B-26 possessed serious and peculiar problems. The cockpit

---

*Colonel Piotrowski believed the esprit of the detachment pilots and their strong desire for mission accomplishment may have cost the lives of two B-26 crews. It was not unusual for pilots to push the aircraft to its extreme limits, sometimes disregarding flying safety standards. [Piotrowski intvw, previously cited.]

lights had a bad habit of falling off or not illuminating the instruments at the very time they were needed most. The gunsight pipper vibrated excessively and, when the .50-caliber guns were firing, the muzzle flashes prevented the pilot from seeing little if anything. To retain some semblance of night vision, the pilot used the old trick of closing one eye during the attack. This, however, did not relieve the problem of acrid powder smoke in the cockpit, or the greasy smear on the windshield from powder blown back from the gun barrels.[33]

Besides poorly located ordnance switches and cockpit glare on the canopy, the T-28 had its peculiar liabilities. To see through the gunsight--the old F-86 sight without the gyro-- required the pilot to stretch his neck forward. But in this position he could not read the top instruments, so necessary in a dive maneuver. So he resumed a normal sitting posture, read the instruments, then again stretched forward to reacquire the target. Only an experienced pilot could perform this ticklish action.[34]

A chief drawback to using parachute flares for illumination was the blinding effect on the strike pilot. This disoriented him as he pulled off the target into the darkness. Shadows cast by the flare and reflections from the clouds also caused vertigo and spatial disorientation.* The offset method of dropping flares somewhat eased this problem. By dropping flares to the side of the target the strike pilot could attack without looking directly into the light, then recover around the flare using it as a constant flight reference. Operating under these conditions demanded that the aircrews be highly competent at reading cockpit instruments.[35]

Farm Gate as an Experimental Laboratory

One of Farm Gate's objectives was to serve as an experimental laboratory for Air Force counterinsurgency operations

---

*Jet crews were making the same complaint six years later. [Ltr (S), Dep Comdr for Ops, 8th TFWg, to 7th AF, 14 Dec 68.]

and doctrine. Toward this end, the detachment investigated and analyzed tactics and equipment that might prove appropriate to its mission. Some were shown to be valid while others, such as dropping 20-pound fragmentation bombs from C-47's were quickly discarded in favor of more acceptable ordnance release methods. One experiment involved night visual reconnaissance by a pair of C-47 flareships. Flying in staggered trail formation, the first C-47 dispensed flares at 40-second intervals while the second aircraft, flying much lower and about 2 minutes behind the first, performed the reconnaissance. Although feasible, this operation was expensive. Night photo reconnaissance was also tried with single and multiple flaredrops. The results were unsatisfactory due to the low illumination rating (1 million candlepower) of the flares.[36]

Farm Gate crews experimented very early with napalm, especially as a strike adjustment point in the absence of a flareship. Using the hamlet's fire arrow as a reference, the strike aircraft would drop one or two napalm cans. As in artillery adjustment, the napalm blaze served as a base point from which the hamlet's defenders readjusted their target information.*[37]

To spread napalm over a wider area several additives were tried. The Madam Nhu Cocktail† added charcoal to the other napalm ingredients in the canister. When the blaze increased but slightly, this experiment gave way to the beer can additive.‡ Empty beer cans were added, the theory being that upon impact beer cans and ingredients would be spread over a wide area. This effort was soon phased out, since the results achieved did not justify the time and effort involved.[38]

---

*By November 1962, due to the enemy's improved antiaircraft capability, this tactic had to be accompanied by a strafing run to pin down enemy gunners. [Draft paper (S), Farm Gate Tactics and Techniques, Jun 1962.]

†Named after Vietnamese President Diem's strong-willed, anti-American sister-in-law.

‡No proof exists that the readily available and endless supply of empty beer cans prompted their use in the experiment.

The majority of successful Farm Gate experiments had to do with ordnance delivery and field testing. Crews soon discovered that, other than napalm, the M-47 white phosphorous bomb was their best weapon. Excellent for jungle use, it penetrated the canopy before detonating instead of dissipating its effects on the top layers of foliage as napalm did. Furthermore, the M-47 afforded the aircraft an extra margin of safety since it could be delivered during a dive.[39]

Farm Gate also reintroduced the World War II Daisy Cutter antipersonnel bomb. The nose fuse in either a general purpose (GP) or fragmentation (antipersonnel) bomb was removed and an old gun barrel or pipe section welded to it. The nose plug was then reinserted into the bomb while a tail fuse with an instantaneous primer/detonator unit was set for a no-delay detonation. After release from the aircraft the pipe would hit the ground first, transmitting the ground shock to the tail fuse. This exploded all or most of the weapon above ground, hurling lethal shrapnel over a wide area. Demonstrating their effectiveness, Daisy Cutters continued in use through 1970.[40]

Other Farm Gate innovations included the placement of two pieces of ordnance on an aircraft's one-piece station, and modification of the T-28 practice ordnance rack to carry four flares instead of four practice bombs.[41]

The Tempo Increases

Coincident with Farm Gate's assumption in December 1961 of night strike operations, the enemy stepped up his attacks on friendly villages and hamlets in South Vietnam and expanded the conflict in Laos. Communist forces launched a spring drive in Laos (6-27 May 1962) which eventually won them control over a large part of that country. Responding to this increased enemy activity, the United States redeployed four additional reconnaissance B-26's to Southeast Asia under code name Black Watch. Two of the aircraft were stationed at Bangkok, Thailand, and the remainder went to Farm Gate. Between 29 May and 21 July 1962 the Thailand-based B-26's (plexiglass noses) flew 50 photo reconnaissance missions over Laos. However, these aircraft were attached to Farm Gate after a 14-nation Geneva conference agreed on 23 July 1962 to guarantee the neutrality of Laos. The following month saw four U-10B aircraft assigned to Farm Gate so that, by the end of 1962, it possessed 24 planes--eight T-28's, four C-47's, eight B-26's and four U-10B's.[42]

RB-26 At Tan Son Nhut AB, 1964

       This small augmentation of aircraft did not seem too significant at the time. In reality, however, it marked the beginning of deep U.S. Air Force involvement in Southeast Asia. Greater appreciation of air support by the ARVN and the Vietnamese para-military forces increased considerably the number of requests to Farm Gate for immediate air support. The detachment flew 187 combat sorties in June 1962 with an increase to 462 in August--still it was not enough. The sustained around-the-clock operations clearly required more aircraft. Moreover, additional requests for Farm Gate air support were generated by the arrival of two U.S. Army helicopter companies (usually escorted by Farm Gate aircraft in daylight hours), increased U.S. Army Special Forces activities, and improved weather in the II Corps area.[43]

       In August 1962, the detachment received some relief. VNAF C-47's began to stand night flare alert assisted by the

C-123's of the USAF Mule Train Squadron.* Thereafter, Farm Gate C-47's gradually relinquished their share of flare responsibilities to the VNAF and Mule Train. Some relief was forthcoming in the strike area as well. In November 1962, the Commander in Chief, Pacific Command (CINCPAC) requested further augmentation of Farm Gate by 17 aircraft--five T-28's, ten B-26's, and two C-47's. President Kennedy approved the request two months later and by February 1963, the aircraft were in place.†44

During the first half of 1963, the T-28's flew 1,416 sorties while the B-26's accounted for 1,495 sorties. These high sortie rates created maintenance problems in Farm Gate's overage aircraft. The T-28's underwent numerous cylinder changes and experienced high oil consumption. In September 1963 the Air Force recommended that the T-28 be replaced with the A-1E, a more rugged aircraft offering better payload, loiter, and range capability. In June 1964 the changeover took place. The T-28's returned to the Special Air Warfare Center at Eglin for training and potential combat missions elsewhere in the world.45

The B-26's in particular were war-weary. Many had served in two wars and survived storage twice. They suffered from cracks, popped rivets, and wing-spar corrosion. Oil coolers, deflectors, and magnetos for these aircraft were in short supply. Often routine postflight inspections would reveal cylinders which needed changing. As one former B-26 pilot recalled, "The wiring was old, moisture and oil soaked, plus frayed by

---

*Mule Train had arrived in Southeast Asia in January 1962, on temporary duty from the 464th Troop Carrier Wing, Pope AFB, N.C. Twelve of the squadron's C-123's were located in South Vietnam, the remainder at Clark AB, Philippines.

†Plans were under way to transfer Farm Gate personnel and equipment to PACAF on permanent change of station (PCS). This action occurred in June 1963; the designation Farm Gate was discontinued and the 1st Air Commando Squadron, Composite, activated in its place. [Ltr (U), AFOMO 62 to PACAF, subj: Activation of the 1st Air Commando Squadron, Composite and Certain Other USAF Unit Actions, 17 Jun 63; hist (S), 13th AF, Jan-Jun 63, p 72.]

constant vibrations. On some aircraft almost half the wiring is dead and leads nowhere. No two B-26's have the same wiring diagram or configuration. Engines were very complex and difficult to move about in remote areas." In short, the Invader had become a "maintenance nightmare."[46]

But it was operational flying throughout 1963 that subjected the Invader to the severest strain. The 40° dive angles, accompanied by rolling pullouts plus full-aileron deflection at high speeds, imposed heavy stress on the aircraft. The marginal flying safety aspects of the airplane were dramatically illustrated in February 1964 before an audience of distinguished Army and Air Force officers at Eglin AFB. On the range, a B-26 of the 1st Air Commando Wing (successor to the 4400th CCTS) was completing a strafing run using flares when it appeared that the wing separated from the fuselage. The airplane disintegrated upon crashing and was enveloped in flames.[47]

Investigation disclosed that, although the aircraft was in a shallow dive (20°-25°), metal fatigue in the left wing caused the crash. The Air Force, therefore, grounded all B-26's and withdrew them from combat service in Southeast Asia 2 months later. The day after the last B-26 left South Vietnam, a rash of wing separations plagued the T-28 forcing a reevaluation of its role as a counterinsurgency fighter-bomber. Thus, 2 months after the B-26's had departed, the Air Force phased out the T-28's as well. Both aircraft were down but not out. After extensive rehabilitation in the United States they would return to combat. Meantime, the A-1 Skyraider and newer jet aircraft assumed the attack role.[48]

Farm Gate's Contribution to Night Operations

During their first 2 years of operation, Farm Gate's air commandos furnished the VNAF with a much-needed night strike capability, but as a laboratory for developing new night tactics, the detachment did not fare so well. Its main contribution was to reintroduce many night tactics used by aircrews in World War II and the Korean War. A case in point is the tactic of dropping napalm on the first run, then strafing back across in the light of the fire. P-61 Black Widow crews used this technique extensively in 1945 during the ebbing months of the air war over Europe. B-26 crews repeated the tactic in Korea. But during the interwar years--for one reason or another--this and other night tactics were forgotten. Through Farm Gate these tactics had to be painstakingly relearned.

The air commandos met singular success in integrating flare and strike aircraft as a potent night-attack combination. Again this was not original, for the B-26 and C-47 had been similarly combined in Korea. But this time the B-26/C-47 tactics would not be lost. Reaffirmed and modified by Farm Gate, they served as the basis for further developments in flare/strike tactics and techniques employed in Southeast Asia.

Perhaps more important was Farm Gate's introducing the VNAF to night strike operations in 1962. An operations inspector of the Thirteenth Air Force Inspector General team evaluated VNAF progress in January 1964. He noted that, while the performance of the VNAF flareships was outstanding, the same could not be said of the strike aircraft:

> Most of the bombs missed the target. The VNAF pilots were making very shallow bomb runs, did not appear to establish a stabilized dive and released bombs at much too high an altitude. With the small bombs being employed, these pilots could have pressed on in for real effectiveness. The superb support provided by the flareship was, for all practical purposes, wasted by the careless, ineffective performance of the fighters.[49]

Despite the inspector's criticism, the performance of VNAF strike pilots had improved since 1962, when Farm Gate first discovered the Vietnamese were either unable or unwilling to fly at night.*

---

*The Farm Gate T-28 section checked out several VNAF student officers who had received pilot training at USAF bases or from the French. These included pilots from the 1st Fighter Squadron proficient in the A-1 Skyraider, and those checked out in the few remaining F-8F Bearcats in the VNAF inventory. None were night qualified. The quality of the first group of VNAF pilots trained by Farm Gate was "either extremely good or very, very bad." [See Pattee intvw, previously cited.]

For two years the air commandos trained the VNAF to the extent it was willing to fly night strike missions. Hence, the reason for the mediocre performance of VNAF strike pilots in 1964 was a simple one. Night operations require experienced and proficient instrument pilots--a type rarely found in the VNAF.

The first group of Vietnamese strike pilots trained by Farm Gate did have over 1,400 combat sorties and from 5,000-7,000 flying hours. Almost all this activity, however, had been conducted by day and in clear weather, for the VNAF paid scant attention to instrument or night flying. Nonetheless, from the beginning of Farm Gate operations it was evident that South Vietnam's survival depended on night operations becoming a way of life for the VNAF as it had for the enemy. As David Halberstam, The New York Times correspondent, noted, "The Vietcong were taught that the night was their friend, the enemy of the white man and his airplane. To operate in the dark became a way of life with the Vietcong: they lived, taught, traveled and fought at night."[50]

(U) In summary, Farm Gate had only scratched the surface. It was a beginning but much remained to be done, especially in developing better methods of detecting and then impeding or halting the enemy's night activities. If it was decided to expand the VNAF, the shortage of maintenance, supply, and flying personnel would make progress painfully slow. Meanwhile, until the VNAF could shoulder more of the burden, the Air Force units that succeeded the air commandos would fly most of the night strike sorties. How the Air Force went about the night operations task, how it tried to solve a myriad of associated problems--these are examined in the ensuing chapters.

II. HAMLET-OUTPOST DEFENSE AND THE BEGINNING OF NIGHT INTERDICTION

Mule Train and C-123 Flare Operations

The original mission of the three Mule Train C-123 squadrons in South Vietnam was to furnish supplemental tactical airlift support for the Vietnamese armed forces, but when the Vietcong intensified night attacks against the hamlets, the Air Force pressed the C-123's into duty as flareships. In September 1963, for example, C-123's from Tan Son Nhut began flying 5-hour night flare missions. By early 1964 these aircraft, together with VNAF C-47's, were conducting nearly all the night flare drops.[1]

Essentially, Mule Train's flareship/strike techniques were Farm Gate's. After the C-123 crew received the geographic coordinates of the outpost under attack, it navigated by mapreading or low-frequency radio to the position. The VNAF navigator usually established and maintained contact with the hamlet by FM radio. He relayed outpost information on the enemy to the fighters, although fire arrows were still used to show the direction of the enemy attack. Language barriers within the cockpit or between strike aircraft and the flareship were still too common for effective communication. The C-123 copilot repeatedly had to relay the information to the fighters. To ease this problem, many crews devised point-and-talk sheets containing Vietnamese instructions on one side and English on the other.[2]

During the early C-123 flare operations Mk-5 and Mk-6 flares were hand-released. Mule Train crews used members of the Army of Republic of Vietnam (ARVN) airborne brigade as flare launchers (kickers), or in a pinch secured volunteers from USAF ground personnel. Problems besetting the crews included unreliable ordnance, preignition, out-of-phase deployment and ignition, and broken lanyards. The greatest danger was the slipstream that flowed around the open aft cargo door during the flare-dispensing operation. At times, this peculiar airflow swept the flares against the aircraft's side or even back into the cargo door area. Meager personal safety equipment heightened the danger. Equipped with only asbestos gloves and a short-handled spade, the flare launcher had to push out flares ignited inside the aircraft. Their burning magnesium was hot enough to melt steel.[3]

A locally-manufactured flare-delivery chute with five troughs solved the dilemma. With the cargo ramp lowered to its horizontal position, this dispenser could be strapped to the ramp's outer edge. Then by lowering the cargo door the ramp opening was reduced, thereby eliminating the slipstream problem and the alarming tendency of flares to return to the airplane. Besides restoring peace of mine to the crew, the chute made restraining straps for kickers unnecessary and reduced their exposure to prematurely ignited flares [4]

Flare Drop from a C-123

As a further safeguard, flare boxes were built to control a chance fire from a malfunctioning flare. Set on roller conveyors these boxes were strapped to the aircraft floor directly opposite the flare chute. When a malfunction occurred the straps were cut, cargo door and ramp opened, and the entire flare box jettisoned. [5]

Early C-123 Flareship Operations

As a rule, the daily mission briefing fixed the exact flare pattern and spacing to be flown by the C-123. Once airborne, the aircraft customarily flew at an absolute altitude of 4,000 feet. To minimize hostile ground fire the interior lighting was almost completely blacked out. Before entering the target area and after checking with the aircraft commander, the loadmaster and his two kickers set the flare fuzes for the desired altitude at which illumination would begin. Just before reaching the target they raised the cargo door, installed the dispensing chute, and set the ejection time on the dispenser generally for 5-second intervals. A warning horn signaled flare release with the interphone as backup. The flareship pilot evaluated wind drfit, weather, terrain hazards, and the enemy position. Afterwards, he repeatedly adjusted the altitude and pattern to keep the target area constantly illuminated.[6]

Awaiting arrival of the strike aircraft, the C-123 contacted the hamlet by FM radio to identify the target position and location of friendly forces. Positive target identification was required by radio, ground fire arrows and/or phosphorous markers. This done, the aircraft put the navigation, position, rotating beacon, and formation lights in bright-flashing position. This aided the rendezvous and enabled strike aircraft to see the flareship during bomb runs and pullouts. The C-123 used the Farm Gate right-turn, racetrack pattern with strike aircraft breaking left after a strafing or bombing pass.[7]

Generally, within 15 or 20 minutes the C-123 flareships and strike aircraft could be over the hamlet or outpost under attack. Nonetheless, the aircraft were too few to prevent the enemy from expanding his night attacks. On most of these forays he captured large stores of weapons and FM radios and proved adept in ambushing ARVN convoys dispatched in relief. As the Air Force began its third year of operatins, it was estimated the enemy controlled, partially or completely, almost half of South Vietnam.[8]

Enemy antiaircraft fire increased alarmingly. During the month of October 1963 the Vietcong hit more aircraft than in all of 1962. Strike aircraft, notably those on night napalm runs under flares, constantly encountered barrage fire. The Air Force therefore changed its tactics. Fragmentation or antipersonnel bombs replaced napalm on many flights, giving the fighters a dive-zoom capability and short exposure under the flares. Because of accurate ground fire, the 2,500-foot optimum-dispensing altitude for the flareship was to become the minimum accepted altitude. Flaredrops from around 4,000 feet became standard thereby losing some accuracy.[9]

(U) Besides revised tactics, the Air Force required a new weapon system, one that could remain airborne for many hours, respond immediately, and pack the firepower to repel these enemy attacks. Seeking to satisfy this requirement, the Air Force improvised once more--modifying the C-47 flareship into the AC-47 Spooky gunship.

The AC-47 Gunship*

Early Development and Employment

Development of the side-firing gunship began in 1964 when the Air Force successfully adapted the General Electric SUU-11A minigun to the old C-47 airframe. The first aircraft was tested initially at Eglin AFB in 1964. A further operational evaluation in South Vietnam during late 1964 and 1965 proved the weapon system's capability for night support of hamlets and Special Forces camps.[10] Gen. John P. McConnell, Air Force Chief of Staff, highly praised the prototype's performance in South Vietnam noting its value in night hamlet defense in the absence of heavier strike aircraft. Although acknowledging the gunship's vulnerability to ground fire, the Air Force chief believed the immediate response characteristics of the gunship far outweighed this handicap.[11]

---

*A definitive study on USAF fixed-wing gunships is being prepared by Lt. Col. Jack S. Ballard, Historian, Office of Air Force History.

AC-47 Gunship

During November 1965, the 4th Air Commando Squadron from Forbes AFB, Kans., arrived at Tan Son Nhut AB with the first gunships. The aircraft had flown the Pacific unarmed, since armament would be installed later in South Vietnam. By the end of the year all gunships carried one or two miniguns. None had the full complement of three per aircraft.*12

The three gatling-type miniguns occupied the space on the left side of the AC-47, formerly the location of the forward cargo door and the first and third windows forward of that door. The pilot fired the miniguns electrically by pushing a button on his control column. He could fire the weapons singly, in pairs, or all three together. Each minigun held 16,500 7.62-mm ball-and-tracer rounds and could rake the enemy with 6,000 rounds-a-minute.13

---

*AC-47's were given several nicknames, the most popular being Puff the Magic Dragon, Dragon Ship, and Spooky. Puff was the call sign of the first prototype gunship in South Vietnam. The 4th Air Commando Squadron chose Spooky as more symbolic of their mission. [Hist (S), 14th Air Commando Wg, 1 Jan-30 Jun 66, footnote 2, p 42.]

The gunship generally carried 48 Mk-24 flares of 2-million-candlepower each. A pneumatic flare launcher was located on the left side of the aircraft in the fifth window forward of the main door. The loadmaster rarely used this device because it often broke down. Instead, as in Farm Gate operations, he threw most of the flares out the cargo door. Despite these minor problems, as 1965 drew to a close, the 4th Air Commando Squadron had flown 277 combat missions, dropped 2,458 flares, and expended 137,136 rounds of ammunition.[14]

Tactics and Techniques

The AC-47 Spooky gunship carried a crew of two pilots, a navigator, flight engineer, loadmaster, and two gunners. On occasion a VNAF observer was added. By 1965, however, the President had modified the rules of engagement to no longer require this observer aboard strike aircraft at night, if the mission

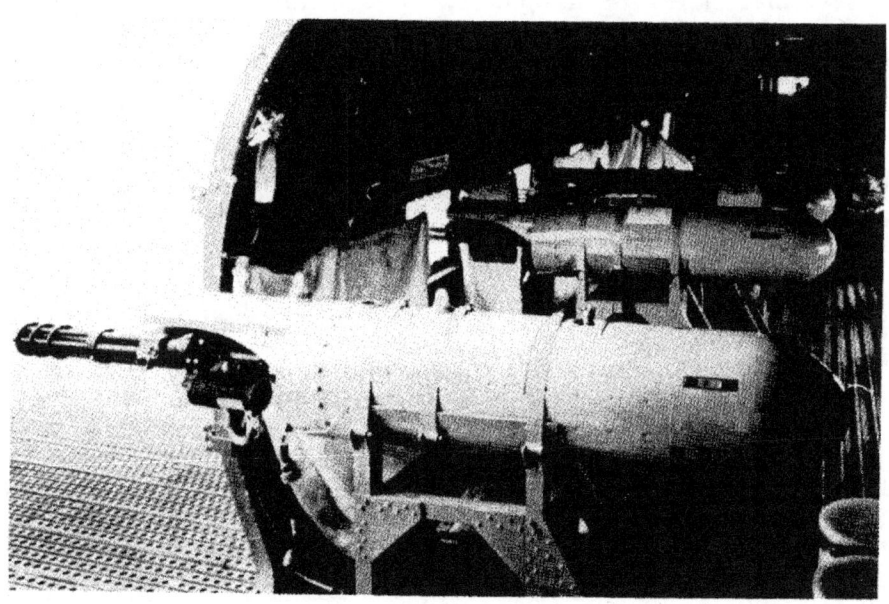

7.62-mm Miniguns on AC-47

was in defense of a hamlet or outpost.*15

   A request from a friendly unit in the field touched off the typical gunship fire-support mission. The unit's call for aid went through ARVN or U.S. Army channels to a direct air support center (DASC--one for each numbered corps area). If approved the Air Force fragged a gunship from airborne alert or ground posture to the target area. En route the crew reviewed all known target information such as type of target, terrain, weather and visibility, and emergency procedures. Flare fuzes were set and the gun-arming checklist completed down to "copilot arming switch."16

   Navigation to the target area continued to be dead reckoning or mapreading, aided by radio (TACAN)+ or vectors from ground radar stations. To help identify the target, the crew kept cockpit lights dim and used large-scale (1:250,000) maps with grid coordinates. The copilot contacted the ground commander on the ARC-44 FM radio to determine his location and defense status, enemy positions, and the type of support desired--either flares or firepower. Frequently, the initial contact was with an airborne forward air controller who supplied Spooky the information. Once in contact, the gunship dropped a flare for positive identification.17

   Most hamlets used the proven fire arrows and flares as marking devices. By 1965, however, several hamlets used

---

  *As late as October 1968, Spooky missions from Pleiku and Binh Thuy carried VNAF interpreters, those from Phan Rang and Bien Hoa did not. Need for an interpreter hinged on whether or not the operations supported the ARVN. Units from Phan Rang and Bien Hoa provided little ARVN support. What they did provide was directed by English-speaking controllers. [Ltr (C), Deputy Chief of Operations, 14th Special Operations Wing, to Dir, DASC Alpha, subj: Vietnamese Observers Aboard Spooky Aircraft, 24 Oct 68.]

  +A tactical air navigation system consisting of short-range UHF radio stations. In the form of a readout on the instrument panel the pilot continuously receives accurate distance and bearing information from the particular station tuned.

strobe lights. If displaying a light would reveal friendly positions, the ground controller talked the Spooky pilot onto the target by directing the gunship in relation to terrain features. Enemy positions were marked by tracer pyrotechnics, white phosphorous, or ground flares. Upon receiving the ground commander's and the DASC's clearance to attack, the pilot usually fired a short burst from one of the miniguns. This confirmed the target and minimized the risk of hitting friendly forces.[18]

After confirming the target, the pilot flew the aircraft straight and level, keeping the target just outside and forward of the left prop dome. He maintained an indicated airspeed (IAS) of 120 knots and a strike altitude between 2,500 and 3,500 feet AGL. The latter was often adjusted for such variables as weather, enemy ground fire, and target acquisition difficulties. As the target passed under the engine cowling, the pilot rolled the aircraft into a 30° bank,* flying a pylon turn. The actual angle of declination was now 42° for the miniguns, had a separate declination of 12°.+[19]

When the gunsight pipper‡ came on target, the pilot fired 3- to 7-second bursts since shorter ones might damage the guns. As he fired, the pilot fed in top rudder consistent with the angle of bank, duration of firing pass, and number of guns firing. Meanwhile, the copilot monitored the gunship's altitude and airspeed. He notified the pilot if the plane approached a dangerous altitude.[20]

Many times the pipper strayed from the target. If it moved to the <u>rear</u>, the pilot stopped firing, turned the gunship slightly <u>away</u> from the target, and repositioned for another firing pass. If the pipper moved off the target toward the <u>front</u> of the aircraft, the pilot <u>steepened</u> the bank and realigned on the target.[21]

---

*The maximum bank angle permitted was 60°. [Hist (S), 4th Air Commando Squadron, 1 Jan-30 Jun 66, II, 1.]

+The 12° declination of the miniguns was an intheater modification. It decreased the angle of bank the gunship had to fly, thus helping the pilot roll into his target. Too, the greater aircraft stability aided flare-dispensing/loading and maintenance of the guns. Finally, the declination decreased the slant range the gun had to fire, so that altitude could be increased with no appreciable operational loss. [Hist (S), 14th Air Commando Wing, 1 Jan-30 Jun 66, p 46.]

‡The center or bead of the minigun's ring gunsight.

At a slant range of about 8,000 feet, each 3-second minigun burst covered an elliptical area nearly 52 yards in diameter. Hence, as the gunship flew its left-hand orbit around the target, the guns swept the enemy with almost continuous fire. In addition, most pilots alternated between firing their guns in bursts and dropping flares.* By 1965 it took from 75 to 100 flares to support one hamlet at night for 2 or 3 hours.[22]

Out-Country Operations

The Spooky's long loiter time fitted it well for night armed reconnaissance, therefore, in late February 1966, the Air Force deployed four AC-47's to Thailand in support of the Laotian interdiction campaign (see Chapter IV). The gunships visually reconnoitered the network of roads and trails of the Ho Chi Minh Trail, over which the North Vietnamese and Pathet Lao infiltrated men and materiel into South Vietnam. The Spookies also served as FAC's to control strikes of other aircraft and, if need be, attacked on their own. Enemy antiaircraft fire, poor maps, marginal weather, hazardous terrain, and political restraints--all complicated this dual role and called forth new tactics and techniques.[23]

As FAC aircraft in Laos, the AC-47 shared battlefield command and control with the C-130's. The Spookies carried UHF, VHF, HF, and FM radio, plus TACAN and ADF (automatic direction finder). Thus, from a coordination/communications standpoint, the gunships proved a good substitute for the new

---

*Parachute flares were expensive, costing almost $75.00 each. [Kenneth Sams, First Test and Combat Use of the AC-47 (S) (HQ PACAF, Project CHECO, 8 Dec 65), pp 4-5.

Figure 2 (U)

airborne battlefield command and control center (ABCCC) C-130's then in the theater.*24

When strike aircraft were fragged, one AC-47 went on station in Northern Laos (Barrel Roll). Among its crew were an operations officer, an intelligence officer, and a Laotian Air Force representative. The AC-47 managed all fighter and FAC aircraft entering the area, including strike aircraft diverted from North Vietnam or Southern Laos (Steel Tiger/Tiger Hound). As the fighters checked in, the gunship assigned them to a specific FAC. It also diverted fighters from assigned targets to more lucrative ones as necessary. In this politically sensitive climate, the Laotian crewmember was the sole person under the rules of engagement who could validate immediate-response targets. Many times a target fell in a gray area. For instance, a truck park located next to a village being contested for by both government and enemy forces. The Laotian observer could resolve any doubt of a target's validity within minutes by calling Vientiane or Savannakhet on the single-side-band radio.[25]

When acting as a FAC, the gunship generally flew at 4,000 feet AGL and kept clear of strike aircraft. The AC-47's pattern depended on terrain, weather, ground fire, wind, and the target itself. The gunship/FAC furnished the fighter target identification, type of ordnance required and direction of its expenditure, location of enemy ground fire, terrain elevation, and emergency instructions in event the strike aircraft sustained battle damage.[26] The AC-47 proved an adequate and necessary substitute as a FAC but it was not well suited to the job. The view from the cockpit was poor. Moreover, the gunship maneuvered too slowly and could not mark the target with ground flares.[27]

Besides controlling other aircraft strikes, the gunships flew armed reconnaissance and attacked on their own. Flying out of Da Nang and Pleiku in South Vietnam as well as Ubon and Udorn in Thailand, the AC-47's navigated blacked out to a specific geographic area. There they dropped flares to detect enemy vehicles moving along the lines of communication (LOC). When a gunship pinpointed a target, it turned around,

---

*Chapter IV treats the ABCCC operation in more detail.

followed the road, and fired at the vehicles as they passed under the prop dome. If the target was a truck park, for example, the aircraft executed a pylon-turn attack.[28]

Another "truck-buster" system linked gunships with indigenous roadwatch teams. Staging from Udorn two AC-47's took off at 1800 and 2400, respectively, following a preset schedule that allowed at least four contacts a night with each ground team. As the Spooky navigated to a team, the Laotian on board contacted it by radio. When a convoy of trucks or other moving target passed, the team notified the gunship which flew along the road dropping flares. Acquiring the target, the AC-47 either opened fire or called for additional strike aircraft. This system destroyed 243 trucks from mid-December 1965 to mid-July 1966, until a buildup of enemy antiaircraft defenses made further AC-47 operations along the Ho Chi Minh Trail too dangerous. After losing four aircraft and 26 crewmembers in 6 months of operations over Laos, the Air Force withdrew the AC-47's and reassigned them to hamlet defense. The refurbished On-Mark B-26's took over Laotian operations from the gunships.[29]

Problem Areas

The design of the AC-47 made it hard for the crew to see ground targets and ground markers. It demanded fine coordination for a flare/gunship to spot smoke from target markers and keep it in view long enough to establish a flare pattern or pylon turn. Starting a ground fire or two for direction reference helped the AC-47 pilot acquire the target and also assisted the strike pilot.[30] High winds further hampered gunship operations causing flare drops to become quite erratic and large wind corrections made it difficult to maintain the pylon turn. The gunsight could not compensate for wind and the use of "Kentucky windage" reduced accuracy.[31]

Vulnerability to ground fire imposed the most severe limits on AC-47 operations. Below 2,500 feet AGL--the lowest permissible operating altitude--the slow-moving gunship came under enemy small arms fire.[32] Again, flares dropped below 2,500 feet hit the ground while still burning, depriving friendly troops of the AC-47's full capability to light up the area. Flares dropped through overcast silhouetted the aircraft against the clouds exposing it to ground fire. Hence, as in Mule Train operations, the minimum acceptable altitude for effective gunship operations remained at 2,500 feet.[33]

(U) In summary, the AC-47 proved an effective improvised weapon, especially in defense of strategic hamlets. It could cruise for many hours and illuminate targets with flares. Its miniguns could rake the enemy with fairly accurate fire, particularly troops in the open. Although later phased out of both the USAF and VNAF inventories, the aircraft continued to be effective in the defense of "Lima Sites" in Barrel Roll through 1970.

C-130 Blindbat Operations

A buildup of American ground and air forces occurred after the Gulf of Tonkin incident in August 1964. As part of it, the Air Force placed portions of the C-130 Hercules fleet on extended temporary duty to South Vietnam. In April 1965, the 315th Air Division dispatched four Hercules transports to Tan Son Nhut to deliver a cargo backlog that in-country resources could not handle. By the end of the year the C-130 fleet had expanded to 30 aircraft, operating from five bases in South Vietnam and one base in Thailand. The Laos interdiction effort, meanwhile, picked up momentum and the Air Force relieved the C-130's operating from Da Nang of airlift duties and assigned them an out-country flareship mission. In March 1966, this operation and six aircraft shifted to Ubon, Thailand.[34]

The C-130's operating in southern Laos were nicknamed Blindbat; those in northern Laos and North Vietnam, Lamplighter. Eventually, however, Blindbat became the accepted nickname for all C-130 flare missions. These aircraft were normal production models with no armor and wet (unprotected) fuel tanks. Hence they flew only in areas relatively free of enemy antiaircraft (AA) guns and primarily furnished night flare support for strike aircraft attacking enemy traffic on the Ho Chi Minh Trail. They also supplied the customary flare support of friendly forces, served as a backup ABCCC, and flew weather reconnaissance as required.[35] The following figure depicts a later C-130 FAC/flareship, fitted with armor and a night observation device:

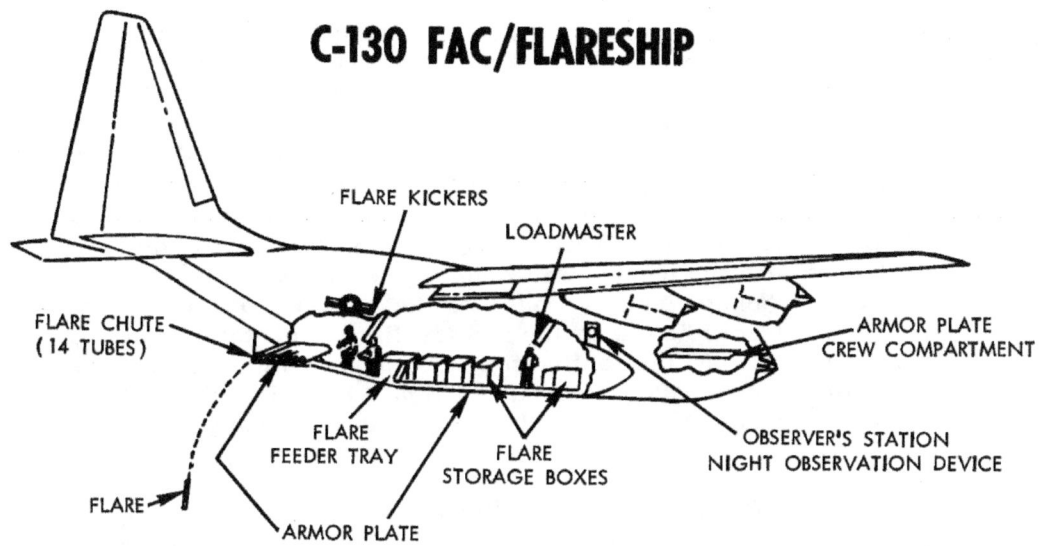

Figure 3 (U)

During this period the Mk-24 parachute flare replaced the old Mk-6. The two timers on this new 1,650,000- to 1,900,000-candlepower flare adjusted parachute deployment and ignition to the uneven Southeast Asia terrain. The Mk-24 fell at the rate of 900 feet a minute, burned around 3 minutes, illuminated a circular area about 1 mile in radius, and could also be rigged to burn as a ground marker.* Moreover, the Air Force continued to use the Mk-6 as a ground target marker (log). The Mk-6's white pinpoint of light lingered for about 45 minutes, resembling a burning log from the air. A C-130 generally carried 250 Mk-24 flares and 30 Mk-6 ground marker logs.36

---

*As a ground marker, the Mk-24 flare burned too briefly and had a high dud rate. Investigations showed the duds stemmed from production defects--one producer's flare dud rate reached 10-15 percent. [Hq PACAF, In-country and Out-country Strike Operations in Southeast Asia, 1 Jan 65-31 Dec 69, II, Hardware Strike Aircraft (S), Oct 70, pp 118-120.]

The typical Blindbat mission during 1965-1967 started at a selected rendezvous point where strike aircraft joined the flareship before proceeding to the target. This point, 35-50 miles from the target, was furnished to strike and flareship units by Seventh Air Force frag order. Here, flying at 20,000 feet and 210 knots indicated airspeed (KIAS), the C-130 flew a right hand pattern. The pattern was designed so its inbound heading enabled the flareship and strike aircraft to start descending into the combat area after join-up. Airborne beacon radar aided the rendezvous. Nonetheless, because of the constant danger of swift strike aircraft colliding with the slower flareship, the C-130 Blindbats turned on their anticollision, topside wing, and fuselage lights. In the dark murky sky these lights helped each pilot make a safe rendezvous. At other times the flareship flew blacked out.*37

As in Farm Gate operations, two fighters normally made up the strike element. The fighters entered the rendezvous area 2,000 feet above the flareship. After join-up they accelerated to 250 KIAS and began descending to 6,500 feet AGL. The strike element stayed high and behind the flareship, usually 2,000 feet above and in the 4:30 or 7:30 o'clock position.+ The fighters kept the C-130's navigation lights constantly in view.38

Upon penetrating the armed reconnaissance (recce) area, the C-130 commander alerted the strike leader to a possible flare drop. A similar notification took place when he detected enemy activity and decided to drop flares or a ground marker. The number of flares to be dropped and the time interval between each release depended on the terrain and type of target. A bridge, for example, required fewer flares than trucks traveling along a main supply route. The flareship dispensed its first stack of 12 Mk-24 flares at 6,000 feet with flare ignition set for 3,000 feet. (As enemy AA defenses grew, flare drop altitudes varied

---

*Join-up techniques employed by specific aircraft are described in this section in very broad general terms. Later chapters will discuss in greater depth jet fighyer-bomber tactics and techniques involving flareships.

+In clock code the dead-ahead position of the flareship was 12 o'clock.

from 7,500-10,000 feet.) Once Blindbat dropped the first group of flares, it began the standard right-hand racetrack pattern. In a successful drop the flares ignited over the target just as the strike aircraft turned on their base leg. After the first pass the strike leader turned left and notified the flareship whether or not further flaredrops were needed. He could also provide a refined drift correction or new targets in the strike area.*39 (See figure 4).

The C-130 Blindbats flew a different mission profile when serving as flareship and forward air controller.+ The flare/controller aircraft left its operating base in sufficient time to meet the fragged time over target (TOT). As a rule, the pilot kept the C-130's enroute altitude at 10,000 feet AGL. About 10 minutes before reaching the recce area, the aircraft descended to flaredrop altitude (5,000-7,000) feet, depressurized, and the pilot alerted the crew for the start of flaredrop operations.40

Upon entering the target area the flareship flew to the fragged target. However, if none had been scheduled the flareship asked the ABCCC for any available target of opportunity. In event the ABCCC had no traffic for Blindbat, the plane reconnoitered on its own such potential targets as roads, rivers, and suspected truck parks. By 1968, the Air Force had equipped the C-130's with a night observation device (NOD), mounted either in the right paradrop door or right escape hatch. This improved starlight scope amplified reflected surrounding light,‡ and proved excellent for detecting truck traffic at night. Two years later, a

---

*During flare release the pilot held the flareship at 250 KIAS. By September 1965 flaredrop altitude had climbed to 8,000 feet. [See PACAF Tactics and Techniques Bulletin 22 (C), 6002d Stan/Eval Gp, 14 Sep 65.] Strike pilots interviewed said that by 1968 flaredrop altitude in enemy-defended areas of Laos had risen to 11,000 feet.

+The 374th TAWg conducted a 1 1/2-day FAC school at Ubon for their crews. [Summary Sheet (S), 7th AF Tac Tng to 7th AF Dir/Ops, Gunship II, 26 Feb 68.]

‡See the C-123 Section of Chapter III for a detailed discussion of the NOD. Pave Way tactics are to be found in the appropriate section of Chapter V.

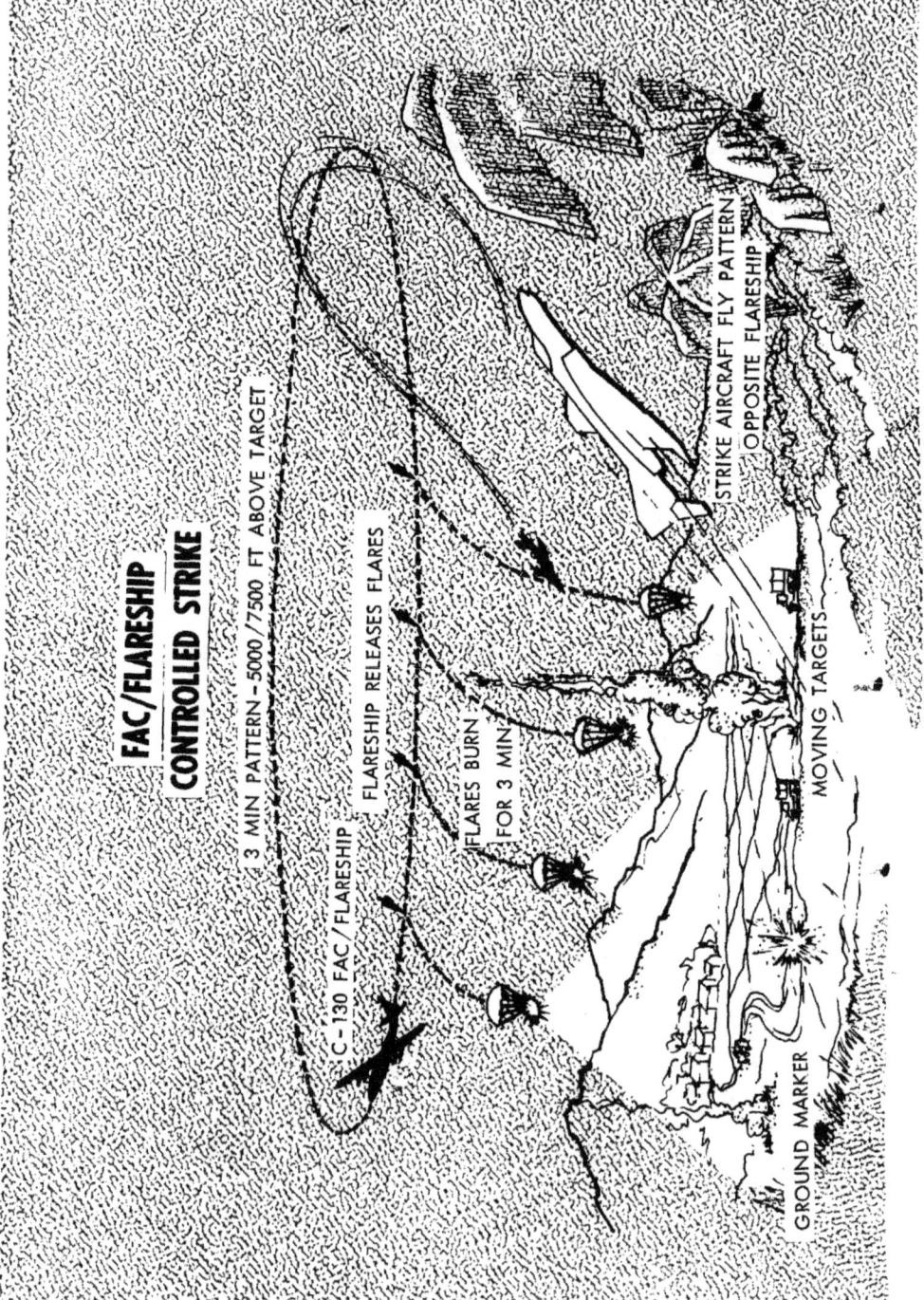

Figure 4

objects and terrain features before returning for visual display on the scope. After transferring the scope image to film, the Mohawk observer developed it in about 3 minutes. Next he scanned the film for the black dots denoting targets, then passed the information to U.S. Army units or the C-130 flareship.[46]

The C-model Spud provided infrared Red Haze coverage. A passive detector, Red Haze emitted no radar pulses for the enemy to discover. Instead, it produced detailed imagery by sensing temperature variations in the terrain and objects on the ground. These heat differences appeared on film that could not be viewed in the aircraft. The Spud observer used his infrared scope for the actual picture, whereupon he radioed target information to Army units, Blindbat, or waiting strike aircraft.[47]

The OV-1C Mohawks lifted off at sundown. Flying at 2,000 feet AGL and 150-250 knots they conducted infrared missions along the LOC's in Laos or other areas of suspected enemy activity. Too low to effectively use TACAN, these Spuds navigated mainly by doppler radar* and mapreading. Moving up and down the roads the OV-1C dropped a marker log at the spot where it received a significant infrared ground return.+ Following behind, Blindbat illuminated the area with a stick of flares and called in strike aircraft to hit trucks or other targets fleeing the vicinity. If a target's validity was questioned--for instance, a target discovered by an OV-1B's SLAR--an infrared C model might cover the same area to secure confirmation. If doubt remained the strike was called off. Frequently an OV-1A--the photo reconnaissance version of the Spud--flew over the area the next day to obtain better information. Another determination as to the target's validity was then made.[48]

---

*A radar system which differentiates between fixed and moving targets by detecting the apparent change in frequency of the reflected wave due to motion of target or the observer.

+For infrared to be effective the Spud had to fly beneath cloud levels. Infrared was ineffective in severe weather. [Montagliani, Army Aviation in RVN, previously cited, p 57.]

Problems Associated with Blindbat Operations

Flaring enemy supply routes often presented a difficult problem to Blindbat crews. Flares dropped parallel to a major highway were commonly on the same path the strike aircraft had to take. This put flares both in front and behind the strike aircraft at the critical bomb-release point. This forced the attack pilot to make his bomb run through the flare pattern, risking collision with descending flares. In some cases, the problem was alleviated by having the flares dropped perpendicular to the strike heading. This not only put the light directly over the target and ahead of the strike aircraft during the attack, but exposed the aircraft to minimum enemy antiaircraft fire.[49]

The use of ground marker logs for target acquisition overcame many disadvantages of the air-launched flares. In forests or mountains, however, the logs were hard to see from all angles and the enemy created confusion by lighting decoy flares. As a countermeasure, the Air Force used the LUU-1B red-burning or LUU-5 green-burning marker. This type of modified Mk-24 flare excelled the white Mk-6 in distinct color and higher intensity. Nonetheless, the difficulty in attaining accurate delivery of ground markers persisted. For example, in areas heavily defended by antiaircraft artillery the C-130 dropped the logs from a relatively high altitude, exposing them to wind drift during descent. It was not uncommon to have a log land one-quarter mile or more from the target. As a result, the strike aircraft could only estimate the target's exact location; so more often than not the enemy's trucks or supplies escaped destruction.*[50]

---

*According to the O-2 FAC's of the 20th Tactical Support Squadron, the Blindbat aircraft also were "very prone to indiscriminate flare dropping" which caused problems to the forward air controller trying to spot the enemy. Premature flaring, they said, lost them many targets and they insisted that: "Flaring must be done just prior to ordnance delivery." [Ltr (S), 20th Tac Air Support Sq to 7th AF Dir/Tng, Tac Tng.] But it should be noted that the Blindbat crews were not flare-trained as were, for example, the C-123 Candlestick crews; they were primarily airlift specialists on TDY rotation to Ubon from bases in Taiwan. The new crews in the rotation were unfamiliar with target geography, FAC methods, various tactical delivery patterns, enemy defenses, etc. This unfamiliarity often caused delays in setting up attacks or resulted in excessive caution due to misidentification of ground fire. The Blindbat experience highlights the fact that night operations require dedicated, full-time units.

The automatic flare dispenser also gave the C-130 crew trouble. Locally manufactured, it was locked in place on the aircraft ramp in the firing position. The crew could use this independent pneumatic system either manually or electrically to drop flares in any combination, sequence, or time interval. In addition, two plywood racks secured to the ramp held 15 prearmed flares. Unfortunately, the flare launcher blocked the secondary bailout exits, the flares struck the fuselage when ejected, and their storage boxes were too heavy.[51]

The Air Force, therefore, installed another flare launcher, known as the LAU-62, in the C-130. Manually loaded and operated, it consisted of 14 semicircular tubes. Twelve were loaded with Mk-24 flares, the remainder were used for jettisoning Mk-24's or releasing Mk-6 marker logs. Spring-loaded retaining bars held the flares in the 12 launching chutes. A steel rod connected each bar to a direct-leverage launch handle on the inboard side of each chute. Storage boxes or racks and a flare-feeding ramp eased movement of the flares to the launcher.[52] Tests in February 1968 found the LAU-62 too expensive, too heavy, and the buildup time excessive to configure it for the average 7-hour mission. Consequently, C-130 crews continued to drop flares and markers by hand.[53]

As the 1969-70 dry season in Laos ended, the Air Force decided to withdraw the Blindbats from service and replace them with a B-57G Tropic Moon III squadron.* Actually, the Air Force was approaching the upper limit of its manpower ceiling in Thailand. If a new unit was brought in, a unit already there had to be taken out. Blindbat, with its limited flare/FAC capability, seemed the logical choice to go. The flare mission had become obsolete and the large C-130's took up considerable ramp space at Ubon. So in June 1970--as the southwest monsoon began in earnest--the Blindbats left Thailand.[54] For all practical purposes the USAF flareship era in Southeast Asia had come to a close.

---

*See Chapter IV. These modified B-57G Canberras were equipped with low-light-level television (LLLTV), forward-looking infrared radar (FLIR), and forward-looking radar/MTI, plus an advanced digital computer system for target tracking and straight-and-level weapon delivery.

Summary

In Southeast Asia operations the flareships proved quite successful in the hamlet/outpost defense role, but only partly so over the Ho Chi Minh Trail in Laos. The explanation lay in the flares. A tremendous light source, they worked as much against the strike crews as for them. The moment flares ignited the element of surprise departed. The enemy either pulled his trucks off the road and under the jungle canopy, or opened up with his antiaircraft batteries. If the flareships delivered the flares inaccurately or some of them were duds, the strike crews found it almost impossible to properly identify the target and effectively deliver the ordnance. Again, the flares swinging during descent intensified ground glare, caused shadows, and disoriented the pilot. Further, the flare light blinded the crews and blotted out the target during final run-in. And on climb-out the pilot suffered vertigo as he flew in and out of the light. Little wonder, then, that most strike crews wanted to hit the enemy's trucks by moonlight to preserve the element of surprise, or solely use marker logs as an aid. [55]

For night strike operations the flareships served merely as a stopgap. The Air Force sorely needed a single aircraft, equipped to spot targets at night and to deliver weapons on these targets. While the night detection/attack gap had narrowed a trifle, much remained to be done. By 1966, only 10 percent of all USAF sorties in South Vietnam and Laos were flown at night.[*] At the same time, the enemy moved 80 percent of his vehicular traffic under the cover of darkness. [56]

(U) In 1952, French Air Force General G. J. M. Chaussin[+] had pointed up the need to strip away the cloak of darkness that shielded enemy movements:

---

[*]During July-December 1965, only 28 percent of the total airstrikes over North Vietnam occurred at night. This percentile climbed in the first half of 1966 due to an increase in Navy--not Air Force--sorties. [Memo (S), Dir/Tac Eval Cen to 7th AF Dir/Ops, subj: Time of Air Strikes Over NVN [ca Feb 66].]

[+]General Chaussin commanded the French Air Forces in Indochina during the Indochina War.

> As long as the air force cannot intervene at
> night with the same efficiency as during the day, it
> will never be the decisive weapon it should be. For
> that, it must be able to navigate in safety and crews
> must be able to <u>see</u>... The teeming Vietminhs on
> the paths beneath the trees really have to be "seen,"
> and this...is extremely difficult even by day.[57]

Technology held the key to the problem. The ideal solution would be a new aircraft of sufficient range and loiter time, combining heavy accurate firepower with the speed, maneuverability, and armor of the jet fighter-bomber. Augmenting these characteristics would be supersensitive devices or "eyes." But ideal solutions often never get off the drawing board or, if they do, sometimes wind up like the World War II Luftwaffe's ME-262--too little, too late!

In early 1966, the Air Force started Operation Shed Light. This high priority program's first phase was to develop new sensors, illumination devices, navigation aids, and visual weapon delivery systems. Some devices, like new flares, would be ready in a year. Others, such as the self-contained night attack (SCNA) aircraft, would take at least 3-7 years.[58]

In Shed Light, the Air Force faced for the first time the serious shortcomings of its night interdiction effort. Determined to go beyond mere improvisation in correcting them, the Air Force set up Shed Light offices at its headquarters, as well as the headquarters of Air Force Systems Command (AFSC) and the Aeronautical Systems Division (ASD). The program received $23.2 million for fiscal year 1966, $81 million the following year. In February 1967, there were 65 Shed Light projects under way; by early 1968 the number had climbed to 100. Projects included such night detection devices as side-looking airborne radar, forward-looking infrared (FLIR), and low-light-level television (LLTV). The Air Force looked to Shed Light for the sophisticated night detection devices to strengthen night interdiction operations-- especially to choke off the enemy logistic flow over the Ho Chi Minh Trail.[59]

III. NIGHT INTERDICTION

The aim of the Air Force's armed reconnaissance and interdiction campaign in Southeast Asia was to impede the logistics flow from North Vietnam into the south. To this end the Air Force attacked the road and trail network and the numerous mountain passes connecting these transportation arteries. This complex lacing of passes, rivers, and trails formed the LOC popularly known as the Ho Chi Minh Trail. The airmen tried to pinch off the flow of men and materiel over the Trail. They cut it at vulnerable points, destroyed supply areas and truck parks, and detected and attacked vehicles, sampans, pack animals, and porters.[1]

(U) This chapter reviews Air Force tactics and techniques employed in the night interdiction campaign in the Laotian panhandle. Beginning 1964 there were two separate and distinct wars being fought in the small mountainous kingdom of Laos. One, nicknamed Steel Tiger,* involved the interdiction of the road/trail network in the panhandle of central and southern Laos. The other, Barrel Roll was in the northeast between Pathet Lao/North Vietnamese troops and Royal Laotian Government (RLG) forces. It primarily pitted friendly Meo guerrillas under the command of Maj. Gen. Vang Pao--himself an ethnic Meo--against Communist regular/unconventional forces. What made Barrel Roll unique was that the United States used air power rather than ground forces to support the guerrillas.+ The Air Force performed the traditional close-support role but occasionally interdicted enemy LOC's and supply depots in the area. In the strategic sense, Barrel Roll was a self-contained action--its target supply lines separate from the LOC network feeding the Vietcong/North Vietnamese insurgency in South Vietnam.[2]

---

*The Air Force waged a similar interdiction campaign against the enemy's LOC's in the panhandle of North Vietnam. Such sorties fell under the operations order governing attacks in the northern area of Vietnam (coded Rolling Thunder).

+This author currently is writing a separate history on "The Secret War" in Laos.

Meanwhile, the insurgency in South Vietnam had grown to alarming proportions by mid-1964. The ARVN had suffered countless defeats and wholesale desertions were common. At the same time, the North Vietnamese had escalated the insurgency into an invasion. To adequately support it, however, demanded a steady flow of supplies. In the beginning, the enemy relied on rather large stocks previously stored in hidden areas within South Vietnam and Cambodia. When these dwindled, he had to establish a permanent feeder network from North Vietnam. Hence the Ho Chi Minh trail became the conduit for supplying enemy forces in the south.[3]

The Ho Chi Minh Trail: Description and Geography

(U) The anti-Japanese guerrillas in World War II, and the Viet Minh during the Indochina War with France, traveled the tortuous trails and footpaths, later to be known as the Ho Chi Minh Trail. Following the 1954 division of Vietnam along the 17th parallel, the trail became an avenue to the south for North Vietnamese agents and Communist-indoctrinated returnees. Eventually this network of jungle trails evolved into a dry-season truck route. In 1964, the enemy's vehicular traffic moved through the Nape and Mu Gia passes in North Vietnam to Thaket, thence to Tchepone and other points in southern Laos. There various feeder lines, including waterways, extended into South Vietnam and Cambodian sanctuaries. By 1965, after immense labor, the enemy added bypasses and turnouts and cut at least 600 miles of new roads, mostly through dense jungle.[4]

Meanwhile, logistic support facilities kept pace with the road network. For example, the enemy set up a major depot area near Tchepone, Laos, and garrisoned it with North Vietnamese units. Camps and way stations--for road workers, equipment, and porters--were secreted under a triple canopy of foliage every few miles. Besides the large amount of human labor they employed to maintain roads, the Vietcong/North Vietnamese also used a surprising quantity of mechanized equipment, from bulldozers to trucks.*[5]

---
*The Vietcong/North Vietnamese used elephants and water buffalo extensively in road building. By 1967 the North Vietnamese employed an estimated 15,000-20,000 laborers in the maintenance, construction, and improvement of roads. [Rprt of Joint Technical Coordinating Group (JTCG/ME) for Munitions Effectiveness (S), 1967.]

Militarily, the Ho Chi Minh Trail had expanded by the end of 1966 into a LOC that posed an extremely difficult target system for effective air interdiction. The trail's Laotian routes contained no major bridges. The most promising chokepoints appeared to be mountain passes, but the ingenious enemy spanned these barriers with many new and alternate roads. He erected camouflage trellises over stretches of road not hidden by natural jungle canopy, and replaced conventional crossings at many streams with underwater bridges.６

In addition, the enemy heavily defended the trail from air attack. During 1966, he built nearly 3,000 gun positions along the LOC's and at road junctions, truck parks, and bivouac areas. The weapons were often relocated to meet changing priorities, surprise unsuspecting aircraft, or prevent strikes against pinpointed antiaircraft sites. To assure flexible and rapid deployment, the guns in all important areas had several prepared positions to fire from--many of them camouflaged. The North Vietnamese even went so far as to construct dummy sites manned by wooden guns.*７

It was against this strongly defended and complicated network of roads, rivers, trails, and footpaths that the Air Force directed its interdiction campaign.⁺ In 1966, the system's total capacity was an estimated 300 tons of supplies a day infiltrated into South Vietnam along with thousands of troops a month. The Air Force conceded that complete stoppage of this logistic flow through

---

*Reminiscent of Gen. John Magruder's deception of Gen. George S. McClellan during the 1862 Peninsula Campaign. A former Shakespearian actor, Gen. Magruder was charged with delaying Gen. McClellan at Yorktown to gain more time for Gen. Robert E. Lee. His soldiers felled, stripped, and placed many trees on dummy gun carriages. Viewing this formidable array of "cannon" from a distance, General McClellan delayed his push toward Richmond, calling for heavy siege mortars. By the time the mortars arrived, Lee was better prepared and Magruder abandoned Yorktown. When the Union Army finally advanced, it was quite chagrined to discover the dummy or "Quaker" guns in the fort.

⁺The roads were one lane with a width of 8-12 feet. Width of the typical trail was 3 feet.

the network was virtually impossible. Nonetheless, it wanted to cut the infiltration of men and materiel from a river to a trickle, and make the cost of supporting the pipeline prohibitive to the North Vietnamese.8

(U) Considering the topography of Laos, however, night interdiction--based mainly on "eyeball" reconnaissance and attack techniques--would be a formidable task. Topography closely affected air operations, and the Ho Chi Minh Trail meandered through some of the most rugged terrain in Southeast Asia if not the world. Except for the Plain of Jarres and the area adjacent to the Mekong River, little of Laos had been cleared for cultivation. Much of the remainder was mountainous or covered by dense tropical rain forest. The multicanopied forests contained trees of varying heights, averaging in some areas 150 feet or more. Sunlight could not penetrate the foliage, and the fairly clean forest floor made for ideal footpaths and even roadways. From the air these routes seemed unusable, when in reality "human ant" movement by foot, oxcart, and bicycle was taking place.*9

(U) Laos and South Vietnam contained the Annamite Chain, a group of rugged and steep mountains. Limestone karsts,+ honeycombed with caves and towering 5,000-8,000 feet were the chief physiographic feature. Usually a karst stood alone, its steeply rounded or vertical sides overgrown with foliage and its top veiled by thick clouds. The karsts were very hard to see at night.10

(U) Monsoon weather dictated not only where and how extensively the enemy could operate his LOC's, but where and how extensively the Air Force could interdict them. During the southwest monsoon, washouts, floods, slides, and knee-deep mud limited movement over the trail. Cloud cover and low visibility hampered the detection of aircraft by enemy gunners. These conditions also restricted takeoffs from airfields in Thailand and made visual reconnaissance of roads and waterways almost impossible. Additionally, airmen had to use all-weather bombing

---
*The Joint Technical Coordinating Group estimated that a well-balanced bicycle could carry up to 200 pounds. A porter could manage 40 to 60 pounds.
+karst--a limestone region marked by sinks and interspersed with abrupt ridges, irregular protuberant rocks, caverns, and underground streams.

techniques that were inherently less accurate than visual methods. Thus, inclement weather hindered and reduced operations on both sides.[11]

Furthermore, to visually acquire and attack targets at night--particularly trucks--was a difficult job even under ideal conditions. An aircraft without a target and acquisition system faced an enormous task in attacking moving vehicles at night. Many times the pilot found the target obscured and turned to the forward air controller for its description. Then the degree of success rested on the quality of illumination and the FAC's ability to locate, mark, and describe the target in relation to visible reference points. Such factors as spatial disorientation, high-density traffic, limited aircraft performance, enemy defenses, and marginal detection devices--all heightened the difficulty.[12]

If a crew did successfully detect and track a moving target, it still demanded a precise attack of almost perfect accuracy to destroy it. The illustrations on pages 53-55 graphically highlight the problems confronting the strike crews. Note that the dive angle, bombing altitude, and airspeed have to stay within specific tolerances to achieve success. Because these criteria proved difficult to meet, a compensating factor such as incendiary munitions had to be introduced. Napalm and similar munitions that would simply start a fire were not enough. Specifically, munitions were required that could provide wide-area coverage, penetrate the multicanopy jungle, and attain a high percentage of kills against vehicles and personnel without the need for extreme delivery accuracy.

The United States Begins Air Operations in Laos

The USAF effort in Laos began in May 1964 when the Joint Chiefs of Staff ordered CINCPAC to use Air Force and Navy aircraft for medium-and low-level reconnaissance over the Plain of Jarres. At that time the area was being fought over by Pathet Lao and loyalist forces. These RF-101 Yankee Team flights originated from Tan Son Nhut and were publicly acknowledged by the State Department. The latter was quick to point out, however, that the Lao government requested the reconnaissance

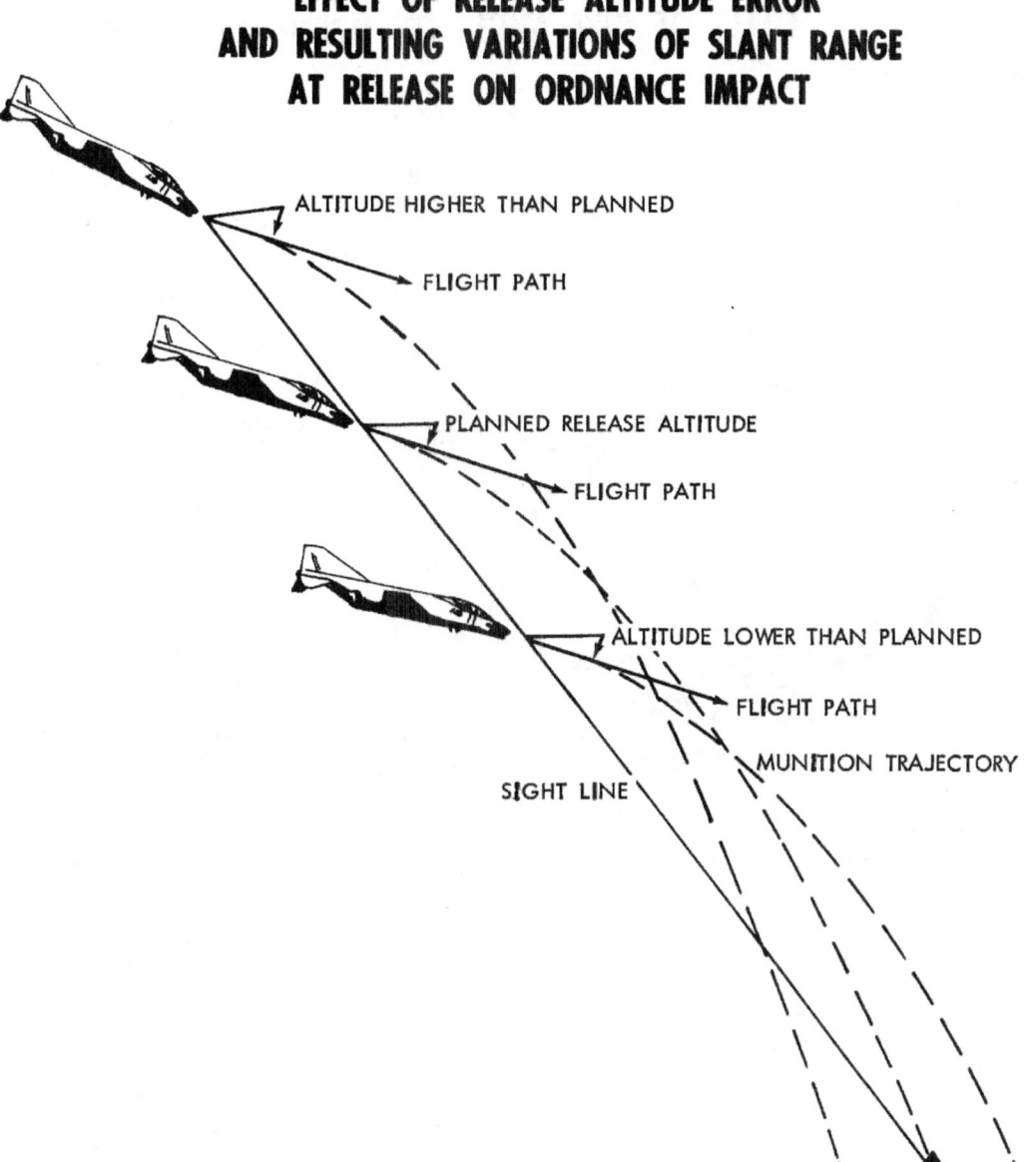

Figure 5

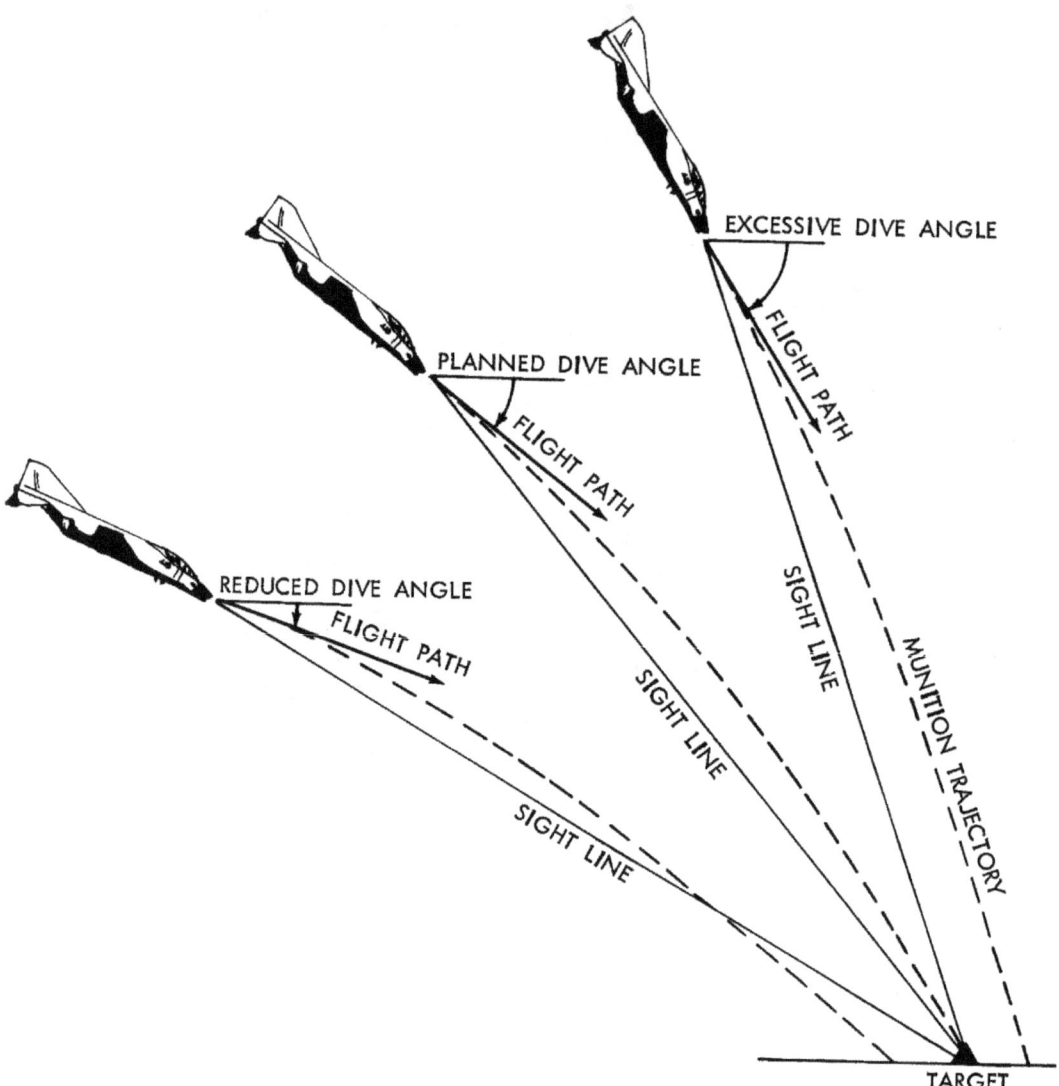

Figure 6

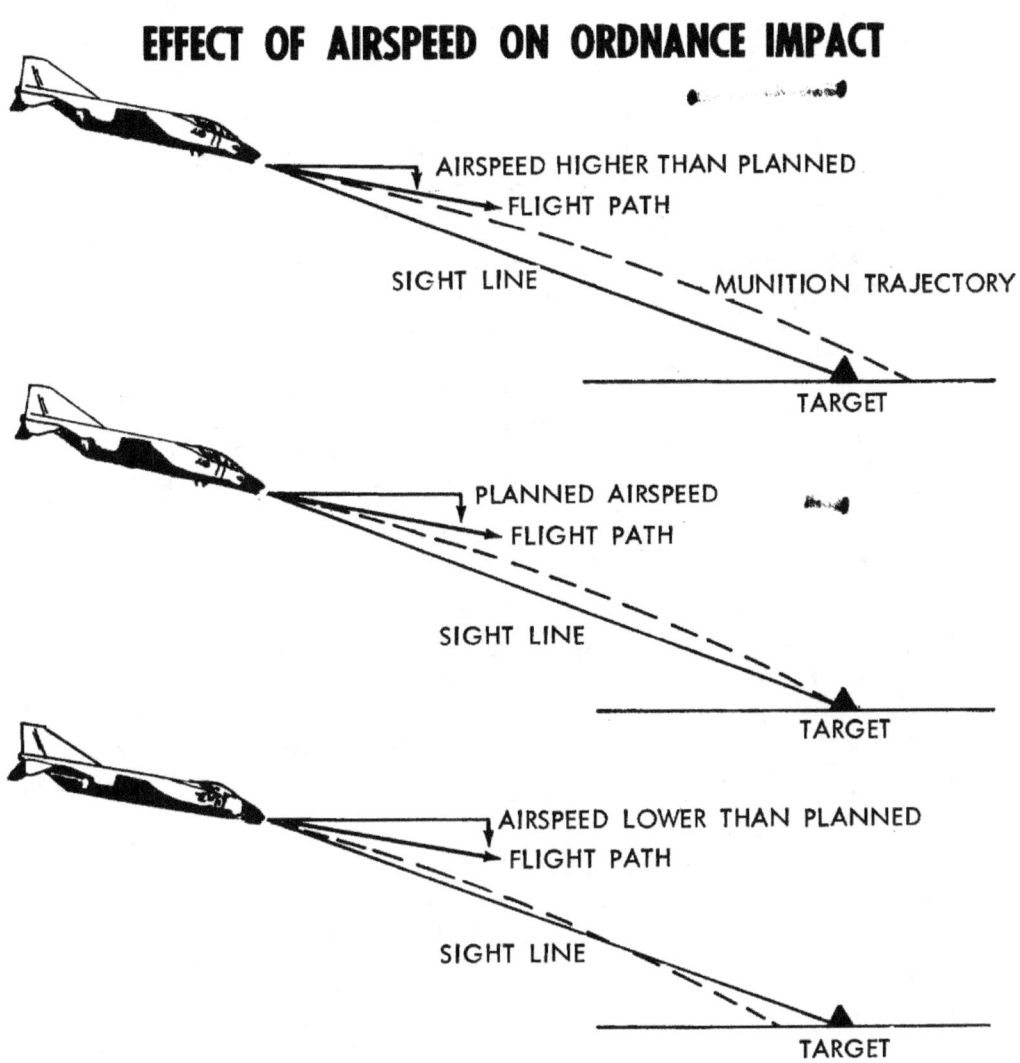

Figure 7

because the International Control Commission (ICC) could not obtain information about recent attacks on neutralist and right-wing forces.*13

Late in May 1964 the JCS extended the Yankee Team missions indefinitely. When two U.S. Navy planes were downed over Laos in June, the armed escorts of reconnaissance aircraft were authorized--with restrictions to return enemy fire. On 18 and 21 November, two USAF Yankee Team aircraft, an F-100 and RF-101, also fell to enemy ground fire. Gen. Maxwell D. Taylor, then serving as the U.S. Ambassador to South Vietnam, discussed the problem with the National Security Council (NSC) and other top U.S. officials. In early December the President approved several very limited and highly controlled measures for exerting pressure on North Vietnam. These included strikes on enemy infiltration routes and facilities in Laos. Nicknamed Barrel Roll, the missions began 14 December 1964.†14

From the outset, the very nature of the out-country war worked against any systematic attack of the Ho Chi Minh Trail. Technically speaking, Laos was a neutral country--a neutrality guaranteed by the Geneva Accords of 1954 and a declaration of the 14-nation Geneva conference signed on 23 July 1962. As Premier, Souvanna Phouma headed a tenuous coalition of leftists, rightists, and neutralists. He quickly found this neutrality in constant jeopardy from Communist-led Pathet Lao violations and North Vietnam's massive infiltration of men and materiel to the Vietcong over the Ho Chi Minh Trail.15

---

*The ICC, created by the 1954 Geneva Accords, consisted of Canada, India, and Poland. Terminated in 1959 upon request of the Laotians, the commission was revived in 1961 to set up a cease-fire in the kingdom. The ICC could either investigate suspected violations on its own or at the request of the RLG. [See testimony of Ambassador Sullivan, 20-22 Oct 69, in Hearings before the Senate Subcmte, Cmte on Foreign Relations 91st Cong., 1st sess., U.S. Security Agreements and Commitments Abroad-Kingdom of Laos pp 426-27.

†Early air operations in Laos were coded Barrel Roll. After 3 April 1965, the panhandle and central area of the country was identified as Steel Tiger. This was the region that became synonymous with the interdiction program.

When Prince Souvanna Phouma reluctantly agreed to U.S. strikes on North Vietnamese targets in Laos, it was with the implicit understanding the United States must not publicly acknowledge its active Laotian role. He did not want to give the Communists any pretext for stepping up the struggle or furnish grist for their propaganda mill. <u>Publicly</u>, Laos must appear to be neutral, despite the overrunning of the Plain of Jarres by Pathet Lao/North Vietnamese forces and their continued threat to Laotian cities and towns.[16]

The North Vietnamese steadfastly denied these blatant violations of the Geneva Accords. Inasmuch as the ICC was unable to check the area under Communist control, nothing could be legally proven. By the same token, any public admission by the United States of its violating the Accords might polarize the Laotian government at Vientiane. This in turn would force Souvanna to publicly disavow the violations and call upon America to cease bombing the trail. To sidestep this situation, the United States refused to comment on Air Force Laotian operations.[17]

The very unique command and control procedures also impacted squarely on American participation in Laos. In 1961, President Kennedy gave all ambassadors direct responsibility for U.S. operations in their respective countries. He excepted only organic military commands reporting through the chain of command to the JCS. Since no such command chain existed in Laos, air operations were handled through the Air Attache to Ambassador William H. Sullivan. The latter established policy in line with Washington guidance and with Souvanna Phouma's approval. Thus, while Headquarters, Seventh Air Force in Saigon controlled USAF resources, only Ambassador Sullivan could validate targets in Laos. This out-country war was soon known as "The Ambassador's War," and the 56th Special Operations Wing at Nakhon Phanom as "Ambassador Sullivan's Air Force."[18]

Many restrictive but essential rules of engagement issued for South Vietnam were used in Laos. Their very nature hampered any systematic interdiction effort. Initially, for example, the rules specified sterile periods between missions. Originally 3 days but later reduced to 48 hours, these pauses were political and intended to counter any impression of suddenly escalating air operations. Later removed, the sterile periods while in force made it very difficult to conduct an effective night interdiction campaign.[19]

Target selection lagged due to the many agencies involved. Since final approval rested with the State and Defense Departments, it often took weeks before a preplanned target could be hit. In many cases, pilots were not even permitted to choose the direction they could fly on a given armed reconnaissance route. Ordnance selection was left to local commanders. At first forbidden, napalm was permitted under special conditions after 15 March 1965. An irksome rule to many aircrews specified that, when the target was obscured, the strike aircraft must either return to base loaded or jettison their bombs in the ocean.* Relaxation of the rules of engagement was painfully slow.+20

Aftermath of Tonkin Gulf: Upsurge in Force Deployments

For the Air Force, the Gulf of Tonkin incidents signaled the beginning of new emphasis on air power in the counterinsurgency war. In August 1964, the Air Force deployed two B-57 Canberra squadrons from Clark AB, Philippines, to Bien Hoa AB, South Vietnam. At the same time, it moved one F-105 Thunderchief squadron from Yokota AB, Japan, to Korat AB, Thailand, and shifted four additional F-100 Super Sabre squadrons to Takhli AB, Thailand. Also, in August, the Thais agreed to allow the launching of combat sorties from their country to include strikes against North Vietnam. This triggered a corresponding airfield/facilities program in both South Vietnam and Thailand.21

On 22 January 1965, the Air Force launched its first night interdiction effort in Laos. Four F-100's, aided by a C-130 Blindbat, conducted armed reconnaissance along Route 7 in eastern

---

*This "no secondary target" restriction resulted directly from the inadvertent bombing of a Laotian village, Ban Tan Vai, on the night of 15 January 1965. [Capt. Melvin F. Porter, Night Interdiction in Southeast Asia (TS) (Hq USAF, Project CHECO, 9 Sep 66), pp 8-9.]

+One most impractical rule forbade armed escorts of Yankee Team reconnaissance aircraft from attacking trucks they might see. These same trucks, if seen by Barrel Roll aircraft, could be struck. [Porter, Night Interdiction, p 62.]

Laos. After spotting no vehicles and expending no ordnance, all aircraft returned safely to Da Nang AB, South Vietnam. This inauspicious beginning set the pattern for the next 2 years of the Laotian interdiction effort. In the first quarter of 1965, for instance, only 25 percent of armed recce strikes were flown at night against major supply routes, although 60 percent of the truck movement occurred during these hours.[22]

The Rolling Thunder campaign against North Vietnam accounted in part for the dearth of armed recce strikes for Laos during this period. As the campaign steadily widened and intensified, it hampered infiltration to the south. These air attacks forced the enemy to travel by night and disperse his units on the march into villages and homes. What had been a leisurely truck ride of 2 to 4 days through North Vietnam was now a 40-day trip with much of the latter part on foot. The longer travel time required additional way stations and exposed the infiltrators to more hardship and disease. Furthermore, the air operations in the north pushed the enemy westward, away from the more exposed coastal routes into the trail corridors of Laos.[23]

In spite of longer travel time and attendant supply disease, and travel problems, Hanoi quickened infiltration of men and supplies down the trail and geared up its road-building program. Soon large battalion-size units were making the trip southward.* In October 1965, to stem the flow, 2d Air Division employed a combination of B-57's and C-130 flareships at night. Over the last 2 weeks in December, U.S. aircraft flew 251 night sorties--a vast rise over previous efforts but still just a finger in the dike. Night interdiction remained woefully weak at the end of 1965.[24]

---

*According to the excellent Rand Corporation study, Infiltration of Personnel from North Vietnam, 1959-1967 (S) (RM-5760, Oct 68), "infiltration" may well be a misnomer since it "has been of battalion-size units along established trails and does not occur in small clandestine groups hacking their way through the jungle at night." The study's authors (M.J. Weiner, J.R. Brom, and R.E. Koon), after exhaustively examining the interrogations of captured enemy prisoners, conclude: "The procedure seems to be more of a planned military movement under conditions of jungle protection."

Why the Air Force flew so few night interdiction missions in Laos was no mystery. The war in South Vietnam and strikes against the North--including its logistics network-- held first claim on USAF assets. While these strikes stretched infiltration time to the south, they also forced the enemy westward into Laos where few air sorties could be scheduled.* Moreover, Adm. U.S. Grant Sharp, Commander in Chief, Pacific, considered armed night reconnaissance secondary to day missions against fixed targets. He believed the greatest blow to infiltration would be to destroy "fixed components of [the enemy's] logistics system and this can best be accomplished during daylight hours." Fixed components included storage buildings, truck parks, fuel and ammunition dumps, and bridges--the standard interdiction targets.+25

The Requirement for Effective Night Training

Not enough evidence supports the contention that sufficient sorties in Laos during 1965-1966 would have secured proportionally better results. Night training at stateside bases simply did not prepare aircrews for the interdiction campaign in Southeast Asia. The first F-105 squadron deployed to Korat AB, Thailand, had no knowledge of the full range of weapons, tactics and techniques associated with the various tasks they would have to perform. Many pilot combat veterans believed too much stress had been put on unrealistic training--dive-bombing, rocketry, and straffing, practiced on closed ranges using downwind base-leg patterns. Most of these pilots were well aware of the need for flying safety on bombing and gunnery ranges. Nonetheless, many believed undue stress on flying safety had stereotyped tactics.26

---

*In late March 1965 this point was stressed by the USAF representative to a conference with Ambassador Sullivan at Udorn. [Msg (TS), CINCPACAF to CINCPAC, 280004Z Mar 65.]

+Later CINCPAC analyzed the first few months of the Laotian interdiction campaign. Admiral Sharp acknowledged armed reconnaissance might be harassing the enemy but wanted any contemplated sortie increase devoted to fixed targets. In fact, he wanted the sorties allocated for armed recce and attacks on route segments and choke-points sharply reduced. [Msg (S), CINCPAC to AmEmb, Vientiane, and COMUSMACV, 260330Z Jun 65.]

The F-105 pilots were not the only group critical of their stateside training.* One F-4C squadron commander noted:

> New pilots continue to arrive with absolutely no night weapons delivery training. This is the most difficult training to try and expose pilots to in a combat theatre. Flares and flareships are at a premium and trying to divert a flare ship for this training sometimes involves weeks. This results in fighter units having, in essence, a pilot that is 50 percent qualified.[27]

As in Southeast Asia, flareships were scarce at stateside training bases. Moreover up to 1966, few strike aircraft could carry and dispense flares--thus aggravating the problem. The Special Air Warfare Center at Eglin controlled the C-47 and C-123 flareships needed for stateside training of strike crews. The Center, however, had barely enough flareships to conduct the primary mission of its air commando wing. The situation worsened in September 1966 when the 4510th Combat Crew Training Wing at Luke AFB, Ariz., stopped giving F-100 classes night attack training, due to a shortage of instructor pilots and supporting flareships. This resulted in three F-100 classes, scheduled to graduate in early 1967, being diverted from strike crew assignments in Southeast Asia to FAC programs or PACAF staff jobs.†[28]

(U) Not only jet aircraft crews suffered from the shortcomings in night training. As late as 1967, out of a total 23 hours of night training, A-1 pilots received but 2 hours in Phase I

---

*In early 1966 TAC's F-100, F-105, and F-4C training course syllabii provided for only two night ordnance delivery sorties per student pilot. [Hist (TS-NOFORN), Pacific Air Forces, 1 Jan 66-31 Dec 66, p 301.]

†Until relaxed in mid-1967, PACAF policy required all FAC's to be graduates of USAF fighter schools. F-100 pilots were therefore used against FAC requirements. Maj. Ralph A. Rowley analyzes the pros and cons of the matter in Forward Air Control in Southeast Asia 1965-1970 (S) (Ofc/AF Hist, not yet published).

operations (aircraft orientation). More important, they spent only 3 hours in Phase II--the critical weapons delivery portion of the course. In those 3 hours Skyraider pilots were expected to fly formation, work with flareships, and become familiar with dive-bombing, strafing, and rocketry at night.*

Human factors also contributed to shortcomings in night training. Some training units showed a natural reluctance to change procedures, because they sincerely believed the training offered crews rotating to Southeast Asia was satisfactory. However, in recounting the training deficiencies of FAC's sent to Vietnam, one pilot observed:

> The people back here [stateside] decided what they [in SEA] needed; we decided over there what we needed. And although we would converse with each other it was, "Oh, hell, he doesn't know what he's talking about." So, we in Vietnam kept training the way we thought it should be done. When their output [O-1 FAC's] finally reached us we said, "These people can't even fly the airplane. What are they doing back in the States?"30

A breakdown in communications between forces in the field and those back home is nothing new in modern war. In this instance the breakdown underlined the need to keep combat crew training/replacement training unit (CCT/RTU) courses up to date, particularly in view of the fluid war situation. Tactics suitable in 1966, when the enemy lightly defended his Laotian areas, proved inadequate a year later when these same areas

---

*The author could not obtain a A-26 training syllabus dated before July 1968. The 1968 syllabus reflected a very realistic training program. Of total training time of 34 hours and 20 minutes the pilots flew 18 hours at night, conducting 12 night missions. The missions for both crew members included delivery parameters of up to 30° dive angles, 190-310 KIAS, 50-4,000 feet AGL release altitude for all types of ordnance. [See Tactical Air Command, Pilot A-26 Syllabus, July 1968; and Tactical Air Command, Navigator A-26 Syllabus, July 1968.]

bristled with antiaircraft guns.* Similarly, the outlook of Southeast Asia veterans assigned to stateside training units changed. After being away from combat for some time one pilot commented:

> Over in Vietnam they're saying, "We need night flying." Seventh Air Force is saying, "We need night flying." We say, "Oh, hell, you don't know what you're talking about!"31

Stateside training needed to be more closely attuned to actual conditions in Southeast Asia. The enemy preferred night activities, so more night training was a must. In January 1966 Secretary of the Air Force Harold Brown had stressed the paramount importance of special night training for crews enroute to Southeast Asia. But training courses could not be revised overnight; it took time to pinpoint the training needs of these crews.32

Meanwhile, after the Gulf of Tonkin incident, rapid deployment of USAF units and the accompanying drain on crew resources put TAC in a quandry. The TAC staff faced the question confronting all military planners over the years--how much training is enough? Up through 1965 the number of crewmembers with Southeast Asia tours was quite small, so TAC lacked the readily available experience to answer the question. Again should crews receive generalized or thorough, detailed training? The 1-year Southeast Asia tours for individuals forced TAC to pump a steady stream of capable aircrews into the theater pipeline. For this reason, TAC opted for training capable rather

---

*Just such a complaint was voiced in 1969. The 609th SOS (A-26) noted that night ordnance delivery training at England AFB, La., was not compatible with the SEA environment. Low altitude training under flares"...is not used in this theater, except under very rare circumstances because of extremely heavy and accurate enemy gun defenses. Consequently, all A-26 aircraft in this theater use the medium altitude glide/dive bombing tactics." [Ltr (no classification), 609th SOS to 56th SOW (DCOS), subj: Training - A-26, 26 Mar 69.]

than expert aircrews, and CCT/RTU courses adopted a generalized training approach. Not until March 1967--when TAC had caught up with PACAF pipeline demands--were more thorough crew training courses introduced. In the interim, combat crews lacking sufficient night training had to receive it in South Vietnam or in the hostile skies over Laos and North Vietnam.[33]

Additional Sorties for Night Interdiction

By mid-1965 the Air Force knew for sure North Vietnamese units were moving in force into South Vietnam. What's more, the enemy's logistic capability had surpassed his requirements and he was stockpiling for future use. Such stockpiling might be the prelude to an all-out offensive in one or more of the corps areas. This could be disastrous considering the weakness of the ARVN in 1965. It was evident the Air Force needed to reassess its air effort.[34]

Much of this stockpiled material moved into South Vietnam at night over the Ho Chi Minh Trail. USAF forward air controllers operating by day in the Steel Tiger area seldom saw any motor vehicles. They did see tire prints along the road and heavy dust on the trees. Indigenous roadwatch teams later confirmed the enemy was hiding under thick jungle canopy by day and moving mostly at night.[35] At first, General Thao Ma, head of the Royal Loatian Air Force (RLAF), doubted the high rate of enemy movement at night. He continued to reserve most of the southern half of Laos for RLAF operations. But after observing the lights of enemy vehicles during a night flight, Ma altered his views. By mid-November 1965 he had given the green light to expanded USAF operations in the Steel Tiger area.[36]

This might have been the turning point of the interdiction effort. On 15 November 1965, Gen. William C. Westmoreland (USA), COMUSMACV, directed his staff and 2d Air Division to recommend ways to better use air power in sealing off the border infiltration. General Westmoreland also instructed 2d Air Division to schedule up to 100 sorties per day into Steel Tiger, and asked the Navy to up its sorties from 32 to 96 per day. He further requested Ambassador William Sullivan to seek Souvanna Phouma's permission for defoliation of key LOC's and B-52 Arc Light participation in the interdiction effort.[37]

Due to the strict rules of engagement, General Westmoreland wanted the recently deployed C-130 ABCCC as an integral part of the operation.* The C-130 ABCCC's removable command and control compartment contained UHF, VHF, and HF radios, and could furnish secure voice communications. As an airborne command post the aircraft could direct and divert strike aircraft to proper targets, particularly those uncovered in Steel Tiger adjacent to the South Vietnamese border. Two RLAF officers on board solved the thorny problem of validating targets. They could certify targets at once or, if in doubt, radio Vientiane or Savannakhet for validation within minutes. The plane also acted as traffic controller, furnishing separation and time between fighters and the FAC's. Furthermore, it could call for additional strike aircraft as needed, function as a communications relay, and contact search and rescue (SAR) centers as well as SAR aircraft.[38]

At a Saigon briefing on 28 November 1965, Secretary of Defense McNamara approved the expanded Laotian air operations requested by General Westmoreland. Called Tiger Hound, the campaign began 1 week later. The special task force, formed at Tan Son Nhut AB, consisted of 10 USAF and 10 U.S. Army O-1 FAC aircraft manned by 30 USAF crews, along with 13 Army OV-1 Mohawks equipped with night sensor equipment.† Other aircraft joining the task force included Marine and Navy F-4B's, AC-47's, Ranch Hand C-123's,‡ B-52's, as well as assorted photo reconnaissance and flare aircraft. Sorties were flown around the clock with the heaviest concentration during daylight hours. In the first 2 months of the campaign, less than 30 percent of the total strikes were at night, even though an estimated 60 percent of truck movements occurred under cover of darkness.[39]

When enemy movements at night rose to 95 percent, the task force responded by fragging more night interdiction sorties. By April 1966, 858 night sorties were being flown against 2,514 day. As the night sorties increased so did the

---

*The first C-130 ABCCC arrived in the theater in September 1965.

†The Mohawks discussed in Chapter II were assigned to this task force.

‡Ranch Hand was the code name for C-123's equipped for defoliation operations.

combat experience level of the aircrews. Hence, in April, strike aircraft destroyed 325 trucks and damaged 205. During that month the enemy featured high road speeds and bold use of full headlights. This push of vehicles lasted until the beginning of the monsoon season. The North Vietnamese paid a heavy price, however--854 trucks destroyed, another 538 damaged.*40

Truck kills also climbed because of the better quality intelligence being furnished task force planners. Information on enemy truck movements was gathered from many sources, including roadwatch teams and photo reconnaissance aircraft. The most important data, however, came from the airborne FAC. Like his strike pilot counterpart, the Tiger Hound FAC performed at peak effectiveness once he had gained some expertise. When familiar with his geographical area of patrol, the FAC in his slow-flying plane could detect camouflaged vehicle tire tracks, recently used fords, new road constructions, and, at times, evidence of recent foot traffic. Truck sightings mounted as intelligence officers correlated the FAC's data with information on the enemy's means of transportation, favorite routes, defense, supply areas, and truck parks.41

The Role of the Forward Air Controller

As the interdiction effort in Laos commenced in earnest, it underscored several factors: the political situation, rules of engagement, limited resources, and the difficulties in night target acquisition. All demanded precise techniques for area reconnaissance and surveillance, as well as thorough grounding in procedures for control of air strikes. To satisfy these requirements the strike control and reconnaissance (SCAR) mission evolved.+42

The many-faceted SCAR function in Southeast Asia had its roots in the Korean War. The Air Force developed SCAR to

---

*During the operation, 22 aircraft were lost to ground fire. [Capt. Melvin F. Porter, Tiger Hound (TS) (Hq PACAF, Project CHECO, 6 Sep 66), p 49.]

+The term "FAC" is used in this work to denote a role that is often considered SCAR. The semantic problem of FAC versus SCAR is well-documented in Maj. A. W. Thompson, Strike Control and Reconnaissance (SCAR) in SEA (S) (Hq PACAF, Project CHECO, 22 Jan 69).]

pinpoint fast-moving targets for attack by F-80's and other jets. Soon visual reconnaissance was added to the SCAR mission. Later, due to poor ground communications, the FAC in Korea took over the responsibility for calling in strike aircraft for immediate close support. By the end of the war, the FAC was flying visual reconnaissance in his T-6 Mosquito, as well as obtaining and controlling strike aircraft. Nevertheless, after hostilities ended the SCAR mission lapsed.*43

      The VNAF possessed limited capability for conducting battlefield reconnaissance and area surveillance. Hence Air Force FAC's and U.S. Army air liaison officers (ALO's), assigned to ARVN units, performed these functions in the Cessna O-1 aircraft. When a FAC detected hostile activity in his area of responsibility, he requested air support. After the aircraft arrived he controlled the air strike against the enemy force.44

      The O-1 used in the Tiger Hound task force was a direct descendant of the World War II L-5 Horsefly. It cruised at 90-115 knots and could stay aloft about 4 1/2 hours. Its short run of 590 feet enabled it to operate from the numerous primitive airstrips dotting the Southeast Asia countryside. Twenty of these "puddle jumpers" supported the early Tiger Hound interdiction effort.45

O-1 SCAR/FAC Tactics--Preplanned Targets

      Since the SCAR/FAC pilot ferreted out and controlled air strikes against the enemy, he was a key member of the night interdiction team. The forward air controller had to know every inch of the terrain he operated over and the maps depicting it. He had to understand the nature and night tactics of the enemy, together with the type of defenses he might encounter while controlling the airstrike. At night, the FAC was frequently the eyes of the strike pilot. Many times the success of the mission hinged on the FAC's accurate description of the target and competent direction of the airstrike.46

---

    *The temporary eclipse of the FAC mission after the Korean War is discussed in Chapter I of Maj. Ralph A. Rowley's Forward Air Control in Southeast Asia, 1961-1964 (S) (Ofc/AF Hist, Jan 1972.)

O-1E Bird Dog Over South Vietnam

(U) Mission preparation for preplanned targets usually occurred the day prior to the air strike. The frag order gave the FAC the type and ordnance of the fighter(s) he would be working. Using his knowledge of the terrain and enemy defenses, the FAC planned the direction of the attack, the breakaway, and any later passes. He kept mission planning flexible and keyed to the fluid insurgency warfare. Onsite reconnaissance the following day repeatedly revealed changes in the target that forced deviations from the mission as first planned.47

(U) Ordinarily, FAC's would reach the target area 30 minutes before the fighters arrived. The classical way to complete the rendezvous was for the FAC to meet the fighters at a predetermined location, then proceed together to the target. The FAC specified a TACAN distance and radial, completing the rendezvous with the use of wing lights or flashing beacon ("Going Christmas Tree!"). Once the O-1 pilot saw the fighters he had to direct their eyes to find him. The most accepted method was clock code, for example, "I'm in your 2 o'clock position, low."48

At times, TACAN's were ineffective due to aircraft distance from the station or equipment malfunction. Then pilots rendezvoused by asking for a vector from one of the control and reporting centers (CRC's), by grid coordinates, or visually through prominent landmarks. Only in extreme emergencies did the FAC drop flares and talk the strike pilots to him. At first flarelight the North Vietnamese drivers pulled off the road, scurried under the trees and disappeared. Thus any chance of catching moving traffic by surprise was lost.[49]

Once the target was located, the FAC had to mark it for the faster, higher-flying strike aircraft. Having no sight or similar device on which to line up on a firing pass, the O-1 FAC pilot substituted a grease pencil mark on the windshield. The technique was to fly the aircraft in an attitude where the rocket pods were level with the horizon. Then, looking straight ahead, the pilot marked the windshield where the horizon crossed the center post. The mark usually fell halfway between the second and third bolt of the center windshield support. This grease mark was invisible at night, so pilots mentally drew an imaginary line between the two bolts for reference. To mark the target, the O-1 carried four or eight 2.75-inch rockets usually configured with a 6- or 10-pound Willy Peter (white Phosphorous) head. The O-1 FAC could also drop wing-mounted Mk-24 flares or logs. In addition, many O-1's carried the U.S. Army's hand-fired slap parachute flares.[50]

The FAC would roll in at 5,500-6,000 AGL and mark the target with a rocket. Next he dropped a flare directly over the target during pullup. If the FAC controlled an aircraft carrying flares, he might make the rocket mark himself then instruct the aircraft to drop flares so as to conserve his own. After marking a target the FAC made doubly sure the strike pilot could identify it properly before he allowed the strike to proceed. Beyond this, control of the attack differed little from one by day.[51]

(U) During the attack the FAC's job was to position himself so he could always see the fighters and target. He could thereby keep the fighters lined up on the target and help them avoid mid-air collisions. Further, by seeing the target he could adjust ordnance release points and observe enemy activity and ground fire. The O-1 FAC used either an outside holding pattern or an inside holding pattern (see figures 8 and 9). Outside holding was best to

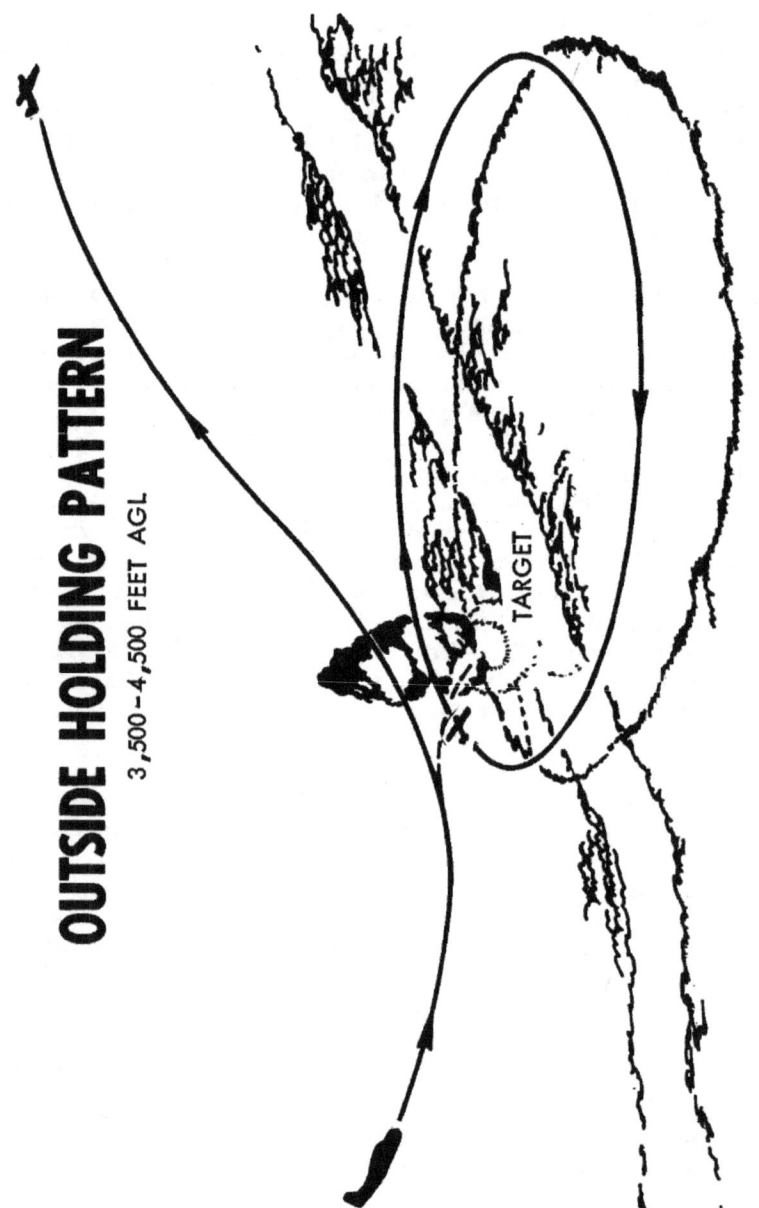

Figure 8

OVERHEAD HOLDING PATTERN

2,000 – 3,000 FEET DIRECTLY OVER TARGET

STRIKE AIRCRAFT WORKS DIRECTLY UNDER FAC

STRIKE AIRCRAFT CAN VARY ATTACK HEADING

USED FOR NAPALM, CBU, AND LOW ANGLE STRAFE

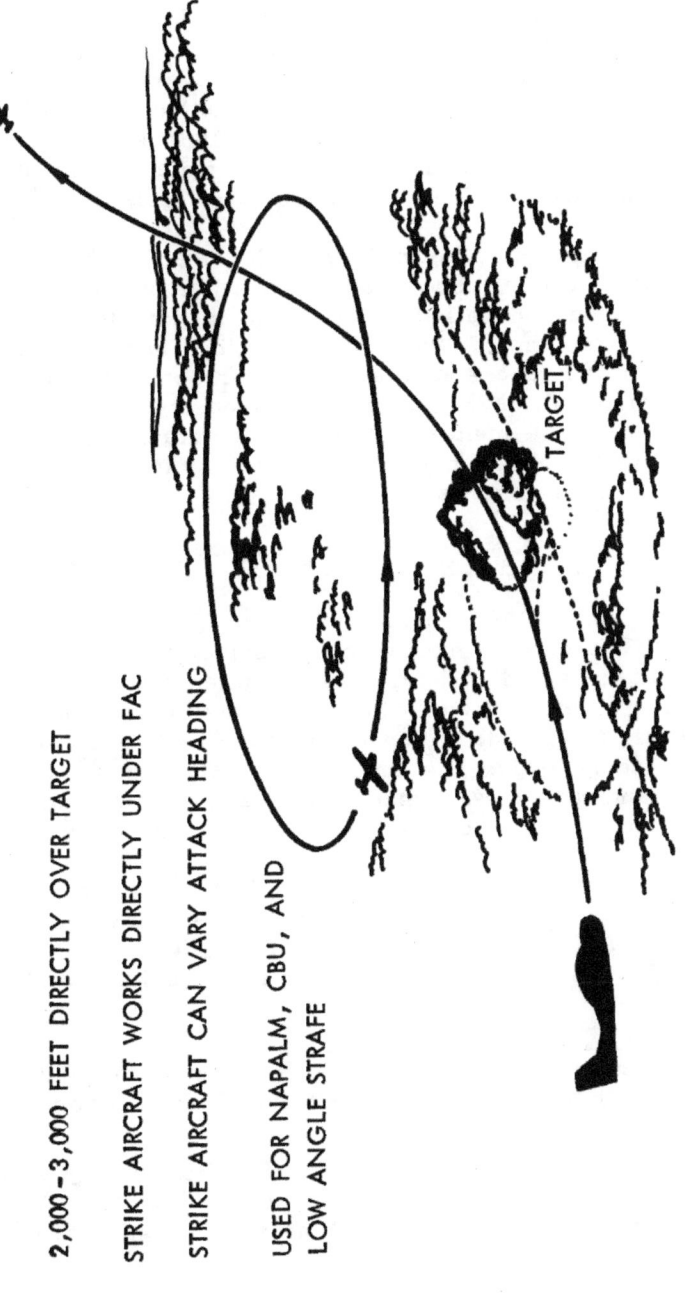

Figure 9

it for use with rifles, machine guns, and recoilless rifles. The Air Force tested several of these devices and found them unwieldy and offering limited viewing. Nevertheless, it installed the rifle version on FAC aircraft in want of something better. An improved USAF version of the starlight scope, the 6-pound AN/AVG-3, reached Southeast Asia in time for the 1967-68 dry season and was installed on various FAC aircraft.[60]

The T-28 Zorro flew behind the O-1 Bird Dog. When the starlight scope discovered a truck, sampan, or similar target, the O-1 flared and called in the T-28 to complete the strike.* In the first 3 months of 1967 truck sightings soared dramatically. Of more than 500 trucks sighted, however, only 70 were destroyed and 45 damaged. Monsoon rains and enemy antiaircraft defenses finally forced the hunter/killer team to curtail operations in June 1967. By that time, however, future employment of the starlight scope had been established.[61]

The Search for a New FAC Aircraft

As a FAC aircraft, the O-1 Bird Dog had definite shortcomings. It was plagued with excessive engine failure. Furthermore, at night and in bad weather, when the pilot had reduced reference to the horizon, the O-1's insufficient instrumentation and cockpit lighting made flying hazardous. While the machine possessed enough endurance time for a FAC mission (usually 3 1/2 hours), it was handicapped with inadequate rate of climb and zoom, not enough top speed, and too few marking rockets.[62]

As a result, a Southeast Asia Operational Requirement (SEAOR)† was submitted outlining requirements for an improved FAC aircraft. The North American OV-10 Bronco was selected to eventually replace the O-1, but first deliveries could not be made

---

*Greater detail on employment of the starlight scope in FAC aircraft will be found in the O-2 and C-123 sections of this chapter and the T-28 section of chapter V.

†The Air Force established SEAOR's in July 1965 to expedite the operational requirements of units in Southeast Asia. The system recognized short- and long-term requirements.

until February 1968. As an interim replacement, the Air Force
bought the Cessna 337 Skymaster and redesignated it the O-2.
This 2-place, twin-engine (push/pull) aircraft had a high wing
and twin tail booms. Its navigational equipment included TACAN;
VHF omnirange (VOR); and identification, friend or foe (IFF).
White lights on the panels, adjustable by rheostat, illumined the
instruments. One of the first units to receive the O-2 in November
1967 was the 23d TASSq at Nakhon Phanom.[63]

O-2 Nail FAC's--Tactics and Techniques

Nicknamed Nails, the O-2's in Southeast Asia served
almost exclusively in the strike control and reconnaissance role.
Early (1967) O-2 missions differed from those of a year later. In
1967, working with Blindbat C-130's, the FAC's marked the targets
with smoke rockets after the flareships had already marked them
with flares or marker logs. Not until early 1968 did the Air Force
permit O-2's to drop marker logs. Thereafter, the standard O-2
load consisted of seven 2.75-inch Willy Peter marking rockets,
two Mk-6 marker logs, and four Mk-24 flares. Since Willy Peter
was a smoke rocket of short life, it was often used along with
flare illumination. Flying at 90-120 knots, the O-2 Nail completed an average mission in 2 hours and 45 minutes.[64]

Cessna O-2A Observation Aircraft

Most O-2's carried two crew members--a pilot and a starlight scope operator who was also the navigator. Premission briefing dealt mainly with the daily intelligence summary, weather, emergency procedures, and rules of engagement. Afterwards, the O-2 took off and navigated by TACAN or mapreading to its general area of responsibility. If the TACAN wasn't working, the Control and Reporting Center's (CRC's) covering that particular area vectored the FAC. Once over the LOC the navigator handled the navigation.65

About 1 to 1 1/2 miles from the LOC, the O-2 navigator completed the first order of business--a rapid visual reconnaissance of the entire fragged area so that opportune targets were not allowed to escape. By this procedure the navigator hoped to detect ground activity before the enemy realized a FAC was in the area. The technique seldom worked. The enemy knew he would be reconnoitered, so at dusk he automatically adopted his night tactics.66

After this first inspection, the navigator rested the scope on the doorsill and searched the area systematically with the starlight scope. (A small windscreen deflected the air and the scope was tied to the operator with a lanyard.) Since the navigator continually peered into the scope he couldn't read the maps or charts. Hence he memorized all headings, times enroute, distances, and fixing landmarks. He used hand and voice signals to indicate directional turns. Instructions such as "Easy right" (10°-15° of bank), "Left turn" (15°-30° of bank), "Hard left" (roughly 45° of bank), and "Roll out," were used. The operation called for close coordination between navigator and pilot. The Nail tactics manual noted: "Yelling, chewing, stamping feet and other such actions are not conducive to effective night coordination."67

Enemy antiaircraft fire set the operating altitudes for visual reconnaissance. Normally, the O-2 FAC team flew between 3,500-4,500 feet, and in heavy gunfire areas--for example, Tchepone--climbed to 6,500 feet. To assess the accuracy of enemy ground fire, many observers adopted a favorite technique of keeping one eye in the scope and the other toward the rear of the aircraft. "If the tracer did not get any bigger, you knew he was on you. You instantly called for a hard bank to the left." Since the aircraft had dual controls, the navigator often performed this maneuver. "Nail pilots were always prepared for this."68

If trucks or suspicious activity was seen, the Nail crew decided when and where to strike. The O-2 contacted the ABCCC which assigned available aircraft and strike radio frequencies. The FAC frequently picked the rendezvous point, commonly a range and bearing from a TACAN. Once in contact with the attack aircraft, the O-2 pilot relayed the rendezvous point, target altitude and description, suggested run-in heading, and a general area briefing. In turn the strike pilot told the FAC how long he could work with him (play time) and the type of ordnance carried.69

Not until strike aircraft arrived or were at least on their way did the O-2 mark the target. Ideally, the FAC dropped the markers a few miles down the road from the trucks and out of the enemy drivers' view (similar to the O-1 tactics discussed earlier). On dark moonless nights the pilot flew upwind of the target and dropped a flare. Flare settings and release altitudes varied but most FAC's preferred 4,000 feet AGL with settings of 10 and 15 seconds on the parachute and igniter, respectively. This usually put the flare over the target after about one-half of its burn time. Next the O-2 executed a right-hand turn, enabling the navigator to keep the target continually in view. After flare ignition the navigator switched to high-powered binoculars because the bright light blanked out the starlight scope. He pointed out the target to the pilot who marked it with a Willy Peter rocket and proceeded to direct the strike.*70

Like his O-1 counterpart, the O-2 FAC preferred holding on the approach side of the target, offset to the side during the

---

*Many crews were not enthusiastic over the use of Willy Peter marking rockets at night. If a pilot took his eye off the target --for example, to cross check engine and flight instruments—he might easily miss the rocket's ignition on impact. What's more, the rocket's smoke quickly dissipated and blended with smoke created by flares, making target acquisition very difficult. Needed was a bright long-burning log that could be delivered by the 2.75-inch rocket. [Ltr (S), Dep Comdr/Ops, 35th TFWg to 7th AF Dir/Ops Analys, subj: Night Weather Operations, 14 Dec 68--hereinafter cited as 35th TFWg ltr--in supporting documents of Lt. Col. Philip R. Harrison, Impact of Darkness and Weather on Air Operations in SEA (S) (Hq PACAF, Project CHECO, 10 Mar 69.)]

the strike aircraft's attack to avoid midair collision.* Most roads patrolled by the Nails ran northwest to southeast, so the FAC held east of the road in the northwest quadrant. This left both running up the road and the west clear. The daylight axiom "see and be seen" did not apply at night, for visibility was limited and strike aircraft ran blacked out. In addition, some FAC areas were but 3 miles long. Fighters in hot pursuit of trucks repeatedly crossed from one control area to another, and sometimes two strikes were on the target at once.71

O-2 Crew Checks Their Ordnance and Aircraft

Being offset from the target, the O-2 gave strike pilots a reference point during pulloff to avoid spatial disorientation. It also gave gunners a jumping illusion that made FAC aircraft harder to hit. The fighter usually flew the classic racetrack pattern, descending down through and pulling back up through the FAC's altitude. After the strike was over, the O-2 circled the area and performed bomb damage assessment (BDA) with scope and naked eye, or gave the strike pilot corrections for

---

*See figures 8 and 9, pp 70, 71.

another pass. To confirm a kill the O-2 had to see the vehicle burn. Otherwise, the pilot got credit for a damaged truck.[72]

On bright moonlit nights the procedures were essentially similar except that the pilot would mark the target without expending flares. This not only introduced an element of surprise, but many strike pilots favored attacking without illumination because it cut the risk of spatial disorientation. Regardless of sky condition, the FAC gave the fighter-bomber's crew the target's position relative to the burning logs or smoking rockets in cardinal points (north, east, south, west) and meters, *if* the distance was not over 50 meters. If it was, he stated the distance in ground reference terms, for instance, "See my mark and smoke? Hit halfway between them." Or "There is a field halfway between my mark and the river. I want you to hit in the tree line on the west edge of the field, one-half the way between the north and south boundaries of the field."[73]

When two aircraft were available to attack a target, the O-2 FAC stacked one well above the other's working altitude. After the first expended its ordnance, it positioned itself above the O-2 while the second was cleared in. Once the second was established in the strike pattern, the first climbed and held above the strike pattern. It was most important the FAC keep adequate lateral separation between the two aircraft as their altitudes were being changed.[74]

Ordnance

To destroy trucks along the Ho Chi Minh Trail, O-2 FAC's preferred the soft (spreading) ordnance such as the M-35/36 Funny Bomb (called Tokyo Fire Bomb in World War II). This weapon (M-31/32 and M-35/36) came in several sizes, all containing incendiary bomblets that ignited on impact. Funny Bombs had clamshell, blunt-nosed casings of poor aerodynamic quality but of excellent spreading characteristics. One bomb could cover almost the length of a football field--three to four times the distance of BLU-27 napalm.[75]

BOMB, INCENDIARY CLUSTER, M36

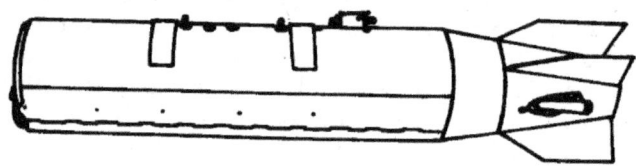

Figure 10 (U)

One of spreading ordnance's biggest pluses lay in its offsetting night bombing problems. In the B-57, for example, the gunner aimed through a fixed-angle, nonsynchronous gunsight. This sight had a 50- and 100-mil ring around the pipper, used for estimating distances from the FAC's ground marker to the aiming point. The B-57 crew--or any other crew for that matter--estimated offset distance based on wind direction/intensity and the FAC's estimate of where the moving truck would be when the ordnance hit. Estimating distances in the black of night proved iffy at best. On the other hand, spreading ordnance could set off numerous fires over a large area and was ideal for destroying convoys and truck parks. During the Commando Hunt III interdiction campaign of 1970, this munition destroyed more trucks than any other.[76]

Napalm, CBU-24 antipersonnel bomblets, and 20-mm machine gun fire ranked high on the list of FAC-preferred ordnance. In attacking trucks, the FAC's cared least for the conventional high explosive (HE) iron bombs because it took a direct hit or very near miss to destroy vehicles. The Air Force continued to use these bombs, however. They came in a variety of sizes, could be carried by all strike aircraft, and were fine for rooting out bunkers or cratering roads.[77]

Until the AC-130 entered the scene,* O-2 FAC's operating along the Laotian trail network considered the

---

*Later chapters will discuss B-57, AC-130 and A-26 operations.

Martin B-57 Canberra and the slow movers[*] the best interdiction aircraft. The conviction rested on the accuracy, long loiter time, and capability of these aircraft to carry spreading ordnance for successfully attacking trucks. Strike pilots did not acquire the ability to hit trucks overnight. Most were halfway through the 1-year tour before they attained it. Crews of the A-1, A-26, and other "low-slow" aircraft held built-in advantages over jet crews. The relatively low altitude and airspeed allowed them to acquire targets that might escape notice of jet crews due to size, smoke, foliage, or camouflage. Moreover, with a shorter turn-radius they could keep the target in sight throughout any repositioning maneuver. Their tracking time was also longer, and being closer to the ground the wind had little affect on released ordnance. Nevertheless, slowness had its handicaps. It kept the recips[+] in range of enemy guns longer, and their response time suffered when compared to the faster jets. This was partially compensated for by their loiter capability which permitted them to be prepositioned.[78]

Gunships had a reputation as truck killers but O-2 FAC's rarely worked with them. They favored conventional strike aircraft and called on the converted transports only when no other ordnance was available. There were two main reasons for this. Several O-2 pilots had inadvertently entered a gunship's propwash and lost control of their aircraft. As one FAC emphatically phrased it, "When he cleared in the area, you got out!" Again, the hunter/killer concept inherent in gunships made teaming with FAC's somewhat redundant.[79]

C-123 Candlestick Operations

An examination of night FAC techniques would be incomplete without a discussion of C-123 Candlestick operations. As previously noted, the first airlift C-123's were used as flareships in 1962. Flare support from airlift aircraft declined as the AC-47 gunship and flare-dedicated C-130's were introduced. Because this mission was vital to the interdiction effort, the Air Force formed a flare-dedicated unit at Nakhon Phanom AB, Thailand-- the 606th Special Operations Squadron of the 56th Special Operations Wing.[80]

---

[*]Relatively slow-moving strike aircraft (e.g., A-1, A-26, AC-119, AC-130), as opposed to fast movers (e.g., F-4, F-105).

[+]Reciprocating engine aircraft.

Aircraft of the 606th consisted of UC-123 B and K models, the latter being jet-augmented. The "U" designation reflected the plane's basic plumbing installed for the aerial defoliation operation (Ranch Hand).* None of the aircraft had radar, cabin pressurization, autopilot, or flight-control boosters. The UC-123 carried its fuel in jettisonable nacelle tanks behind each engine rather than in its wing.†81

By 1968, the 606th primary mission was night reconnaissance and forward air controller/flareship duties on LOC's in neighboring Laos--especially in the Steel Tiger area. The Candlesticks usually flew four sorties a night. The number later increased to nine, eight in Steel Tiger and one in Barrel Roll. Aircraft worked in shifts to continually reconnoiter these roads and trails. Each mission lasted 5 hours with 4 hours over the target area. At sundown, the first two Candlesticks lifted off so as to be over the target area by dark. They remained on station until relieved at midnight by the late sorties.‡82

The C-123 evolved obliquely into a FAC aircraft. The Air Force experimented to compare the effectiveness of the T-28 versus the O-1 in the use of the starlight scope for night visual reconnaissance. For various reasons the scope proved incompatible

---

*Originally, the Ranch Hand squadron contained six C-123's and 69 officers and men. Officially designated Tactical Air Squadron, Provisional One, it arrived in the Philippines in early December 1961 and departed shortly thereafter for Tan Son Nhut. The defoliation program aimed to deprive the Vietcong of ambush cover along roads and canals and to destroy crops. [Hist (S), 13th AF, 1 Jan-30 Jun 63, pp 75-76.]

†This feature paid off when three UC-123's were able to recover safely at Nakon Phanom after receiving direct hits in the wing by 37-mm antiaircraft shells.

‡Availability of night FAC's determined each evening's relief sequence. A C-123 arriving on station at dusk might relieve an O-2 day FAC Covey. In turn he might be relieved by an O-2 Nail, the latter by another Candlestick, and by dawn the C-123 would find another Covey as his replacement. [Intvw (S), author with Maj. Charles A. Beckwith, JSIPS, 1 Mar 71.]

with the T-28.* Improvising, the Air Force placed a locally-
manufactured scope mount near the floor hatch of the Candlestick
flareship. Lying prone, the observer could sweep from 20°
below the horizon to 60° either side of the flight path. Soon the
C-123 and T-28 Zorro formed a hunter/killer team and applied
this technique. Five Zorros rotated in working with the flareship, which took off from Nakhon Phanom and arrived over the
LOC in darkness. When the Candlestick discovered a target, it
radioed the T-28 pilot to allow him sufficient time to position
himself for the strike. Next, the C-123 dropped flares to ignite
at 1,850 feet AGL and burn out around 500 feet. The Zorros
began the attack a few seconds after the flare ignited. This
hunter/killer team operation proved so successful that Seventh
Air Force directed it be established permanently and include the
A-26 Nimrods in the hunter role as well. Thus was born the
Candlestick FAC operation with the starlight scope.[83]

The Candlestick aircraft carried three navigators. One
occupied the normal crew position at his table and kept the aircraft over the road/trail network by using TACAN and specially
annotated maps and charts. He also logged all strike aircraft
worked, targets sighted and struck, and any assessed bomb
damage. The other two navigators operated the starlight scopes.[84]

As the mission started, the table navigator gave the
pilot a heading to the general target area in Laos. After the
Candlestick crossed the bombline, about 50 miles east of Nakhon
Phanom, the loadmasters set up the flare dispenser in the
partially opened cargo ramp. After positioning the ground markers
they stood by for instructions before inserting any Mk-24 flares in
the manual dispenser. Both outside and inside lights were turned
off, save the red cockpit lights which were dimmed. This allowed
the side windows to remain uncovered to aid visual scanning. The
two scope operators moved to their stations and commenced to
recce the road. The flareship worked the entire assigned area
before moving on to secondary targets.[85]

C-123 Scope/Reconnaissance Techniques

On the right side of the C-123, one scope operator lay
prone on a GI mattress and 3/4-inch armorplate. Over the open
floor and slightly ahead of the operator's position was a locally-

---

*See discussion on p 110.

built "doghouse." A starlight scope hung on a traverse rod in this doghouse and pointed out the forward emergency bailout hatch.* From his prone position the navigator could observe through the scope about a square mile on the ground at any one instant.[86]

The Candlestick FAC used the improved Air Force version of the starlight scope. Since it was battery-operated, the crew carried a spare battery and an old U.S. Army scope as well. When the battery failed the spare was used first, then the backup scope. To counterbalance the USAF scope's peculiarities required an experienced operator who could accurately pick out various targets in the scope presentation. For example, both ground fires and truck headlight beams appeared as white spots. Yet, on bright nights, trucks running without lights showed up as black objects, similar to "black bugs crawling down a crack in the floor." Rivers were black, roads white, and trees fluffy cloudlike rolls. The navigator peered through the scope with one eye to keep night vision in the other.[87]

The navigator's mastery of the scope rested on his knowledge of the route. In early Candlestick operations the belly scope operator's position lacked a compass, so the pilot informed the operator of aircraft headings and turns. Later, a compass was added† and the pilot no longer had this job. If the scope operator needed flight information the table navigator furnished it. This rarely happened, however. Like their O-2 Nail counterparts, most scope operators memorized headings, distances, times, and such visual references along their routes as turning points or river bends. For the most part crews flew the same route(s) night after night and knew the area well. If the enemy bulldozed a short bypass or otherwise altered the landscape, the navigator spotted it at once. This extra effort sorted out the good scope operators from the average ones.[88]

Buckled in an adjustable seat, the third navigator sat in the left door. Through a starlight scope, mounted on an automatic weapons support, he scanned the road to the left of the

---

*The doghouse also cut off any stray light that enemy gunners on the ground might detect.

†This auxiliary repeater compass was located on the right bulkhead slightly forward of the doghouse [Beckwith intvw (S), 1 Mar 71.]

aircraft. This was specially useful when the Candlestick circled the target to monitor a strike in progress. Notwithstanding, the 606th seldom used this position due to a shortage of trained personnel.*89

The Seventh Air Force fragged fighters and bombers each night into Laos, tentatively scheduled to strike a certain target or work with a specific FAC. Nonetheless, the ABCCC actually controlled airborne fighter resources, and could divert them to other targets of opportunity. When a hole nav$^+$ picked up trucks or other targets on his scope, the table navigator recorded the TACAN position. Flying between 6,000-9,000 feet the C-123 next tracked the trucks or orbited the fixed target. Meantime, the copilot called the ABCCC for strike aircraft, giving such information as number of vehicles, direction of travel, and TACAN position for the strike aircraft's rendezvous.[90]

The ABCCC controlled many FAC's and strike aircraft. It therefore carefully evaluated each request as to type of target, ordnance available, and to some extent the degree of success that might be anticipated should it release strike aircraft. Each forward air controller calling in believed he had good targets, so this evaluation was no simple matter. In this regard the C-123 copilot "who could sweet talk ABCCC out of ordnance was invaluable." Many times, however, strike aircraft would be assigned to the Candlestick when it entered the armed reconnaissance area. Then it was only necessary to inform the ABCCC before hitting a target.[91]

The Candlesticks (like the O-2 Nails) delayed marking targets until strike aircraft were on hand or at least on their way. Too, they favored dropping the markers a few miles down the road from the trucks out of the enemy drivers' view. This was possible when the C-123 worked with aircraft of long onstation time--the A-1, A-26 or jet B-57 Canberra. The tactic became difficult if other jet aircraft were assigned due to their poor loiter time--as low as 5 minutes in many cases. Little wonder the Candlestick FAC's preferred the slow movers.[92]

---

*Major Beckwith estimated that during his tour the third navigator was available only 25 percent of the time. [Beckwith intvw (S), 1 Mar 71; hist (S), 56th SOWg, Jan-Mar 1969, I, 9.]

$^+$The navigator operating the starlight scope.

Marking and Ordnance Delivery Techniques

After spotting a truck convoy or other moving target, the C-123 flew ahead and made a 90°-270° turnaround or a "hard 180."* Rolling out on about a reciprocal heading, the pilot informed the belly scope operator and the loadmasters who were standing by with Mk-6 logs and a red-burning LUU-1B.† At the scope operator's command, the loadmasters launched the markers out the open ramp door at 1- to 3-second intervals over the target area. Following a 3-minute delay the logs ignited. The aircraft turned around once more and flew back over the burning markers, so the scope operator could fix the target's position relative to them. Frequently, the enemy lit other fires in the vicinity to confuse the FAC and fighter aircrews. This made it necessary at times to further mark the area to make sure strike aircraft had the right target.[93]

Afterwards, the C-123 started a left-hand tracking orbit like that used by a gunship Meantime, the hole nav kept his scope trained on the target. From a perch‡ altitude about 4,000 feet above the Candlestick, the strike aircraft attacked. At this point, a high degree of coordination and proper radio communication between hunter and killer was vital. By 1969 the danger of mid-air collision between aircraft had risen to the point crews feared this mishap more than enemy antiaircraft fire. Thus, prior to the attack aircraft rolling in, the C-123 turned on its fin-mounted rotating beacon (which was shielded from the ground). Furthermore, no strike was allowed to begin unless the fighter could see the FAC.

The Candlestick rarely gave the strike aircraft directions in meters with reference to the burning markers. What might appear a 30-meter distance to the scope operator might be a

---

*An extremely tight 180° turn.

†The short-burning Mk-24 flare was used as a log only during very hazy weather. The green LUU was rarely used, because from the air it looked too much like a white-light Mk-6. [Beckwith intvw (S), 1 Mar 71. The remainder of this C-123 section is based on the Beckwith interview.

‡An airborne position assumed by a fighter/bomber aircraft in preparation for or anticipation of an air-to-ground strike maneuver.

50-meter distance to an F-4 or A-26 pilot. Instead, the FAC used short, precise, ground-reference terms or phrases, easily understood by strike pilots. Ordnance release directions resembled those of the O-2 FAC's, for example, "See where my last two markers are closest together? Bomb between them!" or "Hit one nape* width south of my burning LUU."

Following the FAC's instructions the strike aircraft rolled in. It passed down and under the Candlestick, then up and out the other side. Meanwhile, the FAC maintained a tight left-hand orbit, enabling the scope operator and other crew members to see the target markers and expended ordnance at all times. This attack procedure was repeated if needed.

Enemy gunners quickly picked up the left-hand orbit tactic and began to lead--expertly in some cases--or tail-shoot the Candlesticks. Crew members, including the flight engineer, were on the lookout for enemy AA fire. When seen, "Break right" or "Break left" over the interphone signaled the pilot to change course. It was axiomatic that crews never used the word "Break" in any other context, for to the pilot "Break" meant he

C-123 ORBIT PATTERN

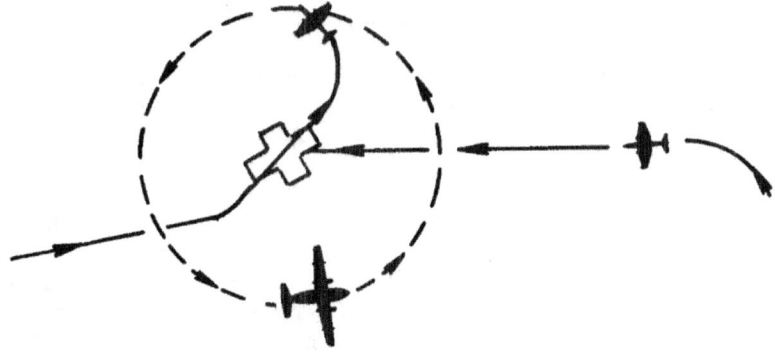

Figure 11

---

*napalm.

should take violent evasive action. As strike aircraft made their pass, enemy AA fire commonly concentrated on them rather than the C-123 but turned back on the FAC once the pass was complete. If this occurred in an area formerly free from enemy fire, the table navigator plotted these new sites for further investigation.

Candlestick FAC's had certain hip-pocket targets in suspected or known areas of enemy activity--truck parks, AA sites, or river crossings. These reserve targets were attacked when the opportunity presented itself. For instance, a U.S. Navy Corsair II, unable to return to its carrier with ordnance, might seek a suitable target to avoid dumping his bombs in the ocean. Having no truck targets that night the FAC might direct the Corsair to an enemy-held but little used staging area. Whether or not the area was active was unimportant, compared to the psychological impact on the ground personnel maintaining the area. Using ordnance to "shake up the bad guys a little, to keep them on their toes" was part of the endless battle of wits between North Vietnamese logistics personnel and USAF strike aircraft. Many times, to the FAC's surprise, a series of violent secondary explosions followed such bombing--a sure sign enemy trucks or supplies were hit. One could never really predict when hip-pocket targets might be active.*

By 1969, heavy AA fire along the Ho Chi Minh Trail posed a formidable threat to C-123 FAC operations. Increasingly, the enemy shot at the Candlesticks and more often the UHF radios of these aircraft picked up the telltale clicks of the enemy's Fire Can[+] radar. When this took place, the C-123's immediately requested the ABCCC to furnish electronic countermeasures (ECM) support. To avoid compromise, the ABCCC never confirmed

---

*Most truck parks were in areas of moderate to heavy foliage, making detection from the air extremely difficult. Often the only clue was a small track 3 miles from the main road that led into a clump of trees. In these parks the cargo was immediately offloaded and separated from the trucks. [Rprt of Joint Technical Coordinating Group (JTCG/ME) for Munitions Effectiveness (S), 1967.]

[+]Code name for North Vietnam fire-control ground radars used for direction of hostile AA fire. A single Fire Can normally controlled from six to eight enemy guns of 57-mm or larger caliber.

to the requester that it was supplying ECM (EB-66) protection. This "trust me" attitude was a little too much for some C-123 crews. They jury-rigged their own ECM chaff dispenser.

This dispenser was a sheet-metal box roughly 12 by 4 by 6 inches. Placed at the right hand of the prone starlight scope operator, the box held from 16 to 20 small red multichannel boxes of chaff. To prevent the 1- to 1 1/2-inch slivers from getting loose in the aircraft and fouling the communications equipment, each little chaff box was secured with a rubber band. A 2- to 3-foot cord was attached to the box and anchored to the bulkhead. When the scope operator, who monitored the radio, heard the Fire Can's clicks, he quickly reached across, grabbed a box of chaff, and threw it out the scope hole beneath him. The attached cord automatically opened the chaff box. This ingenious device actually worked. The scope operator no longer heard the Fire Can's clicks--a sure sign it was either tracking the chaff or had gone off the air. The operator repeated this ECM procedure as necessary.

On 30 June 1971, Candlestick operations ended with inactivation of the 606th Special Operations Squadron at Nakhon Phanom. The 606th had contributed significantly in night operations. Along with the O-2 Nails, its C-123's were the first reliable night hunters employed along the Ho Chi Minh Trail. Yet the whole operation was no more than an improvisation--the mating of the starlight scope with the old Fairchild Provider. Nonetheless, it lasted 4 years and proved highly successful.

In high gear by 1969, the Shed Light program produced sensors and aircraft for the night hunter role far more sophisticated and advanced than the C-123's. The newer AC-130 gunships, for instance, carried advanced starlight scopes, side-looking airborne radar, forward-looking infrared radar, low-light-level television, and fire control computers. By comparison, these advances made the Candlestick operation seem somewhat primitive. Furthermore, these gunships hunted and killed, making it but a matter of time before they replaced the C-123's. Nevertheless, the Candlestick's contribution to the development and implementation of night interdiction tactics assures it a distinct niche in Air Force history.

F-100 Misty FAC

In late June 1967, the 37th Tactical Fighter Wing began operations (code word Commando Sabre) to find out if use of jet aircraft in the FAC/SCAR role was practical. The 2-seat F-100F Super Sabre (call sign Misty) was selected for this mission. During the first year Commando Sabre was a day FAC operation. But, in July 1968, the 37th started a test program to evaluate high-speed aircraft's effectiveness in night visual reconnaissance and forward air controlling. The Misty's primary mission was to detect enemy movement over specified roads and highways in the panhandle of North Vietnam, gather intelligence on night and early-morning traffic, and conduct air strikes as needed. For this mission the jets were configured with two SUU-25 flare pods and the backseater (also a pilot) was given the Army starlight scope. Two flights each night were scheduled into the high-threat areas of Route Package I (RP I) in North Vietnam.*94

The Misty FAC's soon found enemy truck operations in the North Vietnam panhandle strikingly similar to those over the Laotian trail network. The North Vietnamese massed their vehicles in camouflaged parks in RP II until after dark. Around 1900, the convoys moved out at 10-15 miles per hour along selected routes with vehicles spaced about 100 meters apart. Their trip to Delta 74 and other staging areas in RP I took around 9 hours.+ The trucks hid by day and moved south at night, either along Route 137 into Laos or down Route 101 toward the demilitarized zone (DMZ).95

---

*Bombing missions against North Vietnam were coded Rolling Thunder. At first, specific targets were assigned to the Air Force and Navy. In late 1965, however, CINCPAC created six route packages, or areas, to ease air traffic control of armed reconnaissance missions. Weekly assignment of RP's varied between the services. On 1 April 1966, CINCPAC permanently assigned RP I to COMUSMACV; RP's II, III, IV, and VIB (the area in and around Haiphong) to the Commander in Chief, Pacific Fleet (CINCPACFLT); and RP's V and VIA to CINCPACAF. Thus through COMUSMACV the Seventh Air Force became responsible for the lower panhandle and most of northern North Vietnam. [7th AF Handbook (S), Sea Interdiction, 1 Apr 70, p 80.]

+A well-concealed truck park near Delta 74 could hold up to 200 vehicles. [Lt Col John Schlight, Jet Forward Air Controllers in SEASIA (S), (Hq PACAF, Project CHECO, 15 Oct 69), p 16.]

The southbound trip usually lasted 3-5 days, dependent on the number of trucks trying to infiltrate. During 19-23 July 1968 over 300 fully loaded trucks--carrying an estimated 600 tons of supplies according to intelligence sources--passed over these roads to the southern LOC's.* The return of the empty vehicles to RP II took about 15 days. The difference lay in the smaller convoys--often single trucks--and the more dispersed destinations in RP II than on the southern journey.[96]

The Misties could gather intelligence on enemy traffic, but night visual reconnaissance with the starlight scope was a different story. The enemy moved at night but solely in poor weather with no moon--virtually negating the scope's usefulness. Trucks traveled without lights or used a soft blue headlight not visible above 5,000 feet. Whenever flares were dropped near a moving truck, the driver took the usual actions. He either speeded from the lighted area before strike aircraft arrived, or pulled off the side of the road and hid under the trees.[97]

After a few weeks of operations it became obvious that Misties had achieved only moderate success. Possessing little navigational capability the aircraft relied on TACAN fixes and pilotage to locate targets and rendezvous with strike aircraft. Moreover, the FAC's operating altitude was just too low for the jets. Below 2,000 feet the latter often lost TACAN lock on and had trouble keeping radio communications with Invert+ and other GCI sites.[98]

When enemy fire downed two Misties during 16-17 August 1968, the night flights ended. A review of the program pointed up the problems of jets as FAC's. Besides limited navigational capability, the F-100F lacked enough on-station time for efficient visual reconnaissance. It consumed the bulk of its typical 4-hour mission en route to and from home base or tanker refueling tracks. This left only about 1 1/2 hours for visual reconnaissance. In addition, the Air Force had no accurate target-marking device for the Misties. The aircraft could not drop with any consistent accuracy

---

*Considering the enemy's effective countermeasures, probably much more traffic flowed into the staging areas than was discovered.

+The control and reporting post at Nakhon Phanom RTAFB, Thailand.

the long-burning markers used late in the program for pinpointing targets, chiefly trucks. Furthermore, the aircraft could carry but two SUU-25 flare pods of eight flares each--a meager supply barely adequate to do the job.[99]

Nor did the starlight scope work as expected. Satisfactory in an O-2 or Candlestick, the scope crowded the small F-100F cockpit, and its field of vision was restricted. Cockpit lights reflecting off the dome canopy constantly destroyed the scope operator's night vision. In sufficient moonlight or at dusk the scope picked up trucks, even those driven without lights. But with no moon the scope's value diminished.[100]

In a final report the Commander, 37th Tactical Fighter Wing, concluded "lower performance aircraft with longer on-station time, [improved] starlight scopes, flares, shorter, turning radii and lower speeds can better provide [FAC] services at night."[101]

OV-10 Bronco Operations

Under code name Combat Bronco the first OV-10 Broncos were deployed to Bien Hoa AB in July 1968 for evaluation by the 19th Tactical Air Support Squadron. By November, more OV-10's had arrived and several units began equipping with them. The Bronco--the first totally-new combat aircraft introduced and evaluated in Southeast Asia--held distinct advantages over the O-1 and O-2 FAC aircraft.*[102]

Additionally, the OV-10 carried four M-60C 7.62-mm machine guns, each holding 1,600-2,000 rounds and located in the sponson that protruded from beneath the plane's fuselage. Five ordnance stations could carry 3,600 pounds of additional stores. Night configuration consisted of 2,000 7.62-mm rounds, 14 LAU-59 rockets, and 24 Mk-24 flares. Two crew members were provided.[103]

---

*Two engines with improved single-engine capability over the O-2; visibility--pilot and observer stationed well forward of the engine; armor plating--328 pounds distributed in back of seats and along the aircraft's bottom; more marking rockets and flares; faster--cruising at 150-180 knots and diving at 400 knots; greater zoom capability after marking targets; zero-zero ejection seats--the chute opened immediately as the pilot ejected; night and all-weather instrumentation.

Cessna O-2 (left) and OV-10 Bronco Over Thailand

Evaluation of the OV-10 spawned no new FAC tactics. The Bronco's techniques in target illumination, marking and airstrike control remained those employed by previous FAC aircraft. The one notable exception--night airstrike control using artillery illumination--stemmed from the U.S. Army's need to support its firebases at night. Situated in isolated areas, these bases were susceptible to nocturnal mortar and sapper attack, just as hamlets and outposts had been in the early years of the war. OV-10's assisting in the firebase support usually operated from one of five forward operating bases (FOB's). The FOB's possessed short runways, marginal ground operating conditions, and an austere maintenance environment.[104]

When working with an artillery firebase, the FAC described the target to the strike aircraft, then radioed the artillery commander. The battery, commonly 155-mm howitzers, fired a flare toward the enemy on a trajectory parallel to the fighter's attack heading. The flare shell, set to ignite at 2,500 feet AGL, was timed to coincide with the strike aircraft turning base leg. As the last fighter of the flight pulled off the target, the FAC radioed the battery to fire another flare. As a variation, the battery fired three rounds spaced at 1-minute intervals, affording illumination for target acquisition and marking by the Bronco crew. After marking the target, the OV-10 climbed to 3,500 feet AGL and began single-flare illumination at 180 knots IAS. Dispensed at 2-minute intervals, the eight flares (austere base loading) gave 16 minutes of illumination--more than enough time to conduct the strike.[105]

By the close of 1968, it became apparent the O-2 excelled the Bronco in night operations. The OV-10's tandem cockpit and twin-boom design afforded an almost panoramic scene from the front seat but severely restricted the view of the observer seated in the rear. Horizontally, for example, the Bronco scope operator had a 55°-60° field of vision compared with 120° in the O-2. Vertically this limited view was even more pronounced. Here the OV-10 observer lacked about 15°-20° of being able to see straight down, whereas in the OV-2 or Candlestick he could do this unrestricted. Thus the OV-10 had to offset to a greater distance from the road, restricting the scope operator's tracking of roads into heavily wooded areas. Too, the Bronco's props caused distortion and the canopy glare off the front part of the cockpit hampered operations.[106]

The 23d Tactical Air Support Squadron at Nakhon Phanom partially overcame these night handicaps by modifying the Bronco. A night observation sight (NOS) was installed on a flexible mount in the camera port, and a biocular viewer fitted to it. A test program (29 Oct-15 Dec 1969) in the high-threat antiaircraft areas of Laos proved the modification successful and developed night reconnaissance techniques and strike tactics for its use. Both Seventh Air Force and PACAF supported a proposal to supply 12 NOS units and 12 biocular viewers for field modification to the Bronco. Due to the high costs ($1.2 million), however, the Air Force scrapped the proposal in favor of Project Pave Spot--a direct-view device with a laser target designator.[107]

155MM HOWITZER ILLUMINATION FOR AIR STRIKES

155MM HOWITZER BATTERY LOCATED PARALLEL TO STRIKE RUN-IN HEADING

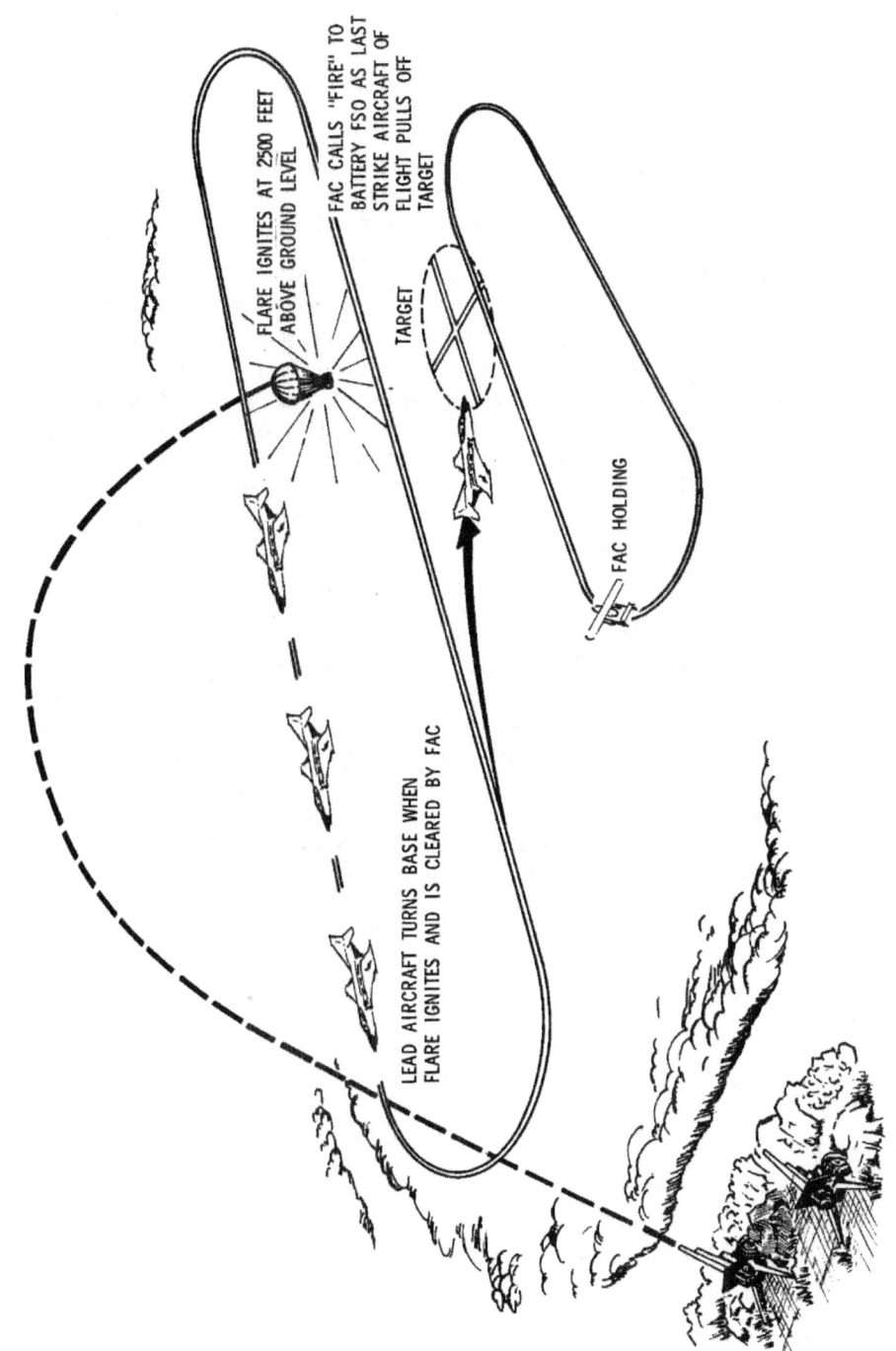

Summary

Employment of forward air controllers in the Laotian interdiction war differed sharply from their use in South Vietnam. In Laos, the FAC's directed most tactical air strikes against LOC's, truck parks, storage areas, and enemy troop concentrations. In South Vietnam, they chiefly controlled close air support missions. Along the Ho Chi Minh Trail, the FAC's real value was ability to uncover targets at night, mark them, and direct air strikes against them. The key element remained "detection" and the enemy's nature and tactics as well as the terrain worked against it. Still the Air Force had to find and attack the enemy or his logistics flow would move south unhampered. Hence the strategy of the entire Southeast Asia war hinged on denial of supplies, equipment, and personnel reinforcements to the enemy.

To do this the Air Force improvised from tools at hand. This time it was the Army's starlight scope--originally intended for use with rifles and crew-served infantry weapons. The Air Force mounted or hung the scope in a variety of FAC aircraft and added a navigator to operate it. Soon, OV-10 and other follow-on crews discovered they could not adequately carry out their missions without a properly positioned starlight scope. This same instrument--updated and linked with new sensors and armament--served as the eyes of the war's foremost interdiction weapon--the AC-130 Spectre gunship.

IV. THE SLOW MOVERS

The Douglas A-26

In midsummer 1964, the historian of the 34th Tactical Group prematurely noted:

> The B-26 "Attack Bomber" was through in SEA. This reliable old plane from WW II, Korea, SEA 1954 through SEA 62-64, had finally reached a point where it had to be put to rest. In this manner, the B-26 finished its role in providing capability for crews to resist many forms of aggression.[1]

Stationed in South Vietnam, the Group historian was unaware of stateside decisions for continuing the B-26 in the Air Force inventory.* The Air Force had already awarded a contract to On-Mark Engineering of Van Nuys, California, to completely refurbish 40 B-26's into the K model, Counter-Invader. By January 1964, the Special Air Warfare Center had tested the first of these aircraft.[2]

The new B-26--so new the FAA certified it as a zero-time aircraft[+]--mounted 14 fixed .50-caliber machineguns. Three were in each wing (later removed) and two rows of four each were in the nose. The eight external pylons could carry 4,000 pounds of armament and the strengthened wings allowed for more fuel. Larger and more reliable engines replaced the older power plants. Like the old Farm Gate B-26, the new model had a reconnaissance nose package that interchanged with the solid nose unit.[3]

Under code word Big Eagle, the Air Force deployed eight of these retreads from England AFB, La., to Nakhon

---

*Not everyone was enthused over modified or refurbished B-26's reentering the theater. In his End of Tour Report, 25 November 1963, to Gen. Jacob E. Smart, CINCPACAF, Maj. Gen. Rollen Anthis, Commander, 2d ADVON, said: "The aircraft is still a B-26, and in my opinion cannot be viewed as more than an interim answer."

[+]An aircraft that had not logged any flying time.

Phanom. The aircraft's designation B-26 was changed to A-26 in deference to the Royal Thailand Government's wishes.*4 At first, the A-26's operated in the Cricket (panhandle) area of Laos, conducting night armed reconnaissance and interdiction--a role destined to make them famous in Southeast Asia. These early flights were flown by blacked-out single-ship elements. They covered the various LOC's at random to surprise the enemy and at the same time prevent his predicting the next air strike. In bad weather, level bombing was carried out by using MSQ-77 Combat Skyspot equipment.+5

In 1966, the Ho Chi Minh Trail was still not heavily defended. Thus tactics for the A-26 (call sign Nimrod) called for attacking unsuspecting targets from a low-altitude reconnaissance

A-26 at Nakhon Phanom AB, Thailand

---

*The Royal Thai Government did not want "B" aircraft on Thai soil since "B" (bomber) would denote offensive aircraft. On the other hand it accepted "F" (fighter) and "A" (attack) aircraft because they could be construed as defensive.

+This equipment is discussed in chapter VI.

posture (1,500-1,800 feet AGL). The aim was to gain the element
of surprise and prevent trucks or other moving targets from
escaping and hiding. After the initial pass the A-26 dropped
flares and continued the attack. If the target was not destroyed,
and the ABCCC could send follow-on aircraft, the Nimrod remained in the target area and acted as FAC.[6]

November was the time of year the North Vietnamese/
Pathet Lao resupplied and strengthened their forces before taking
the offensive. Hence the Seventh Air Force began fragging four
Nimrods each night into the Barrel Roll area of Laos. The plan
was to strike at the enemy in his bivouac areas before he dispersed to attack Royal Laotian Government forces. Enemy
vehicular traffic was also a chief target and roadwatch teams
supplied much of the truck movement information. This integrated operation turned out fine. In one week (2-9 November 1966)
Nimrods destroyed or damaged 67 trucks--results so gratifying
that an A-26 detachment soon operated as a permanent part of
the 606th Air Commando Squadron. By 1967, the A-26's and the
T-28 Zorros formed a new squadron, the 609th.[7]

Before the AC-130 Spectre gunships came on the
scene, the A-26's were the best truck killers in Southeast Asia.
The Nimrods and their FAC counterparts covered the same areas
night after night, which bettered their chances for detecting and
attacking trucks. Many crewmembers believed, nonetheless, the
A-26's effectiveness grew out of its being part of a night-dedicated,
hunter/killer unit--the 56th Special Operations Wing. In the 56th,
strike crews and FAC's lived and worked together. This fostered
a close-knit feeling and a common spirit in which teamwork--so
vital in night operations--became the hallmark. Inasmuch as
FAC's and strike aircraft were often fragged to the same areas
in Steel Tiger or Barrel Roll, they briefed and planned the
missions together. Radio call signs, signals, code words, tactics,
and other matters were worked out on the ground beforehand. In
light of the results this type of organization produced, it is no
wonder Ambassador Sullivan held its members in such high
esteem.[8]

The Seventh Air Force did not confine the Nimrod's
excellent hunter/killer ability to interdiction targets. At times
it fragged the A-26's to Barrel Roll for close air support of

General Vang Pao's Meo guerrillas, or to defend a Lima Site*
or STOL (short takeoff and landing) site from being overrun by
the enemy. Many Nimrods would up an evening's work by serving as a FAC for other strike aircraft. Regardless of mission,
the combination of long loiter time, range, endurance, payload,
and flexibility made the A-26 a formidable night weapon.[9]

(U) Flexibility of the A-26 discouraged "standardized"
tactics as the Air Force uses that term. Much of Nimrod's
combat success rested not on tactical doctrines, per se, but on
aircrew ability to apply specific flight techniques. This skill came
only after flying combat for some time and was acquired for the
most part by trial, error, and experimentation. Furthermore, a
tactic that worked for one crew might not be readily accepted by
another. Certain techniques, however, were common to all A-26
crews. These are described below.

A-26 Characteristics Affecting Night Operations

The design characteristics of the A-26 had a direct
bearing on tactics. The aircraft had been designed for use in
World War II for straight-and-level attack. In South Vietnam,
where there was relatively light enemy fire, this tactic sufficed
but it courted disaster in face of heavy enemy AAA fire along the
Ho Chi Minh Trail. Consequently, tactics were modified to fit
conditions.[11]

The Nimrods usually conducted visual reconnaissance of
the Trail off to the side of the road and without flares.+ The
A-26 was not the best aircraft for this job since the engine nacelles
blocked the pilot's view of the ground. To compensate the pilot had
to fly with an angle of bank and maintain it to keep any target in
view. This was both difficult and hazardous because his eyes were
off the cockpit instruments. Here the navigator proved invaluable,

---

*Lima Site--Aircraft landing sites in Laos used as bases and
resupply points for anti-Communist guerrillas.
+The A-26 carried flares on missions in support of the Meo
Army in Barrel Roll. [Intvw (S), author with Lt. Col. Mark Richards,
USAF, 16 Mar 71. Colonel Richards, an A-26 pilot, flew more than
135 night missions in 1968.]

for he could monitor the artificial horizon indicator and warn the pilot if the bank became too steep.[12]

In addition, the navigator set the armament switches (which the On-Mark modification had been moved to the front panel). The navigator also handled the radios to and from the reconnaissance area but not on the strike itself. When on visual reconnaissance, the right side was his responsibility since it was out of the pilot's view. During takeoff, landing, and attack he monitored the instruments. In Southeast Asia, a few navigators learned to fly the plane from the right seat to make an emergency landing in case the pilot was incapacitated. In short, A-26 navigators discharged most all duties commonly associated with B-26 copilots.[13]

Most Nimrod pilots found the nose guns of little use except to suppress flak. Problems that had plagued the Farm Gate crews cropped up in the A-26--poor ammunition, cookoffs* common, windshield smeared with expended powder, and acrid smoke filling the cabin. The gunflash extending about 20 feet in front of the aircraft had caused Farm Gate pilots to lose night vision temporarily. In Laos, this was far more serious because the cone of fire gave enemy gunners an excellent target to track.+ Moreover, the .50 caliber guns required lower altitudes and decreased range for effective application. As the defensive ground fire in Laos increased, use of the guns became more unacceptable in view of the probable results. Consequently, Nimrod pilots saved their guns for last, content for the most part to lob their fire from a distance rather than zooming through.[14]

---

*Ammunition firing as a result of being allowed to rest in the chamber of an overheated weapon.

+Yet, one historian noted, "A new type of .50 caliber ammunition arrived in early October. This new type was said to have completely eliminated flashing, barrel explosions and projectiles lodging in the gun barrels."[Hist (S), 56th Air Commando Wing, 1 Oct-31 Dec 67, p 53.]

A-26 Night Visual Reconnaissance

The typical night visual reconnaissance mission consisted of single-ship sorties, staggered in takeoff times to continuously cover key LOC's. Enroute to Laos the A-26 flew at 7,000-8,000 feet AGL and once over the Mekong River doused all lights. The Nimrod radioed the ABCCC which handed it off to a FAC. Rendezvous with the latter--ordinarily an O-2 Nail or C-123 Candlestick--was made through a combination of TACAN range and bearing, voice communication, and shielded rotating beacon.[15]

Once in contact, the FAC briefed the A-26 on type of target, highest terrain elevation and location, preferred run-in heading, and other essential information.[16] At times, however, the FAC's had no targets immediately on hand for striking. Since the Nimrod possessed its own hunter/killer capability, it frequently covered the northern half of the reconnaissance area while the O-2 or C-123 reconnoitered the southern portion with the starlight scope. Both aircraft maintained radio contact. If one found a lucrative target the other joined up in less than 5 minutes.[17]

Visibility determined visual reconnaissance altitudes. Missions in Steel Tiger were chiefly flown around 6,000 feet AGL, with the Nimrod offset about 3/4-1 mile to the side of the road. If a truck convoy was spotted--and time permitted--the A-26 immediately turned on a base-leg heading. At 170 knots IAS it aligned the target with the bottom side of the engine nacelle--rolling in quickly to surprise the enemy drivers. The Nimrod dove at the established $25°-35°$ angle and held that dive angle and heading constant while allowing the pipper to drift beyond the target.* As the latter disappeared under the nose and after

---

*After flying about 2 months the pilot knew ordnance characteristics and how to aim so well that he used the gunsight pipper only for azimuth alignment. [Richards intvw (S), 16 Mar 71.]

dropping about 3,000-4,000 feet, the A-26 released the ordnance.*
After the release a 2 1/2-G pullup yielded a bottoming-out near
2,500 feet AGL. When working with an O-2 FAC the Nimrod
often dropped napalm as a marker. This afforded the pilot a
dry run and some idea of the wind. To prevent predictability
and confuse enemy gunners the aircraft flew the second run 90°
or 180° to the first.[18]

If the Nimrod's roll-in was too far back from the truck
convoy, a more shallow dive angle was required. Conversely if
too close, a very steep dive was called for. Pilots tried to shun
both extremes. The shallow dive angle forced a lower release
altitude and exposed the crew to enemy AA fire longer.+ On the
other hand, the steep dive exerted undue stress on the A-26 airframe. Whatever the dive angle, A-26 pilots always tried to hit
the lead and the last truck for this could stop the whole convoy.[19]

If the crew believed the chances good to stop a truck
convoy with the first release, it frequently strung out ordnance by
dropping at spaced intervals. Crew teamwork was a must. After
the pilot released the first station the navigator quickly activated
the armament selection to another station. The pilot then depressed the release button on his steering column to pickle‡ each
follow-on drop. Compressed within a few seconds, these actions
exacted a high degree of crew skill and coordination.[20]

---

*Napalm and iron bombs were released at about 4,000 feet
AGL and M-31/32 ordnance at 3,000 feet.

+In June 1968 severe A-26 and T-28 losses in the 609th
induced the Seventh Air Force to impose a 5,000-foot bottoming-
out altitude. To kill trucks, however, A-26 crews chose to
wink at this directive. This may have accounted for the restriction being lifted in January 1969. [Hist (S), 56th SOWg, Jan-
Mar 1969, I, 68.]

‡To release a bomb or expend ordnance by depressing a
buttom (pickle).

For attacking trucks, most A-26 crews first favored "Funny Bombs," then napalm and cluster bomb units (CBU's).* The latter ordnance was fine for area coverage or attacking gun emplacements. Nimrod crews shared the FAC view that iron bombs were poor for hitting trucks, like "dropping a firecracker in a sponge." Moreover, danger existed in releasing ordnance below the minimum recovery altitude based on bomb blast. Many times the shock waves "rattled the old bird like a honey bucket full of marbles."21

A-26 Trolling/Flak Suppression Operations

Flak suppression was conducted in conjunction with or following an interdiction strike. The A-26 flew very low (1,500-2,000 AGL) along key LOC's or close to known truck parks. When enemy gunners fired, the crew noted the gun position, turned around, and attacked the emplacement with napalm or "hosed 'em down with the guns."22

In addition, trolling was conducted by two Nimrods. One flew low and slow, the other positioned 500 feet above. As the lead aircraft moved through the hail of enemy fire, the second swooped down and attacked the position. Then the daisy chain began as the aircraft reversed positions, the second aircraft assuming the lead. The A-26's usually conducted trolling missions when devoid of all ordnance save their guns.23

---

*The historian of the 56th Air Commando Wing noted that M-31/32 "Funny Bombs" were in short supply and unit morale "dropped to a low ebb during the 'Hard Bomb' interlude but shot up dramatically when M-31 and M-32 ordnance became available." [Hist (S), 56th Air Commando Wg, 1 Jan-31 Mar 68, p 48.]

B-57 effectiveness likewise owed a great deal to fire bombs M-35/36. Production of these bombs was allowed to end in 1967, so no new supplies were available for the intensive dry-season interdiction campaign of 1968. [Ltr (S), Dr. Lee A. DuBridge, Science Adviser to the President, to SECDEF, (no subj), 26 Jun 69.]

An improved version of the bomb (M-36E1) was placed in production in early 1969 when CBU-53/54 proved inadequate. [Talking paper (S), Brig Gen A.G. Riemondy, Dir/Sup & Svs, DCS/Sys & logs, (no subj), (penciled notation indicates paper briefed to Air Force Chief General John D. Ryan on 17 Sep 69).]

A-26 FLAK SUPPRESSION

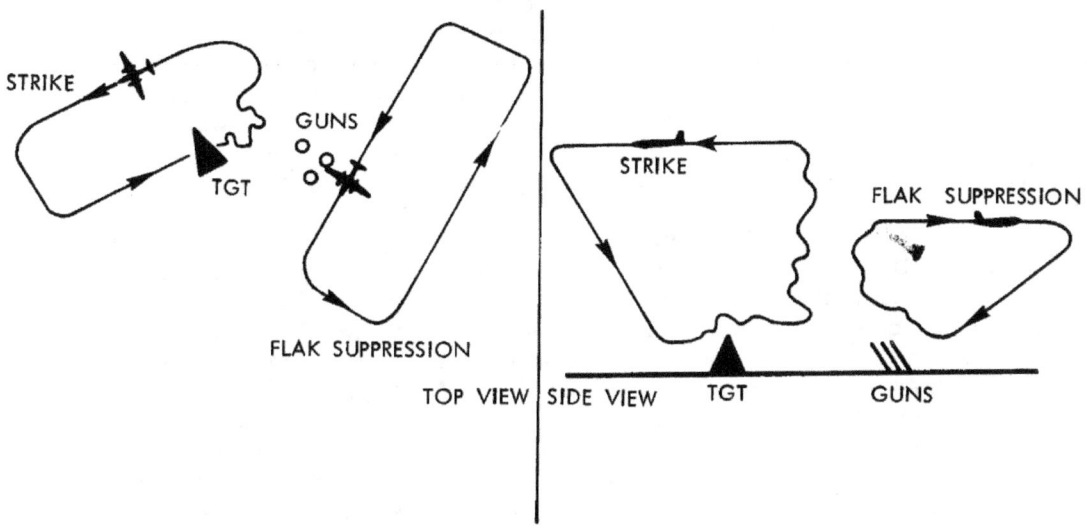

Figure 13 (U)

The A-26 also carried out flak suppression in support of a C-123 on bomb damage assessment or a strike aircraft such as the B-57 making an attack. In the latter case, enemy gunners rarely fired on the inbound pass but waited until the Yellowbird was up and away. Since the enemy needed tracers to align fire on the jet, the A-26 was able to locate and suppress the AA fire with its guns.*24

---

*Aggressive gunners loaded many tracers, fully realizing possible consequences. Those who did not stood a lesser chance of hitting aircraft--or being hit. [Intvw (S), author with Maj. Kenneth E. LaFave, Hq USAF, 12 Mar 71.]

A Seventh Air Force intelligence summary showed that the number of AAA guns in Laos more than doubled from mid-October 1968 to mid-November 1969. About 550 guns were seen at critical road junctures and truck parks. [Hist (S), 8th TFWg, Jan-Mar 1969, p 23.]

The enemy employed the 37-mm gun extensively for barrage fire. It had a 1.6-pound high-explosive warhead and a maximum effective range of 5,600 feet. However, it fired only 80 rounds per minute, and at night its tracer fire could be accurately tracked and avoided. Crewmembers considered the enemy's 14.5-mm ZPU machinegun more dangerous than his 37-mm. Crewed by four to five men, the ZPU had an effective range of 4,600 feet and could accurately pump out 150 rounds per minute. [Hist (S), 56th SOWg, 1 Jul-30 Sep 68, p 29.]

To counter the Nimrod's flak suppression tactics the North Vietnamese constructed many dummy gun sites in open areas near a timberline.* When the aircraft dove to attack a dummy site, concealed weapons among the trees opened up. A second A-26 started an attack on this gun emplacement, only to find another battery--diagonally across from the one he was firing at--now trying to shoot him down. Facing such odds it was better to retreat and live to fight another day.[25]

Many A-26 crews were convinced the enemy monitored their UHF radio conversations with the FAC. They cited the many occasions when upon calling "Turning base" the enemy gunners opened up on them. Chances of surviving flak traps grew slimmer all the time and no one wanted to alert enemy gunners. So rather than announcing a heading the A-26 pilots often said "Am going from California to New York," i.e., proceeding west to east. Comparing this with a north-south truck route the FAC knew the A-26 was on its base leg. Crews similarly disguised other headings, believing the technique helped keep them alive.[26]

Eventually, however, the Nimrod era closed. After nearly 4 years of operation from Nakhon Phanom, there were only a few A-26's left in the USAF inventory. Following inactivation of the 609th Special Operations Squadron, the remaining four A-26's returned to the United States.[27]

From the time of the Big Eagle deployment in June 1966, the 609th flew 7,159 combat sorties--almost exclusively at night-- for a total of 19,763 combat flying hours. During this period Nimrods were credited with destroying 4,268 trucks and damaging 696. This meant one truck destroyed for each one and a half sorties flown. To this tally could be added 201 enemy gun positions. No aircraft, except the AC-130, chalked up a better truck-killing record.[28]

(U) One of the finest compliments paid the Nimrods came from Brig. Gen. Wendell L. Bevan, the former commander of the

---

*The upper limit of tree growth in mountains or high latitudes.

432d Tactical Reconnaissance Wing at Udorn. Although he commanded a jet wing, the General noted the 609th was

> "A one of a kind" outfit--[producing]. . . under conditions where our more sophisticated weapons systems were stymied. Their loss signals the end of an era for the grand old A-26 and the crews who flew it.... They literally "wrote the book" on how to kill trucks at night and in the most hostile AAA environment we have encountered.[29]

T-28 Zorros

The T-28 also experienced revival and demise at Nakhon Phanom, where 12 of these single-engine aircraft formed part of the original Big Eagle detachment. The Zorro bore only a skin-deep resemblance to its Farm Gate predecessor. It possessed a more powerful engine, reinforced wing, self-sealing wing tanks, protective armorplate, and a variety of communications equipment-- VHF, UHF, FM, TACAN, and SIF/IFF.* Additionally, the armament switches--located on the old T-28 between the pilot's feet-- now graced the front panel.[30]

The T-28's flew armed reconnaissance, interdiction, flare support, and--in a pinch--FAC missions. In early 1967, the Zorro's normal combat load for a night mission comprised two fixed .50-caliber machineguns, each with 630 rounds; rockets; and incendiary/general-purpose bombs. The aircraft could carry only 3,500 pounds, less than half the A-1 Skyraider's maximum weight capability. Nonetheless, to deliver its diversified ordnance combinations required the T-28 to spend from 1 hour and 40 minutes to 2 hours and 40 minutes on target.[31]

During this period the Seventh Air Force fragged Zorros on single-ship night sorties with takeoffs spaced 1 hour and 15 minutes apart. The T-28 teamed with O-1 and O-2 FAC's equipped with the starlight scope. Either a C-130 Blindbat or the Zorro furnished any needed flare support.[32] The 56th Special Operations Wing briefed T-28 and FAC crews together, assigning

---

*selective identification feature/identification, friend or foe.

them a specific area to recce singly or as a team. If the briefing showed enemy trucks in the area, the crews worked as a hunter/killer team. The Zorro flew 500-1,000 feet above and behind the FAC, making "S" maneuvers and orienting on the O-2's rotating (and shielded) beacon. When trucks were sighted, the T-28 quickly attacked from this position and achieved at times an element of surprise.[33]

On routine armed reconnaissance the hunter/killer team split up, the FAC flying to one end of the LOC and the Zorro to the other. Keeping proper altitude separation the aircraft started back toward one another from opposite ends, seeking to box in the trucks. If vehicles were seen, conventional rocket-marking tactics followed. Due to the aircraft's limitations, most T-28 pilots considered it a "plug" and not a heavy strike aircraft. Tactically this meant the pilot tried to hit the first and last truck of a convoy to prevent any escaping or pulling off the road. If he corked the bottle (stopped the trucks) the pilot immediately radioed the ABCCC for more heavily armed strike aircraft to finish the job.[34]

Type of ordnance dictated release altitudes for the T-28 as it did for the A-26. To deliver its two M-31/32 Funny Bombs the Zorro rolled in from 7,000-9,000 feet AGL, dove at a 60°-70° angle, and released at about 4,500 feet. This produced a bottoming-out altitude around 2,500-3,000 feet. T-28 pilots, however, failed to share A-26 crew enthusiasm for M-31/32 fire bombs. This flatnosed, garbage can-shaped ordnance made the aircraft hard to maneuver and demanded the high dive angle--not relished by pilots used to conventional attack techniques. As one pilot put it, "The T-28 was not a Stuka dive bomber." Little wonder most Zorro pilots preferred to drop both M-31/32 bombs on the first pass.*

---

*The T-28's bottoming-out rule was the same as the A-26's--3,500 feet. Actually the Zorros "rarely operated above it!" [Intvw No. 2 (S), author with Maj Charles Brown, Hq USAF, 9 Apr 71.]

Phosphorus Bombing

The T-28 pilots liked the 100-pound white phosphorous bomb best, followed by CBU. They also dropped flares as bombs. Since a truck wasn't considered hit--just damaged--unless seen to burn, Zorro pilots often skip-bombed flares into a convoy on their second pass. By doing this they sought to ignite a truck leaking or dripping gasoline.* In addition, like the A-26 crews, they held off using their .50-caliber machineguns until last because of the muzzle flashes.

Night or day the T-28's seldom served as foward air controllers. The Zorro carried only four Mk-24 flares and no Willy Peter marking rockets. When out of ordnance the T-28 would FAC until an O-1 or O-2 could take over. Additionally, it did the job now and then for a T-28 or A-26 from Nakhon Phanom having ordnance still on board. As FAC, the Zorro employed O-2 tactics.

---

*A-26 crews frequently skip-bombed flares into the jungle next to a road to reveal trucks that might be hidden under the foliage. [Technical Report ASD-TR-67-17 (S), AFSC, Low Altitude Recce/Strike Techniques, Problems, Dec 1967.]

The Zorros experimented with the starlight scope, operated by a second crewmember in the rear seat. The test compared the relative effectiveness of the T-28 versus the O-1 in night visual reconnaissance. Zorro scope operators ran into the same problems that later troubled F-100 Misty FAC's. The scope's limited field of view, fore and aft, restricted the T-28 to an orbital pattern for visual reconnaissance. Moreover, the bulky scope crowded the rear seat and caused crew discomfort. Besides, the operator suffered eye fatigue from the reflected light off the plexiglass. Opening the canopy at low speed didn't help much, for wind blast and noise completely blanked out interphone and radio transmissions. The T-28's only advantages over the O-1 lay in longer loiter time, more flare capability, and greater speed for wider coverage in a single flight. In light of these findings the experiment was abandoned.[35]

From its maiden sortie on 9 January 1967 until final phaseout in early 1968, the T-28 flew 3,876 missions losing only four aircraft in combat. Engine failure in January 1968, however, caused two aircraft to crash and the fleet was grounded 3 days for engine inspection. In addition, severe structural problems and strengthened enemy defenses in Laos militated against the T-28 staying in the Air Force's Southeast Asia inventory. By March, the Air Force had decided to phase out the Zorro in favor of the A-1 Skyraider. When the last T-28 combat mission was flown on 9 June, only three of the aircraft were left.* Nonetheless, the Zorro did not die. In tribute to its predecessor, the A-1's of the 22d Special Operations Squadron at Nakhon Phanom adopted the old call sign.[36]

The Douglas A-1 Skyraider

(U) The A-1 Skyraider was no stranger to Nakhon Phahom or the out-country war in Laos. The aircraft had furnished close support in South Vietnam and since 1966 one Skyraider squadron-- the 602d--had operated in Laos as part of Ambassador Sullivan's Air Force. Older than the T-28, design development of this Douglas fighter-bomber began in early 1944, as a replacement for the Dauntless shipboard scout and dive bomber. After service

---

*The three T-28's were eventually handed over to the RLAF.

in the Korean War, the A-1 reached South Vietnam and other nations by way of the vast American military aid program. Eventually, the Skyraider entered the USAF inventory as a counterinsurgency fighter-bomber replacement for the Air Commando B-26's and T-28's.[37]

An excellent gun platform, the Skyraider flew 30 knots faster and had nine more ordnance stations than the T-28. Besides four M-3 20-mm cannons, the A-1 carried rockets, torpedoes, mines, and other stores on external racks. A relatively slow speed enabled the aircraft to better acquire targets and bomb more accurately than the jets.* Auxiliary fuel tanks boosted the A-1's endurance and loiter time over the fast movers, especially at low altitude. On the other hand, the Skyraider maneuvered sluggishly when heavily loaded--maximum climb rate being between 200-300 feet per minute and turn radius about triple that of a clean configuration.+ The slow cruise and escape airspeed of the A-1 and other aircraft at Nakhon Phanom made them vulnerable for barrage fire from larger (23-mm to 100-mm) AA guns.[38]

Of the three A-1 squadrons in the 56th Special Operations Wing only the 22d SOSq had solely a night mission. Flying the A-1E/H, the squadron interdicted enemy supply lines and furnished close air support for friendly forces. Secondarily, it served as FAC for jet aircraft fragged to Barrel Roll. Other A-1 squadrons, however, flew night missions. The 602d SOSq carried out search and rescue--strictly a daylight operation--yet often loaded flares to support General Van Pao's army in Barrel Roll. In 1969 the 1st SOSq flew night escort for AC-119's and AC-123's. Nevertheless, these two squadrons primarily conducted day operations.[39]

---

*The Joint Munitions Effectiveness Manual estimated the A-1's accuracy to be 30 percent better than the jets. [Strike Ops in SEA...Strike Aircraft, pp 118, 120.]

+Clean configuration or clean aircraft--an aircraft without extra fuel tanks, ordnance, and other external stores.

A-1 Armed Reconnaissance

      Armed reconnaissance missions for all aircraft operating in Southeast Asia commenced in the briefing room. Here the A-1 pilot received his assigned area, weather, changes to the mission profile, emergency procedures, specified escape and evasion areas, and required actions upon bailout and crash-landing. An intelligence officer briefed the ground-fire threat along the route and target area. He covered highlights of the previous night's activities--where trucks were seen and hit, the BDA, and where trucks might be expected that night.*40

      Two planes commonly carried out armed reconnaissance in Steel Tiger.† When cleared, the lead pilot took off and his

A-1E Skyraider

---

   *If the mission was to support troops-in-contact (TIC), he explained where the good guys and bad guys were, and what had occurred. [Intvw (S), author with Lt Col Herman J. Methfessel, JCS (C-C), 26 Apr 71. Colonel Methfessel flew more than 100 night combat sorties in 1968-1969.]

   †The U.S. Navy A-1 also used a two-ship cell for night armed reconnaissance. The wingman flew 200 yeards behind and 500 feet above the leader. [Rprt (S), Summary of Air Operations, SEA, XV, 7-20 Jan 66.]

wingman quickly followed. The flight joined up a minute later as the wingman cut off the lead's turn out of traffic. Once over the Mekong River, the flight went into tactical formation--the wingman about 1/2 mile out to the side and 500 feet above the lead who usually flew at 6,500 feet AGL.[41]

The A-1 Zorros, unlike the A-26's, were not allowed to self-FAC* in Steel Tiger. Hence they operated with O-2 Nails, C-123 Candlesticks, and the C-130 Blindbats. For navigation the Zorros relied on TACAN or radar vectors from GCI sites. The aircraft flew blacked out, the lights being turned off at the bombline. After joining the FAC the A-1's orbited nearby while the FAC methodically searched the LOC. When suitable targets were spotted, the FAC marked them and called in the Zorros.[42]

The lead A-1 dove at a 45° angle from about 7,000 feet and dropped ordnance at 4,500-5,500 feet AGL. This first drop--frequently napalm but sometimes a flare--marked the target further and gave the wingman a better view as he delivered the initial strike load. Many A-1 pilots favored napalm for marking since flares caused spatial disorientation and created a milk-bowl effect when reflected off clouds.[43]

The FAC watched the strike and gave immediate restrike information to follow-on aircraft for the next pass. The process went on until the target was knocked out or the A-1's were "Winchester" (out of ordnance). During the attack, armed reconnaissance might quickly change to flak-suppression. Often this took place when enemy gunners fired on the lead aircraft--usually as it pulled off the target after the first pass. Instantly the wingman--orbiting the target 500-1,000 feet above--struck with napalm or a 750-pound VT-fused bomb.[44]

Aircraft crews operating along the Ho Chi Minh Trail knew how hard it was to find and identify active flak sites at night

---

*Self-FAC--to act as its own forward air controller. The A-1's of the 602d SOSq (call sign Firefly) and 1st SOSq (call sign Hobo) could single-ship (fly singly) and self-FAC in Barrel Roll. [Msg (S), 56th SOWg to 7th AF Dir/Ops, 020612Z Nov 68, subj: FAC Procedures and ROE, document T-53 in Thompson, Strike Control and Reconnaissance (SCAR) in SEA.]

As gun emplacements multiplied, it became impractical to destroy the guns. Instead, aircrews silenced them temporarily by killing, injuring, or driving the guncrews to cover. Even if the Zorro's didn't force the evacuation of a gun emplacement, a 100-foot miss with a 750-pound VT-fused bomb injured the gunners physically and psychologically. Most important the bomb's tremendous explosion damaged the hearing of the guncrews. In the North Vietnamese air defense scheme this was critical, since at night the gunners fired at the sound of an aircraft's engines.* A-1 crews were keenly aware the enemy's impaired hearing lowered chances of aircraft being shot down. They also knew the bomb's stupendous bang cowed many gunners and caused them to stop firing and hide until all aircraft had gone. In this respect, pilots of the 22d Special Operations Squadron felt a special pride --they "were never chased off the trail."45

The A-1 Zorros conducted armed reconnaissance with O-2 Nail FAC's, using intelligence information from Igloo White sensors. Igloo White (formerly nicknamed Muscle Shoals) employed airdropped acoustic and seismic sensors to watch for movement of enemy trucks and personnel along infiltration routes. EC-121R aircraft picked up information from activated sensor strings and relayed it to the infiltration surveillance center at Nakhon Phanom, manned by Task Force Alpha (TFA). Air strikes controlled by TFA and using sensor information were dubbed Commando Bolt.46

Task Force Alpha fed the computer with information from activated sensor strings to come up with the time trucks would arrive at a certain point. TFA gave this estimated time of arrival (ETA) and the point's coordinates to the Nail FAC and the blind-bombing site at Nakon Phanom known as LID. LID vectored the FAC and two A-1's (or other aircraft) to the fixed point. The

---

*The enemy's homemade sound-detection equipment was quite reliable. It consisted of two megaphones mounted on a hollow bamboo rod. Inside the rod were two baffles that directed the sound toward the center. Attached at the rod's center were earphones. This cleverly designed, extemporized detection gear was mounted on a wooden base and could be changed in direction and azimuth. [Intvw (S), author with Maj. Richard Starnes, Hq AFSC, 8 Mar 71.]

hunter/killer team sought to arrive in the area the same time as the trucks. If the Nail spotted the trucks, he dropped two groundmarkers and a flare before turning upwind. The lead A-1 released napalm on the road to stop the vehicles. The wingman followed up with Mk-36 Destructor land mines.*47

The A-1, unlike the A-26 and T-28, did not phase out of the USAF inventory. Rather it was gradually removed from the night interdiction role, as more effective night truck-killers such as the AC-130 and AC-119 gunships proved better suited to the task. The Air Force inactivated two special operations squadrons-- the 602d in December 1969 and the night-dedicated 22d several months later. Attrition of the A-1's finally reached the point where their activities had to be cut back. The Zorros retained, however, their missions of close support in Barrel Roll as well as armed helicopter support. In the latter role the A-1's became the mainstay in clearing the enemy from rescue areas so SAR operations could successfully proceed. Notwithstanding, by mid-1970 "Old Reliable" could no longer claim a night interdiction mission.[48]

A-1 Tropic Moon

As a direct outgrowth of the Shed Light R&D program, the Air Force deployed four specially equipped A-1E aircraft to Nakhon Phanom in January 1968. A main aim of Shed Light was supplying sensors for night detection and attack. By joining the sensors with an ordnance release system the aircraft could strike a target once it was picked up. Low-light-level television became one of the program's first sensor developments. In December 1966, Eglin AFB received for testing an A-1E fitted with the Dalmo-Victor, pod-mounted closed circuit LLLTV system. The TV pod nested under the wing on the left inboard station. It contained two cameras having image intensifiers and highly sensitive tubes. Wide-angle optics of the first camera covered an area 40° wide by 30° high. The telephoto lens of the second, a narrow-view camera, magnified an area 8° wide by 6° high.[49]

---

*U.S. Navy-developed, the Mk-36 was a high-drag (slower falling) version of the 500-pound GP-bomb. It detonated when any metallic object entered its magnetic field. [7th AF Handbook (S), SEA Interdiction, 1 Apr 70, p 65.]

On the A-1E, two monitors and operator controls were mounted on the right side of the cockpit's aft compartment, with a repeater scope installed above the copilot's instrument panel. This arrangement proved impractical, however. So on SEA-deployed aircraft one monitor ended up in the center of the pilot's instrument panel in place of the gunsight. Additionally, two monitors were located on the console directly in front of the navigator/observer (who now occupied the copilot's position.) Crewmembers could select either the narrow- or wide-view presentation for viewing. Further, on the pilot's monitor the electronically generated crosshairs of the wide-view display were boresighted* to the aircraft. This allowed the display to function as a gunsight. The display also contained the narrow-view, line-of-sight (LOS) box. This box showed up where the narrow-view camera was pointed when inside the 30° by 40° area depicted on the wide-view camera.[50]

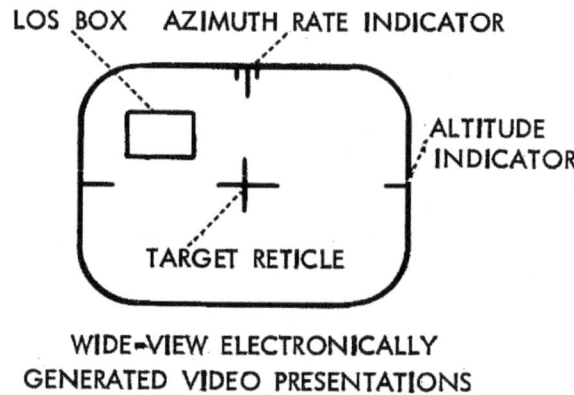

WIDE-VIEW ELECTRONICALLY
GENERATED VIDEO PRESENTATIONS

Figure 14

---

*Boresight line--an optical reference line used in harmonizing guns, rockets, or other weapon launchers.

To choose a wide- or narrow-view presentation the pilot flipped a switch on the throttle, whereas the navigator could monitor both displays simultaneously. Using a tracking handle the navigator could position both cameras from 30° above to 110° below the horizon. The narrow-view camera could swing from 100° left to 80° right of the aircraft heading. In contrast the wide-view camera could move only up and down. The navigator chiefly controlled camera movement but the pilot could gain control of the wide-view camera's depression angle through an override switch.[51]

The system was designed for automatic tracking with the narrow-view camera, <u>provided</u> the target was of high contrast and the aircraft flew straight and level. An electronically generated tracking box, adjustable in size and ratio, was displayed in the center of the narrow-view monitor. When the target was located the operator selected autotrack, placed the tracking box over the target, and released the action switch on the hand control. This kept the narrow-view camera on the target within the limits of the camera's side-to-side swing.[52]

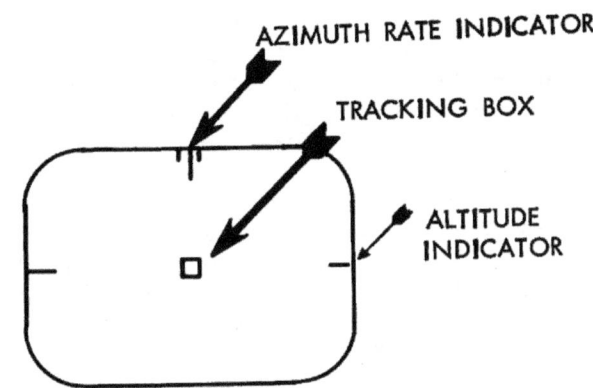

NARROW-VIEW ELECTRONICALLY
GENERATED VIDEO PRESENTATIONS

Figure 15

The LLLTV tests at Eglin, conducted at 2,500-3,000 feet AGL, showed that truck-size targets could be tracked only if sufficient light surrounded them. A quarter-moon was considered minimum light for effective truck-killing. Moreover, television by its very nature failed to present a true portrayal. Too often the navigator sweated to interpret a hazy, drab, distorted picture of the target--only to see the scene swallowed up by dark shadows.[53]

Nevertheless, LLLTV opened up possibilities for lower-light-level operations. The four A-1E's and six crews (coded Tropic Moon I) were to evaluate the sensor equipment in combat by detecting, locating, and striking targets along the Ho Chi Minh Trail. If the aircraft failed to find targets with LLLTV, they were to request a FAC from the ABCCC. They would then operate as standard A-1E's.*[54]

Tropic Moon Armed Reconnaissance--Steel Tiger

First flights of Tropic Moon I aircraft into Steel Tiger originated from Nakhon Phanom in February 1968. The normal schedule specified three A-1E sorties a night with takeoff times staggered to slightly overlap coverage in the reconnaissance area. More important, takeoffs had to conform to moon phase so enough light would be available. To speed up fragging, Tropic Moon I kept its own moon charts. The Seventh Air Force used this chart information and current weather evaluations to develop the frag.[55]

The A-1E's navigated to the reconnaissance area by TACAN with backup from GCI sites. The aircraft normally reached the operating area--in the vicinity of Route 9 and Tchepone, Laos--in 40 minutes. There the navigator searched for terrain features to establish position. This done, the aircraft reconnoitered the LOC with time on station from 1-2 hours. The pilot flew

---

*Tropic Moon crews were highly experienced. Maj. Gerald C. Schwankl, for example, was a former A-1 instructor pilot at Hurlburt Field (an adjunct of Eglin AFB). His navigator, Major Bernard S. Flynn, had spent most of his career in SAC as a B-47/B-52 navigator-bombardier. [Intvw (S), author with Maj Gerald C. Schwankel, Hq AFSC, 6 May 71.]

parallel and to the right of the roadway at 4,500-5,500 feet AGL and 140 knots IAS.56

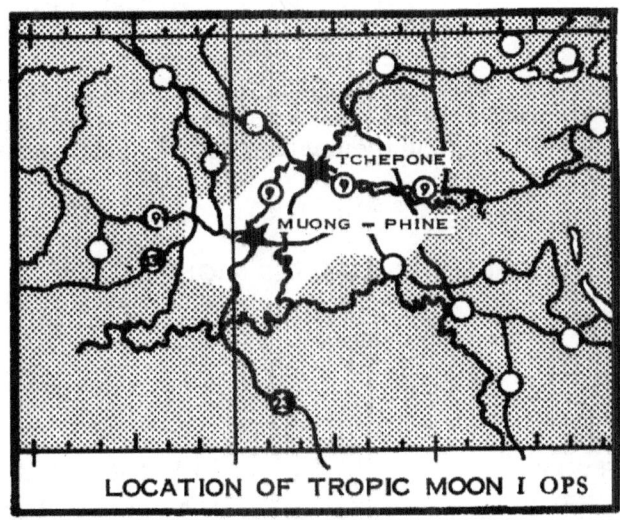

Figure 16

Visibility dictated the offset distance from the roadway. If vegetation was low and the moonlight bright enough, this distance might be as much as 1.5 miles. On the other hand, too little light and constant haze--created by slash-and-burn agricultural techniques--frequently shrunk this distance to about 1/2 mile. In diminished light the wide-view camera was useless. The crews relied almost entirely on the narrow-view camera. It, too, was handicapped because the high roadside vegetation demanded steeply depressed camera angles. Be that as it may, given reasonable ground visibility and enough surrounding light, LLLTV held promise as a night detection device.57

Upon detecting a target, the crew noted the aircraft's relation to it through the narrow-view camera then checked the depression angle. The navigator tracked the target with the TV as the aircraft maintained a left-hand base-leg turn. On attack the A-1E dove at a 20°-30° angle and released ordnance when the proper combination of sight picture, dive angle, airspeed, and altitude was reached. Ordinarily, the aircraft dropped the ordnance at 3,000 feet and bottomed out at 1,500 feet. Since the A-1E's flew singly, they commonly received one free pass at the target for the enemy gunners believed them to be FAC's and not strike aircraft.* After that, however, the gunners were alerted and aircrews limited themselves to two more passes.58

TYPICAL SELF-CONTAINED NIGHT ATTACK

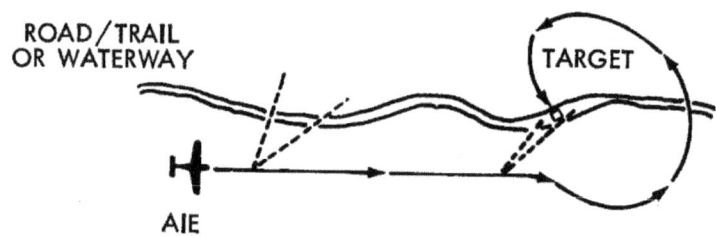

Figure 17

If Tropic Moon I aircraft spotted no trucks along the LOC, they oftentimes "motored" to a road junction and set up their orbiting left-hand pattern. Many times the formidable AA defenses around such areas as Tchepone forced the A-1E's to climb higher. This heightened the slant-range visibility problem. The wide-view camera could not resolve truck-size targets beyond 4,000 feet slant range, so the narrow-view camera had to

---

*The A-1E's might release napalm on the first pass to better mark the target for the second pass. [Schwankl intvw (S), 6 May 71.]

take over. On its TV display a small rectangle covered the target during automatic tracking (figure 14). Thus, as the aircraft gained altitude, detection and tracking capability fell off sharply.[59]

The mixed ordnance load of Tropic Moon I aircraft resembled that of other A-1's. It included M-31/32 Funny Bombs, finned napalm, fragmentation and VT-fused bombs, and Daisy Cutters (antipersonnel bombs). The aircrews considered M-31/32 bombs the best truck killers, finned napalm a close second, and hard bombs last. Tropic Moon I aircraft carried no rockets, however, because at Eglin AFB the ignition plume of a rocket had burned out one camera (approximate cost $20,000).*[60]

TV Armed Reconnaissance in South Vietnam

Proper evaluation of the LLLTV system required straight-and-level flight plus attack in an area free of heavy AA fire. Hence the Air Force moved the Tropic Moon aircraft on temporary duty to Bien Hoa AB, South Vietnam. The move meshed with the Laotian wet season which limited strike aircraft operations. In the south the A-1E's interdicted barge and canal traffic on the LOC's leading from Cambodia to Laos as well as those in the Mekong Delta area.[61]

In the Delta area Tropic Moon I aircraft took more hits than in Laos. Nonetheless, the crews searched the Delta at 2,000-2,500 feet AGL and attacked straight-and-level at around 500 feet AGL--exactly as the LLLTV system was designed to work. The contrast of targets against the canals, the wake of the boats--all sharpened the TV picture and allowed autotracking. Even the persistent drizzle did not degrade the picture as much as haze from Laotian farmers' fires formerly did. As a result, 83 percent of A-1E missions in the III and IV corps areas of South Vietnam sighted targets, destroying or damaging almost half of them.[62]

---

*Even though the TV camera's eye closed if too much light entered, it couldn't close quick enough to escape light from high-velocity rockets. [Schwankl intvw (S), 6 May 71.]

In Steel Tiger the A-1E's had carried flares for other strike aircraft as well as BDA. In South Vietnam, however, they carried them either to supply sufficient light for the LLLTV or to serve as flareship in support of hamlet or outpost defense. If flaring, the A-1E climbed to 10,000 feet AGL and dropped the flare to ignite at 7,000 feet.*63

Progress in the Delta operation pleased A-1E aircrews. Notwithstanding, the overall performance of the LLLTV system was not as effective as it was designed to be. Picture quality was better in Southeast Asia than in the United States, but the system still would not autotrack except on high-contrast targets. Furthermore, the unexpected heavy AA fire in Laos forced the crews to develop tactics for which the system was not intended. Subpar performance was the result.64

Despite these shortcomings the Air Force was convinced the system merited further development. An improved LLLTV was to be mounted in the B-57 along with MTI radar, FLIR, and an automatic weapon delivery system. Meantime, the Air Force ended the Tropic Moon I program on 1 December 1968. It removed the LLLTV from the four A-1E's thereby returning them to standard configuration. The sensors were shipped back to the United States but the aircraft remained at Nakhon Phanom as part of the 56th Special Operations Wing.65

---

*Flaring along the Trail in Laos caused enemy trucks to pull off the road, making it harder for TV to pick them up. Flaring also blanked out the scope temporarily, preventing both target acquisition and BDA. [Msg (S), 7th AF to CINCPACAF, 200245Z Apr 68, subj: Tropic Moon I.]

V. THE FAST MOVERS AND THE GUNSHIPS

The Martin B-57, developed in 1953 from the English Electric Canberra, holds several distinctive firsts in aviation history. It was Great Britain's first jet bomber, the first combat aircraft of foreign design since World War II to be adopted by the United States for operational service, the first of a long line of USAF jet aircraft used in South Vietnam, and the first Air Force jet to drop bombs in the Southeast Asia conflict.*[1]

The B-57B was an extensive modification of the British Canberra to better fit it for the interdiction role. The Air Force had greatly strengthened the aircraft to allow the full range of high "G" maneuvers necessary for tactical delivery. In addition to the rotary bomb-bay door, space for eight .50 caliber or four 20-mm machineguns was added. Load capability was increased to 10,000 lbs. by the addition of eight external wing stations. The B-model was introduced into the Tactical Air Command in 1954 but after 1959 the Pacific Air Forces became sole operator of the aircraft.[2]

The tempo of combat in Vietnam quickened during April-June 1964. In respone, the Air Force reassigned the 8th and 13th Tactical Bombardment Squadrons of the 3d Bombardment Wing from Yokota AB, Japan, to Clark AB, Philippines. These squadrons later deployed on 60-day rotational temporary duty to Bien Hao, South Vietnam. In July 1965 they moved to Da Nang and in October 1966 to Phan Rang. In January 1968, the 8th changed from a TDY to permanent status and the 13th was inactivated due mainly to combat attrition. On 15 October 1969, the last B-57B's

---

*The RF-101's had flown in South Vietnam since 1961. The B-57's and some SAC U-2's, however, were the only jet aircraft in-country until June 1965 when the Air Force deployed a squadron of F-100's. [Hist (S), 34th Tac Gp, 1 Jan-8 Jul 65.]

left South Vietnam for storage in the United States.*3

The early missions of the B-57B Yellowbirds were
(1) close support, and (2) day and night interdiction of the Trail.
Gradually, however, as the complexity of the war changed and
the interdiction mission grew, the Yellowbirds became exclusively
night attack aircraft. By 1967, they and the A-26's had killed

B-57 over Phan Rang AB, South Vietnam

most of the trucks destroyed along the Trail. One reason for
this success was that many pilots had numerous hours in the
B-57B. Several had also flown night interdiction sorties in the
B-26 during the Korean War. Moreover, the in-and-out rotation
of crews every 60 days maintained an information flow within the

---

*Initially, in 1964 and early 1965, the B-57 crews were not
fully qualified for night operations. An intensive training program
in the Philippines was begun in January 1965, however, so that by
mid-year half the authorized number of crews (28) had qualified for
night combat. The program was severely handicapped after June
due to a severe PACAF-wide flare shortage. [Hist (TS-NOFORN),
Pacific Air Forces, 1 Jan-31 Dec 66, pp 323-25.]

two squadrons, enabling crews to identify weaknesses and modify tactics accordingly. With 24 sorties scheduled per day against 23 crews, some pilots accrued over 300 missions. As one B-57B pilot noted, "We were tired--but proficient."[4]

The B-57B's construction and flying characteristics suited it ideally to the interdiction role. Its long tailpipe reduced the engine's noise and the jet plume at night. The broad wing enabled the aircraft to maneuver like a much slower plane while maintaining far greater speed. Unlike other jets, the Canberra's slower run-in speed made target acquisition easier. It pulled out of a dive without the usual mushing associated with the fast movers. The aircraft could carry over 9,000 pounds of ordnance and work a target--depending on distance and load--anywhere from 20 to 60 minutes.[5]

Like the A-26, a great deal of the Canberra's utility grew out of teamwork and coordination between pilot and navigator. In night operations the rugged terrain, marginal weather, enemy defenses, and an old-fashioned gunsight made night dive-bombing a dangerous and complex business. It demanded almost perfect crew coordination. The 2-man crew allowed the pilot to concentrate on flying the aircraft. The navigator handled all radio calls between external control sources, Forward Air Controllers, maintained position of the aircraft, armed the guns for each pass and called airspeed, altitude and angle of attack to the pilot for each bomb run. In addition to "another set of eyes," the navigator capability allowed the pilot to give his undivided attention to destroying the target.[6]

B-57 Tactics

In Route Package I of North Vietnam, the Canberra crews were permitted to conduct armed reconnaissance without a FAC being present. Here the pilot offset to the side of the road and began his "eyeball" reconnaissance with a series of S-turns at 250 knots IAS and 4,000 feet AGL. The B-57B, however, was not an ideal aircraft for visual reconnaissance. Its speed, the large wing blocking the pilot's view to the rear, the lack of any detection devices--these severely hampered a visual mission. Crews quickly realized the Canberra would be better off working with a slower-moving FAC equipped with the starlight scope and carrying sufficient flares and ground markers. As a result, when B-57B interdiction missions began in Laos, a FAC supervised them.[7]

Seventh Air Force normally fragged Canberras as single-ship sorties into the Steel Tiger area of Laos. Using TACAN as the chief navigational aid, the B-57B's climbed to 24,000-28,000 feet (depending on weight carried) and radioed the FAC about 100 miles from the target area. Approximately 50 miles from the FAC the aircraft began a controlled descent to arrive over the target area at 10,000-12,000 feet. The B-57B perched between 8,000-10,000 feet while the FAC marked the target. Once it was established that crews of both aircraft saw the target, the Canberra rolled in at 6,000-8,000 feet AGL. Next it dove at a 30°-45° angle and released ordnance between 4,000-6,000 feet AGL. After bottoming-out around 3,500 feet AGL, the aircraft executed a 4-G pullup followed either by jinking or a climbing turn. On the first pass the B-57B might drop napalm as a marker, then make a high as eight passes--subject to type of target and enemy defenses.[8]

The Air Force also tried the B-57B in the two-ship flak-suppression role used by the A-26. Crews of both aircraft coordinated tactics during the pre-takeoff briefing, and were scheduled into the target area 10 minutes apart. While the first Canberra attacked a target, the second--the suppressor--flew a circular pattern above until it spotted enemy gun defenses. When this occurred, the suppressor cleared with the first aircraft and the FAC and attacked the gun position. Although these tactics proved useful, it was the consensus of Canberra crews that overall effectiveness of the B-57B force was diluted by having two aircraft on the same target.[9]

Inasmuch as their main targets were moving trucks, the Canberra crews strongly favored the M-36 Funny Bomb. Any one of this bomb's 182 thermite bomblets could destroy a truck or at least leave a fire from which further aiming corrections could be made. Not only the B-57B crews but most all combat crews in Southeast Asia considered the M-36 the best truck-killing munitions in the USAF inventory.* From April 1968 on, however, supplies

---

*This statement is based on the author's interviews with many combat crewmembers who interdicted the Trail.

of the Funny Bomb were exhausted until production resumed in mid-1969.10

Deprived of Funny Bombs, the Canberra crews substituted other ordnance. One satisfactory combination included BLU-27's (800-pound napalm cannisters) mounted on the wing pylons, together with M-117's (750-pound general-purpose bombs) in the bomb bay. Despite its effectiveness against vehicles and personnel, napalm covered only one-fourth the area fire bombs did, and it required more precise delivery. As for the M-117's, they lacked the fuze-extenders that would have achieved a more effective fragmentation pattern.11

Mating CBU-24 fragmentation-cluster bombs with napalm didn't work out too well. CBU might stop a truck but it wouldn't destroy it nor would it leave a fire from which pilots could correct their aim for the next strike. Furthermore, only two of the weapons (vice four M-117's) could be carried by the Canberra.* Attempts to restrict the CBU-24's dispersal pattern and increase the bomblet density by lowering the release altitude failed. Hence with the Funny Bomb not available the crews preferred the BLU-27/M-117 ordnance combination.12

B-57 Tropic Moon II

As a further step toward a self-contained night attack aircraft, the Air Force modified three B-57B's and deployed them to South Vietnam in December 1967 for a 90-day test and evaluation. The aircraft--coded Tropic Moon II--were fitted with new night-detection devices. Foremost was the Westinghouse LLLTV with a zoom lens, installed in a pod on the left inboard station of the Canberra. In its stateside test this TV detected moving targets at a slant range of 3,000-6,000 feet under starlight and 8,000-10,000 feet under a one-half to three-quarter moon. It was expected to permit firing on the first pass, thereby eliminating the circular orbit that had characterized A-1E aircraft of Tropic Moon I.13

---

*Four M-65's (1,000-pound GP bombs) frequently were substituted for the M-117's.

Other devices included stabilized optics, a laser ranger, a weapon-delivery computer, plus associated electronic displays and controls. When the LLLTV picked up a target, the laser ranger fed the computer slant-range information (airspeed, bombing altitude, and weapon ballistics were preset). After the TV started tracking the target the computer automatically dropped the bombs. This system, like that of Tropic Moon I aircraft, was designed for straight-and-level attack.14

The Tropic Moon II aircraft flew two sorties each night from Phan Rang AB to the Mekong Delta, the principal targets being sampans on the waterways and trucks along Route 4. Seventh Air Force plans called for the three B-57B's to operate 3 weeks in the Delta, fly close support for 1 week in war zones Charlie and Delta, and complete the remainder of their 90-day TDY in Tiger Hound. An early short round*--it hit a police headquarters --changed all this. The Tropic Moon II crews went to Laos sooner than expected.15

In Tiger Hound and along the truck routes leading to Khe Sanh, the B-57B's of Tropic Moon II ran into problems almost identical to those faced by Tropic Moon I aircraft. Given the area's weather and visibility, the tactic of flying at 3,500 feet AGL and 275 knots IAS was too low and too fast for first-pass target acquisition. The crews acquired most targets at about 9,000 feet slant range--too late to maneuver to complete the bomb run before automatic computer release. Most observers of the test and evaluation consider this system marginal at best, so it was returned to the United States.†16

---

*short rounds--The inadvertent or accidental delivery of ordnance sometimes with resultant death or injury to friendly forces or noncombatants.

†After being briefed on Tropic Moon II's results, Gen. John D. Ryan (then CINCPACAF) concluded that not only was this system marginal but he was tired of "us buying everything they send us." [Trip rprt (S), 7th AF (Plans) Trip Rprt--Tropic Moon LLLTV, 10 May 68.]

Tropic Moon III--The B-57G

In September 1967--two months before operational deployment of the three Tropic Moon II aircraft--a Shed Light General Officers' conference had selected the B-57 as the interim SCNA aircraft until the F-111 was fully operational. On 28 November 1967, the Air Staff approved modification of 16 B-57B's for Tropic Moon III. These modified aircraft eventually became B-57G's.[17]

The Air Force equipped the modified Canberras with LLLTV, FLIR, forward-looking radar/MTI, plus an advanced digital computer system for target-tracking and straight-and-level weapon delivery. It added a laser ranger to furnish the computer accurate slang-range information. As defensive measures it included radar homing and warning (RHAW) and ECM equipment. The aircraft's ceramic armor and foamed-filled, explosion-proof fuel cells (tanks) further protected the crew.[18]

B-57G Canberra

Tactics required B-57G aircraft to operate at 2,000-3,000 feet AGL and at airspeeds of 200-300 knots IAS. Since the sensors were forward-looking, the systems operator directed the aircraft so as to keep the aircraft following the road. Upon discovering a suitable target the pilot lined up the bomber for attack and selected his weapon. At the proper point the ordnance released automatically.[19]

The B-57G's key sensor was forward-looking radar (FLR). Theoretically, it could detect jeep-size targets traveling at 3.5 knots at ranges of almost 8 miles, if the object was within 10° of the ground track. When the navigator located the target on the FLR he placed the crosshairs on a rough approximation of the aiming point. This turned the LLLTV and FLIR at the target and sent steering information to the pilot on his flight control indicator (FCI). The navigator tracked the target in automatic, computer, or manual mode. He used LLLTV and FLIR to supply additional refining information when the target came in range of these sensors. The lineup and release sequence mentioned in the preceeding paragraph followed.[20]

In October 1970, eleven Tropic Moon III aircraft deployed to Ubon, Thailand. After a few weeks operation it became evident the G models were not going to be as successful as anticipated. They wrestled the same problems that had beset earlier Tropic Moon aircraft. Working characteristics of the sensors dictated tactics geared to an operating altitude and airspeed that placed the bomber under the nose of enemy gunners and allowed them too much tracking time. The flak forced the aircraft to higher levels (6,000-8,000 feet AGL) and correspondingly downgraded the sensors' effectiveness. At these altitudes, for instance, the MTI encountered scope strobing* and no video output.[†21]

The FLR detected objects beyond its designed slant range of 9,000-12,000 feet and picked up many things the LLLTV missed.

---

*repeated intense flashes of light of short duration.

†Out of 573 sightings no MTI detections were ever recorded. [Rprt (S), USAF TAWC, TAC, Final Report B-57G SEA Combat Evaluation, Mar 71, p 8.]

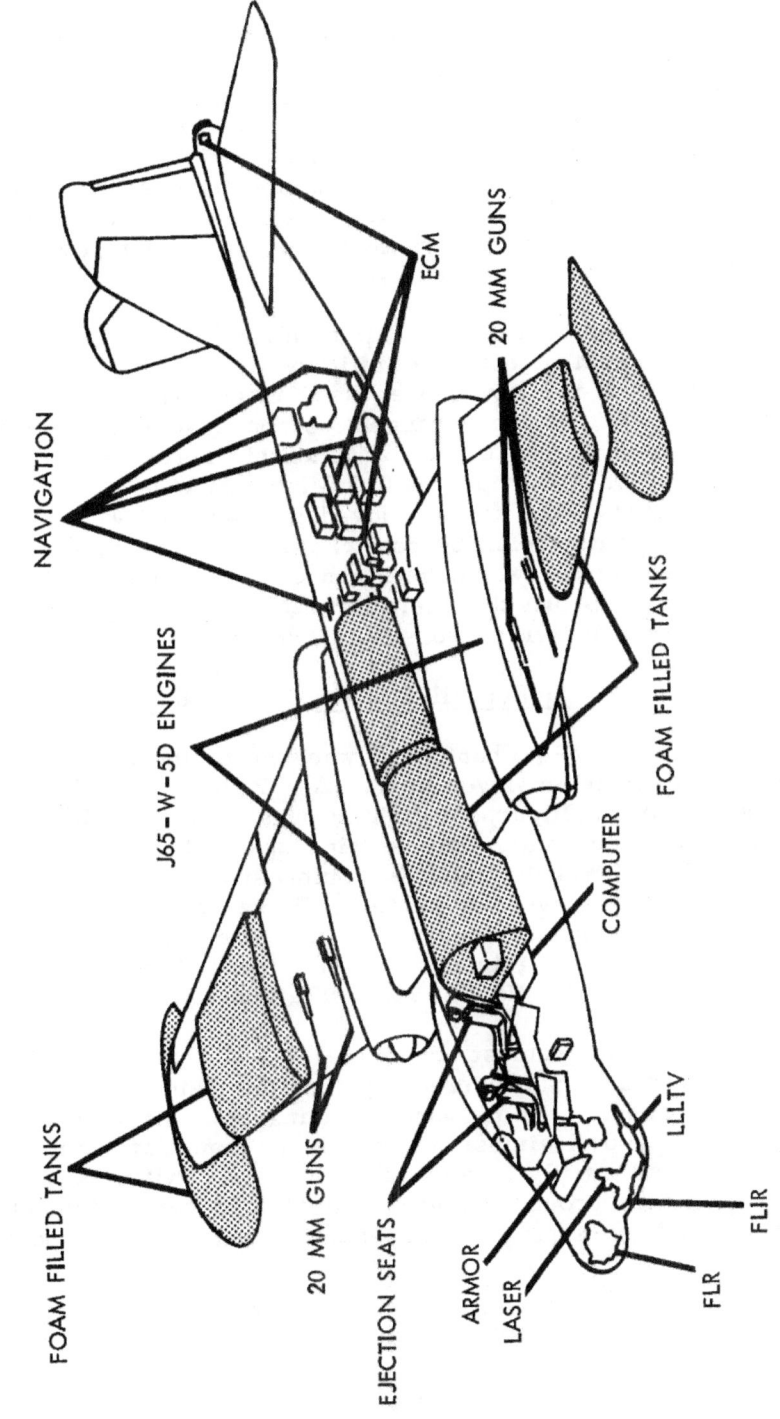

Figure 18

Nonetheless, this slant range--acceptable in controlled stateside tests--was insufficient in combat. Frequently the crews could not get lined up for a bomb run before the point of release had been passed. This required the pilot to fly a teardrop, race-track, or random-turn pattern in an effort to reacquire the target. It was often too late. Enemy drivers had spotted the aircraft and driven off the road to hide. The need for a reliable cuing device or sensor capable of operating at higher ranges and greater distances was obvious.22

(U) Tropic Moon aircraft highlighted an important factor in the procurement of complex military weapons and hardware, some of which had never been used in combat. Due to the long leadtime in developing advanced weapon systems, their future success often depended upon a relatively static battlefield. But in Southeast Asia along the Ho Chi Minh Trail the operational environment changed. The enemy moved in many AA weapons and an area once lightly defended now bristled with defenses. Revised and altered tactics would help redress this balance, but it could do little to improve the operational characteristics of sensors. Only new and better sensors could do that.

McDonnell-Douglas F-4 Phantom II

(U) The F-4 Phantom II was one of the most versatile combat aircraft employed by the Air Force in the Vietnam War. This 2-seat* multipurpose fighter began life as a U.S. Navy shipboard interceptor, only to wind up as the Air Force's standard land-based fighter in Southeast Asia. Here the C, D, and E models served as fighters, fighter-bombers, and high-speed photoreconnaissance aircraft. After the 1968 halt in the bombing of North Vietnam, the Air Force directed most Phantom sorties against the Ho Chi Minh Trail and its defenses.

The foremost advantage of F-4's and other jets lay in their speed and maneuverability that let them operate in heavily defended areas. Enemy gunners using optically-sighted AA artillery found it almost impossible to manually track these planes that sped so swiftly in and out of range. Swiftness allowed the jets to attack ground targets at night with some element of surprise, and to respond to requests for immediate support.23

---

*The crew consisted of two pilots or a pilot and a navigator. The guy-in-back (GIB) performed navigator/observer duties.

F-4E Phantom

On the other hand, speed handicapped the fast movers, especially in their night armed reconnaissance role. The jets had inadequate sensor detection equipment. When not under FAC direction they relied solely on "eyeball reconnaissance" while speeding in the black of night. Their greater speeds and steeper dive angles required ordnance to be dropped from a higher altitude, thus degrading accuracy. The aircraft needed a sizable area for turning and maneuvering, which restricted low level operations in such mountainous areas as Laos and North Vietnam. Limited fuel capacity and lack of continuous air-refueling support reduced the range and onstation time of the jets. The F-4, operating in a 200-mile range, could loiter only 20 minutes before expending ordnance which took another 20 minutes. Air refueling could extend onstation time another 40 minutes to 1 hour.[24]

It was fairly evident that jet aircraft could not match the slow movers in truck-killing and interdiction. The F-4C, for instance, possessed no effective nonvisual system for delivering conventional weapons. Its manually-depressed reticle*

---

*reticle--a system of lines, dots, crosshairs, or wires, in the focus of an optical instrument.

bombsight was reminiscent of World War II aircraft. Moreover the aircraft was without a "heads-up display," so the pilot had to divide his attention among cockpit instruments, bombsight reticle, and the target on the ground. The F-4D eventually enhanced night strike capability with its weapon release computer set (WRCS) and improved radar. Nevertheless, all versions of the F-4 lacked night detection devices, as well as adequate forward-firing munitions until introduction of the E model with its nose-mounted gun. Both the C and D versions of the fighter had poorly designed interior lights, requiring the pilot to mask many of the instrument/cockpit lights in order to operate at night.* Exterior wing lighting was also unsuitable for safe night formation flying. Considering all these conditions, it is surprising the Phantom performed as well as it did.[25]

C-130/F-4 Flare-Strike Tactics

Despite its inherent flare capability the F-4 usually worked with various FAC aircraft. In 1966 the Phantom flew many missions with C-130 Blindbats. When fragged with these aircraft, a pair of F-4's rendezvoused by TACAN or airborne radar in the target area 2,000 feet above the flareship. (Base altitude of the flareship, dependent on terrain, often reached 10,000 feet.) Unless cleared at once for attack the Phantoms set up a holding pattern if they had enough fuel. When immediately cleared one F-4 descended on the side of the flareline opposite the flareship, while the second F-4 remained high. Once established--either above or below the C-130's altitude--the pilot circled the area and identified the target before beginning his strike. Below the Blindbat's altitude the F-4 could attack from any direction, but above it was permitted to work only the left-hand side of the flareline. Meantime, the C-130 flew a right-hand pattern at 160-230 knots IAS and 6,000-8,000 feet AGL, with flares fuzed to ignite at 2,000-3,000 feet AGL. After the first Phantom completed its pass the flareship cleared in the second fighter.[26]

---

*The 497th Night Owl Squadron (8th TFWg) at Ubon, Thailand, locally modified their cockpit lights with a rheostat that could dim or brighten selected instrument lights. [Intvw (S), author with Col. Carl H. Cathey, Jr., HQ USAF (Ops), 2 Jul 71. (See footnote 35 for a resume of Coloney Cathey's SEA experience.).]

C-130/F-4 FLARE-STRIKE TACTICS

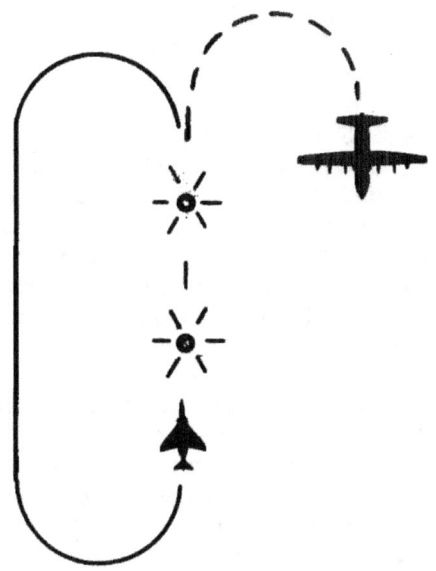

Figure 19 (U)

F-4 Armed Reconnaissance/Lightly Defended Area

By mid-July 1965 there were 184 F-4 aircraft in the Southeast Asia theater. Because the F-4's carried flares, armed reconnaissance quickly became one of the Phantom's main missions. Each mission began in the wing or squadron briefing room. Here the crew carefully chose a route to and from the target. Not only the defenses, airfields, and GCI coverage of the enemy governed this choice but the number of checkpoints as well. Sufficient checkpoints were essential to offset the serious night-navigation problems of jet aircraft. The slightest miscalculation in night navigation could lose the target. Hence the crews realized they had to fully use TACAN and "old-fashioned dead reckoning"* as backup for the F-4's inertial navigation system (INS)

---

*dead reckoning--finding one's position by means of a compass and calculations based on speed, time elapsed, effect of wind, and direction from a known position.

and radar. The INS's design limitations produced a 3- to 5-mile error for each hour of flight. Designed for air intercept, the radar presented a substandard picture when used to "map." Even the WRCS and improved radar of the F-4D did little to enhance night navigation. For these reasons the crews stressed mission planning and painstaking study of truck routes.[27]

The favorite formation for armed reconnaissance consisted of two aircraft. The lead F-4 served as a flareship, the second as killer. This arrangement was favored over one of four F-4's mainly because it was easier to control. At night it was very hard for pilots to see one another while working a target. Furthermore, the requirement to maintain different positions, the increased number of radio calls, and the intrinsic dangers of night flying in a congested area--these militated against any small advantage (more ordnance) offered by a four-ship formation.[28]

The lead Phantom carried the SUU-25/A flare dispenser (a modified LAU-10 Zuni rocket launcher) that used the Mk-24 flare. The dispenser carried eight flares--two in each of its four tubes. Each time the pilot pickled the dispenser tube it released a _minimum_ of two flares. From a drop altitude of 3,500 feet AGL and a 20-second ejection and ignition setting, the flares burned from 150-180 seconds and produced 2,000,000-candlepower illumination. Most crews dropped below this altitude, however, in order not to descend below the flares. Then, too, flares would still be burning on the ground and could be used as markers. A typical load consisted of eight SUU-25/A dispensers (64 flares) mounted on racks under the aircraft.* It was this flare capability of the Phantom and its lack of night detection sensors that prompted F-4 units to develop their own hunter/killer teams and accompanying tactics.[29]

En route, the second F-4 was offset 15° in azimuth and from 5 to 7 miles behind the lead F-4. Intercept radar

---

*Later the 8th TFWg used the SUU-42 dispenser, which had a high Mk-24 dud rate. Another load repeatedly employed consisted of either two fuel tanks outboard with three SUU-25/A's centerline, or a centerline fuel tank plus one outboard fuel tank with three SUU-25's loaded outboard on the opposite wing. The inboard stations then carried either bombs, rockets, or CBU.

F-4 TWO-SHIP CELL

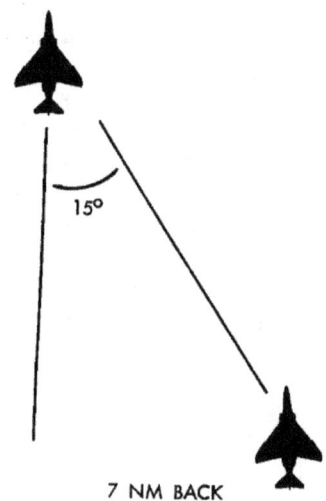

Figure 20

maintained position between aircraft. Altitude was usually 25,000 feet and airspeed around 420 knots.*30

Once the pilot of the lead F-4 determined he was in the assigned reconnaissance area, lights on both aircraft were turned off and proper attack procedures agreed upon. Aircraft altitude and airspeed varied with the flare settings. Most drops took place on a straight-and-level track at 3,500-5,000 feet AGL and 450 knots IAS. Many times the lead employed the double-pickle pattern, dispensing four flares in pairs, 10 seconds apart. After the second drop, the lead held the heading for 15 seconds before making a 180° left turn (figure 19). The 10-second pickle interval, plus the 5 to 7 miles the second F-4 trailed, brought both aircraft over the target area just as the first flare blossomed. The

---

*F-4 crews considered dead reckoning the best navigation method for <u>short</u> legs. The Phantom's radar was poor for mapping but good for <u>low-altitude</u> identification of rivers, valleys, ridge lines, and peaks. [Manual (S), 8th TFWg, Night Combat Tactics, 10 Sep 66.]

Phantoms were then on reciprocal headings and opposite sides of the flareline. In addition, the heading on which the flares were dropped established a reference line. The aircraft used this line to keep track of one another by calling out clock-code positions. The first flare became "6 o'clock" and the last flare, "12 o'clock" (figure 20). The flares also served as a reference point for objects sighted, for example, "Trucks 4 o'clock to number three flare." Before attacking a target, however, the second aircraft called the direction of the intended strike and received confirmation from the lead Phantom.[31]

F-4 TWO-SHIP ATTACK TACTICS

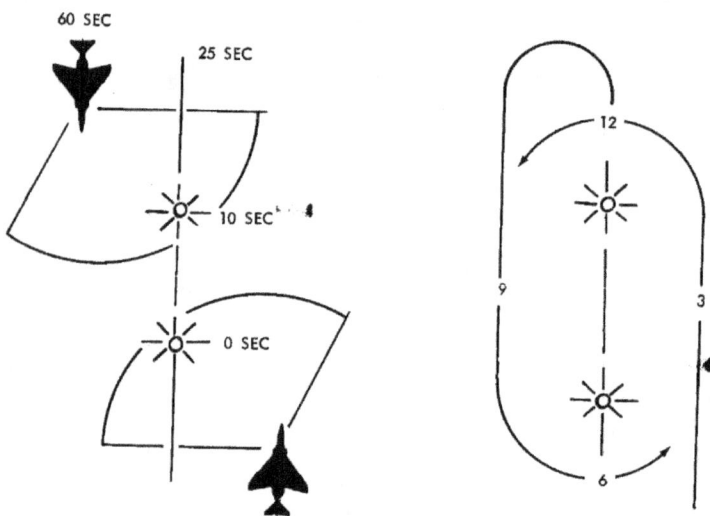

Figure 21 (S)

On occasions the lead F-4 flared and continued on for 2 or 3 miles before flaring again. The second F-4 searched the area of the first flaredrop while the lead reconnoitered the area of the second release. If either crew spotted lucrative targets, the other Phantom could be called in to help.[32]

Experiences of F-4 crews echoed those of other Southeast Asia veterans of air combat. Phantom crews found that flares alerted enemy defenses. Truck drivers immediately pulled off the road at first flarelight. A pilot observed that if the F-4's navigation erred "one could be within one mile of an objective and be completely confused when the flares are lighted and the objective is not immediately acquired." Likewise flares could be dangerous to crews delivering ordnance, for to dive below them gave the enemy more aircraft to track. Moreover, the sudden transition to and from flarelight could cause disorientation, loss of night vision, and vertigo in aircrews.[33]

The 2-man F-4 crew, like that of the A-26 learned to counter disorientation, loss of night vision, and vertigo. The "guy in back"(GIB) of the Phantom crew could monitor solely on instruments the ordnance delivery and the aircraft's recovery. (He had previous instructions to assume aircraft control when some specific altitude, pitch, or angle of bank was exceeded.) The GIB helped the aircraft commander to accurately deliver ordnance by monitoring airspeed and dive angle, cross-checking for proper switch positions, and calling out weapon release altitude. Meantime, the aircraft commander in the front seat could concentrate completely on tracking and maintaining the correct sight picture.[34]

Dive toss--the favored method of ordnance delivery--was later adopted for all attack environments. Dive toss used air-to-air radar and the WRCS. During the bomb run the GIB operated the radar in the AIR-GRD (air-ground) mode to provide a drift-stabilized boresighted antenna. Next he locked on the radar ground return, which fed slant-range data into the WRCS computer and the optical bombsight. At this point the pilot placed the bombsight pipper on the target, pushed the bomb-release button, and began a wings-level straight-ahead pullup of 2-3 G's. When the aircraft reached the proper range the WRCS released the ordnance automatically. If properly maintained, the dive-toss system was more accurate than the manual dive-bomb one. Nevertheless, the straight-ahead wings-level pullup presented enemy gunners ideal tracking for aimed or barrage AA fire. Further, the release of bombs during a pullup of 2-3 G's resulted in an increase of hung ordnance. It also lengthened the bomb patterns on the ground, reducing kill probability for pinpoint targets.

Gross errors were not at all uncommon using dive toss, so it was not used for close support. Until late 1968, the F-4 wings employed dive toss off and on, but almost entirely in lightly defended interdiction areas.[35]

In November 1968, the first Phantoms of a new F-4E squadron touched down at Korat AB, Thailand. (The F-4E's replaced a squadron of F-105's in the 388th Tactical Fighter Wing.) During the F-4E squadron's stateside training the aircrews gained considerable experience in dive toss and maintenance personnel came to know the system's equipment. Soon the 388th was demonstrating the validity of dive toss in combat--posting an enviable circular error average (CEA) of 160-170 feet. Not to be outdone, the other F-4D wings reemployed the system--using the second F-4D of the two-ship formation for flak suppression. By 1969 dive toss had become the chief ordnance release system for all F-4 wings engaged in night interdiction in Laos.*[36]

F-4 Armed Reconnaissance/Highly Defended Area

By mid-1969, few lightly defended areas remained along the Ho Chi Minh Trail. The Rolling Thunder campaign, with its air strikes against the LOC's in North Vietnam, had been scrapped in October 1968. The enemy responded by moving many of his Hanoi/Haiphong-based weapons south, including those of larger caliber. The gunners came south with their guns, and USAF and U.S. Navy pilots soon noted the more accurate and better disciplined fire.[37]

The Air Force devised two flare/search patterns for this hostile environment, both with the view of illuminating the area only once. To do this the target had to be near an easily defined initial point (IP), so the first pass over the target could drop the flares with some precision. Using the first flare pattern the pilot of the lead F-4 dispensed 16-20 flares in a straight-line dense pattern, parallel to and 1-2 miles away from the target. As the

---

*Training and deploying F-4E personnel as a squadron kindled a high unit spirit. As a case in point, each F-4E arriving in Korat had the old Flying Tiger P-40 shark's mouth painted on its nose.

flares blossomed they tended to draw enemy fire away from the strike aircraft.38

F-4 PARALLEL FLARE PATTERN

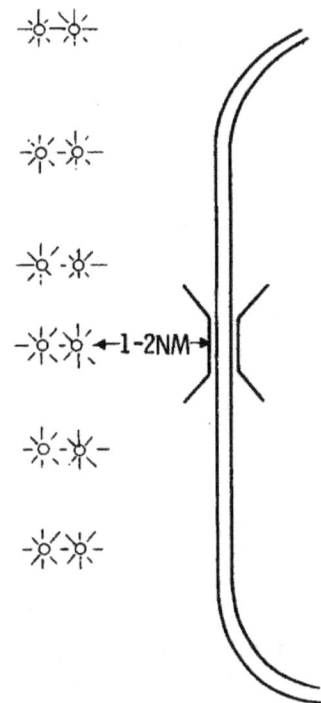

Figure 22

When following the second flare pattern, the pilot of the lead F-4 dispensed flares 1-2 miles back from where he believed the target was. Between each pickle he turned the aircraft 15°-20° while maintaining basic direction and a groundspeed of about 420 knots. After 32 flares were dropped in this manner, there was a good chance the target would be illuminated. Strike aircraft then made short passes across the fringes of the flare-light, not trying to see more than a short segment of the road on a single pass.39

F-4 SHORT-PASS FLARE PATTERN

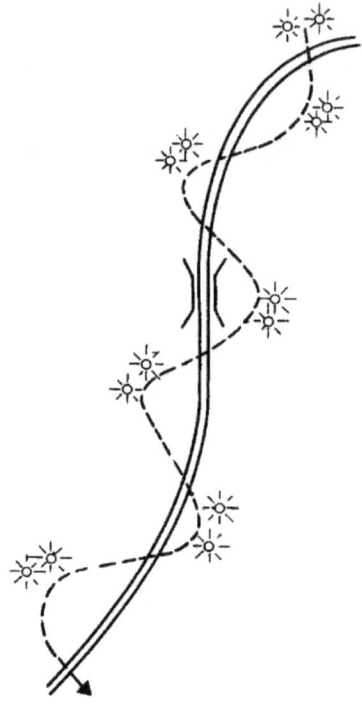

Figure 23

The chances of killing trucks under these conditions were marginal. The wind blew the flares, making it hard to put them directly over the target. From the higher altitudes the flares gave too little light for crews to detect pinpoint targets at the desired roll-in altitude of 9,000-11,000 feet AGL. Often pilots descended into heavy AAA fire, acquired the target, and climbed back to roll-in altitude--burning up valuable fuel in the process.[40]

Hence, most F-4 crews favored working with an O-2 or C-123 FAC. Frequently, however, they were fragged to operate on their own, due to dense air traffic in the reconnaissance area. Two Phantoms--spaced 30 seconds apart--would fly at 100-200 feet AGL over the LOC's, seeking to acquire targets by moonlight or surprise.[41]

F-4 delivery techniques hinged on enemy defenses, ordnance aboard, aircraft speed, and to a certain extent on the intensity of available light. For instance, in lightly defended areas the F-4 could attack almost straight-and-level, recovering at least 500 feet above the highest terrain located within 3 nautical miles of the target track.[42] The Phantom crews of the 8th Tactical Fighter Wing followed the ordnance delivery guidelines in the table below. Note that the M-117 high-explosive bomb could be dropped at either 400 or 450 KCAS (knots, calibrated airspeed) and with either a 30° or 45° dive angle. Release altitudes and mil* settings were changed to accommodate the characteristics of specific ordnance.[43]

400 KCAS DROP

Type	Dive Angle	Release Altitude	Recovery Altitude	Mil Setting
M-117	30°	3,300	2,000	121
	45°	4,750	2,500	99
CBU	Level	--	400	212
	Level	--	1,000	235+3"

450 KCAS DROP

Type	Dive Angle	Release Altitude	Recovery Altitude	Mil Setting
M-117	30°	3,900	2,000	106
	45°	5,300	2,500	80
CBU	Level	--	400	208
	Level	--	1,000	235+3"

For low-level missions, the F-4 crews employed CBU-2 ordnance. This weapon was actually the BLU-3 fragmentation bomb, mated to the 19-tube rear-firing SUU-7 dispenser. Upon ground impact the CBU-2 expelled 250 16-grain steel spheres into the air. It was chiefly an antimateriel weapon. Unfortunately, it required straight-and-level flight through the delivery phase and for two seconds after releasing the pickle button.

---

*mil--1/6400 of 360°.

This munition was also known to damage the dispensing aircraft if these flight conditions were not met. In addition, many incidents were reported of the SUU-7 dispenser damaging the leading edge of the wing when jettisoned. As for napalm, the Phantom crews preferred BLU-27 because of its honey-like consistency (Napalm B) that adhered better and destroyed more. Being complex, these napalm weapons were filled at the factory and shipped as a single unit instead of being filled in the field.[44]

Jinking--rapidly changing an aircraft's heading and altitude--was widely used to evade <u>aimed</u> gunfire. To avoid stereotyping this tactic, positive and abrupt changes were made in a random pattern. A rule of thumb followed by F-4 crews was for the jinking interval (in seconds) to be two-thirds each one thousand foot of altitude. Thus, a Phantom at 15,000 feet jinked every 10 seconds. The lower the altitude, the more frequent the maneuver. Against <u>barrage</u> fire, jinking extended the time the aircraft was exposed so in this instance speed was the best defense. But speed ate up fuel, shrunk time over target, and required frequent trips to a tanker--if one was at hand.[45]

Crews were strongly discouraged from performing their own BDA since it often spatially disoriented them. At first the crews followed this dictum. However, as they became familiar with their operational areas, the tendency of pilots to perform BDA on their own (a holdover from combat crew training at Davis-Monthan AFB, Ariz.) reasserted itself. At this point, a good antidote was strong AA fire or temporary loss of aircraft control.[46]

The lead F-4 did not use afterburner except for a quick spurt (and ignition glow) to help the second F-4 join up. Most crews departed the target area by their own radar or a TACAN bearing. Crews of the 432d Tactical Reconnaissance Wing, for example, rendezvoused near Nakhon Phanom TACAN on their way back. There they used flashlights to check one another's aircraft for hung ordnance before proceeding on to Udorn.[47]

F-4 <u>Loran</u> Bombing/Commando Bolt

In May 1969 a new F-4 mission extended the flexibility and employment of tactical air power. Known as Flasher or Commando Bolt, it teamed loran-equipped, specially modified F-4 Pathfinders with standard F-4 fighter bombers. Utilizing intelligence information from Igloo White sensors, these aircraft were to interdict enemy LOC's in darkness and bad weather. After a year's stateside training, the 25th Tactical Fighter Squadron of loran-equipped F-4's had deployed to Ubon AB, Thailand, in May 1968 and became part of the 8th Tactical Fighter Wing. The 25th's dedicated mission was to dispense anti-infiltration sensors at high speed. The sensors needed to be accurately placed so that Task Force Alpha at Nakhon Phanom could closely track and monitor enemy infiltration. To assure this accuracy the 25th's F-4's were equipped with the Shed Light-developed ARN-92 Loran D sets.[48]

Designed for precise navigation, the Loran D set included a computer, map display, and instrument display coupler. It provided the pilot a readout of his present position, cross-steering correction, as well as the course and distance to any target. At first, like many new avionics, the Loran D set suffered peculiar maintenance problems and frequent loss of signals. By May 1969, however, these problems were mostly overcome and the 25th's F-4's (the "Assam Draggins") could drop sensor strings with an accuracy of 330-660 feet.[49]

Each spring brought bad weather to Steel Tiger. The low ceilings and poor visibility hamstrung operations of gunships, A-1's, and the few remaining A-26's. On the other hand, these conditions aided North Vietnamese infiltration down the Trail. In 1969 the Air Force still had not found a way to harass enemy "movers" during the monsoon weather. So it turned to the 25th's F-4's to fill the void by keeping constant pressure on the LOC's.[50]

The sensor strings were the heart of Commando Bolt. When the infiltration center at Task Force Alpha detected trucks moving through the sensor fields, it computed an ETA for a preplotted Loran point. Flasher aircraft--a Loran-equipped F-4 and a pair of conventional Phantoms--would already be orbiting a predetermined point in Southern Laos, awaiting target information from the TFA. Upon receiving the information the Flasher aircraft departed their orbit to arrive over the target at the predetermined time.[51]

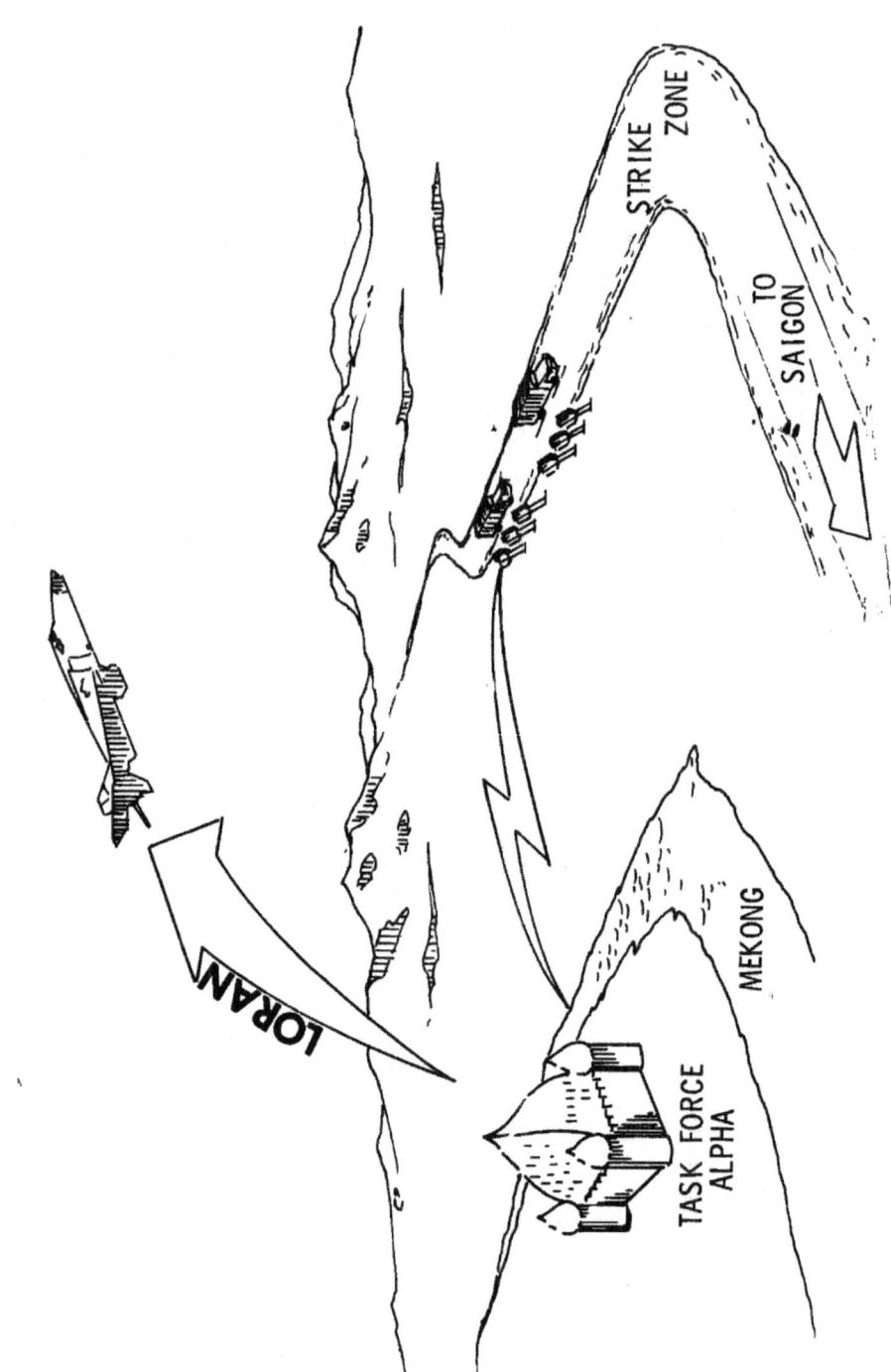

Figure 24

Commando Bolt operations required precise timing and navigation. They also called for the closest crew coordination, particularly when the Loran-equipped F-4 maneuvered into position with its wingmen. To place the maximum ordnance on the target, all aircraft--at time of delivery--had to be stabilized on track at an altitude of 4,000-9,500 feet AGL and an airspeed of 480 knots IAS. To satisfy these criteria the leader flew straight-and-level for at least 2 minutes prior to ordnance release. This allowed the wingmen to move into close formation, stabilize for delivery, then release ordnance on the Loran-equipped F-4's tone signal. The long level flight path gave enemy gunners plenty of tracking time, exposing Commando Bolt missions to heavy barrages of AA fire.[52]

Most Flasher teams employed CBU-24 ordnance, adding napalm in April 1970 due to its excellent area coverage. After ordnance release all aircraft left the target area. Usually the Loran aircraft cycled back to a tanker, refueled, and rendezvoused with the next element of aircraft to be led to a release point. Since many Flasher crews relied on follow-on reconnaissance or FAC verfication for BDA, it was hard to determine the Loran C system's precise effectiveness.[53]

Pave Way

In September 1966, the Air Force set forth a requirement for a laser* target designator system with which a FAC could accurately and covertly mark a target. The strike aircraft would carry pod-mounted laser seekers that locked on the energy return from the target.[54] Eventually two systems evolved. One used the F-4 Pahtom as the "illuminator"; the other, the C-130 Blindbat. Both methods employed F-4's carrying 2,000-pound Mk-84 bombs with laser-seeker kits in their noses. When

---

*acronym for light amplification by stimulated emission of radiation. Laser light is most often invisible or infrared. It differs from ordinary light in that its individual light rays are all the same wave length and all are in step. Hence its energy is not dissipated as the beam moves out--thus permitting an intense concentration of light energy. [Trends, Indicators, and Analyses (S), DCS/Plans & Ops, Apr 69, pp 1-17.]

an F-4 released a Pave Way bomb within a certain area called the "basket," it homed in on the laser beam reflected from the target. Targets were preselected and included fords, bridges, road bends, switchbacks* down a mountainside, and other nonperishable targets.[55]

The F-4 bomber/illuminator team worked at slightly higher altitudes than the F-4/C-130 combination. The optimum release altitude for Pave Way was 12,000 feet. The delivery F-4, therefore, rolled in at 18,000 feet with a 30°-50° dive angle. Meantime the laser-equipped F-4 flew a curved track at 12,000 feet and kept the laser beam on the target. At 20,000 feet slant range a change in bank angle as little as 1° displaced the center of the laser beam about 350 feet on the ground. Consequently little evasive maneuvering was possible.[56]

The laser-equipped C-130 Blindbats worked in a somewhat different way. The C-130 passed the geographic coordinates to the F-4 which computed a Loran release point for the selected heading. The Blindbat flew a 7,000-8,000 foot AGL right-hand orbit, simultaneously tracking the target with the night observation sight (NOS), and laser. The Phantom rolled in and while in level flight released the weapon at the computed Loran coordinates (see figure 21). The size of the release basket compensated for any errors. Variations had the Blindbat illuminating an area with flares or working with as many as three bombers. At times the blacked-out C-130 worked below a cloud-deck (the laser illuminator could not "see" through clouds) while the F-4 worked above. First Southeast Asia tests and evaluation of this weapon system took place in early 1970. The results pointed to the system's immense possibilities.[57]

AC-130 Development and Equipment

The AC-130 Gunship II proved to be the most effective aircraft for night interdiction of targets in Southeast Asia. The Air Force developed this converted Hercules transport as a follow-on to the AC-47 in the classic role of close air support (site defense) and as an interdiction weapon along the

---

*zigzag roads in a mountainous region.

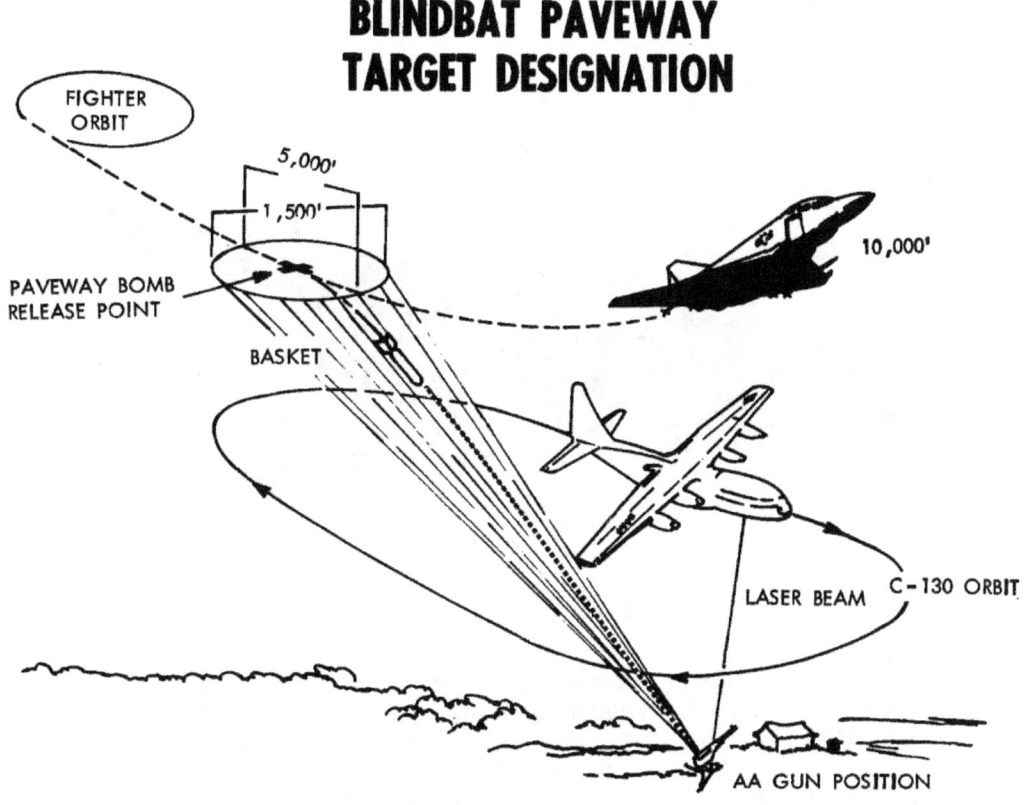

Figure 25

Laotian LOC's. To aid in truck detection the aircraft was equipped with several electronic sensors. Chief among them were a large starlight scope called the night observation device (NOD) and a forward-looking infrared (FLIR).*58

---

*Additionally the aircraft carried side-looking radar to search, acquire, and track X-band radar operated by friendly forces at isolated Laotian sites. This side-looking radar could not detect vehicular traffic. [Hist (S), 8th TFWg, Jan-Mar 1969, p 37.]

AC-130 Gunship

The NOD was an electrically stabilized light intensifier (40,000:1, later 60,000:1) and bigger than the starlight scope in FAC aircraft. A yoke mounted at the crew-entrance door on the left side of the AC-130 supported the NOD. Like its predecessors the scope was ineffective unless sufficient surrounding light--moonlight, starlight, skyglow--was available.[59]

The FLIR system consisted of a mechanical and optical scanner. It was mounted in the wheel well fairing while the operator's station was in a cargo-section booth. The FLIR could detect hot objects such as truck engines, fires, and vehicle surface heat. Detection range varied with the humidity and foliage as well as the differences in size and temperature of the target from its background. Truck-size objects, for instance, were commonly spotted as high as 20,000 feet. Furthermore, while the NOD could lose a target if it disappeared under a tree, the heat seeking capability of the FLIR could continue to track. Moreover it could assess damage by detecting fire and explosions.[60]

In addition, Gunship II carried a 40-kilowatt xenon lamp/illuminator mounted on the cargo-ramp door. A selector switch allowed the operator to select visible light or covert infrared/ultraviolet radiation through use of internal mirrors or filters.*61

AC-130 GUNSHIP DETECTION DEVICES

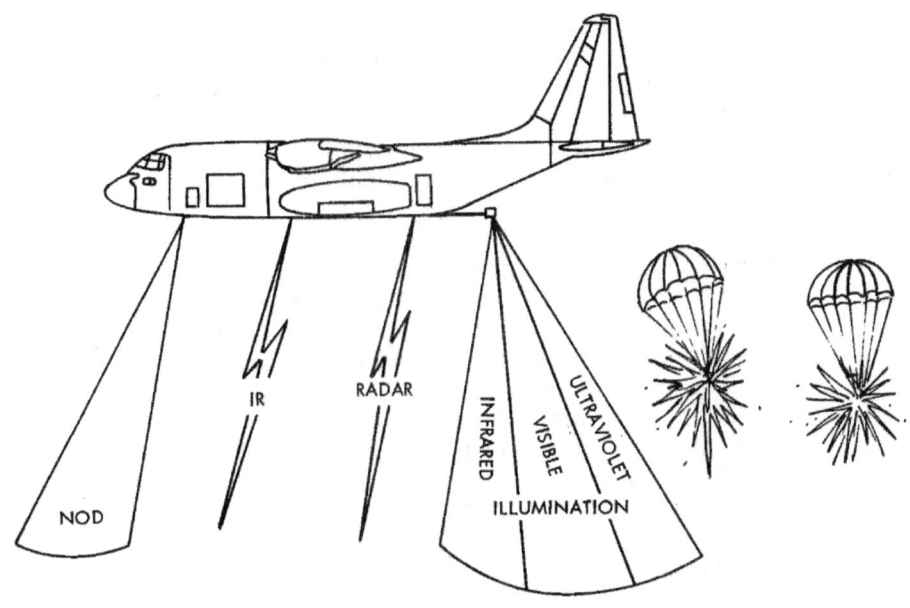

Figure 26

The AC-130's four 7.62-mm miniguns and four 20-mm cannon, like the primary sensors, were situated on the left side of the aircraft. These guns were extremely effective antipersonnel weapons and chiefly responsible for the gunship's success as a truck killer. The minigun could sustain fire at 3,000 or 6,000 rounds-per-minute; the 20-mm gatling, 2,500 rounds-per-minute. Every AC-130 carried about 15,500 rounds of 7.62-mm and 8,000 rounds of 20-mm ammunition.62

---

*xenon--a heavy, colorless, inert, gaseous element used in specialized electric lamps; kilowatt--a unit of power equal to 1,000 watts.

The gunship's AN/AWG-13 analog computer tied sensors and ordnance together. It received inputs from the NOD, FLIR, and beacon radar and established a line-of-sight to a designated point. It solved the approach-guidance problem, supplied azimuth steering signals, and corrected fire-control equations for wind, airspeed, and altitude. All the pilot needed to do was put his gunsight pipper on the target reticle and commence firing.[63]

The AC-130 surpassed the AC-47 in modification and extra equipment. It had foam-filled fuel tanks, radar homing and warning (RHAW) equipment, some protective armor, a pneumatic flare launcher, and a 40-kilowatt searchlight. The latter, operated manually or by remote control, was especially efficient in support of friendly ground forces in contact with the enemy.[64]

During 20 September-1 December 1967, the Air Force conducted the first of two Southeast Asia evaluations of the prototype Gunship II. Evaluation missions normally lasted 5 hours and encompassed airborne alert in support of friendly forces in South Vietnam and interdiction in the Tiger Hound area of Laos. Returned to the United States for modification, the prototype was again in Ubon, Thailand, by February 1968. Meanwhile, the Air Force directed that seven more C-130A's be modified into gunships and tagged for Southeast Asia.[65]

When the prototype AC-130 (Spectre) returned, the yearly monsoon weather in Laos restricted its armed reconnaissance role. Notwithstanding, in only 43 missions the AC-130 sighted 847 vehicles and damaged or destroyed 319 of them. Next, the gunship went to Tan Son Nhut, South Vietnam, to help counter the rocket threat to Saigon. When this threat abated, the AC-130 flew interdiction missions against the enemy's boat, sampan, and truck traffic on the rivers, canals, and roads of South Vietnam. During this period, several U.S. Special Forces camps turned to Spectre for fire support. On three occasions the gunship flew special missions in the DMZ searching for helicopters. By the time the weather began to clear in Laos, however, significant maintenance problems with the AC-130's sensors (many were handmade) cropped up. Seventh Air Force was concerned since continual sensor breakdown would compel Spectre to operate as a conventional AC-47.[66]

The Air Force organized the first AC-130 unit--the 16th Special Operations Squadron--at Ubon in October 1968 and placed it under the 8th Tactical Fighter Wing's control. By the end of the year the tired prototype returned to the United States and four new AC-130's were in place at Ubon.[67]

AC-130 LOC Interdiction Tactics

Seventh Air Force usually fragged a gunship to an area or along specific route(s) with authority to attack any valid target within the area or along the route. Combat experience had shown that the smallest search area should be at least 20 miles long by 7 to 10 miles wide. This allowed enough room in which to vary search patterns, maneuver escorts (when used), and permit the AC-130 to execute evasive maneuvers and other variations in tactics. Similarly, combat experience set the altitude at 4,500-5,500 feet AGL and the airspeed at 145 knots IAS.[68]

The AC-130 relied on three basic patterns in armed reconnaissance missions--random search, parallel search, and spiral search. These patterns (detailed below) showed a significant evolution over the old AC-47 pylon-turn maneuver and revealed that the Spectre had borrowed certain fighter and FAC techniques. The type of pattern chosen hinged on the AAA threat, terrain features, LOC width, height of trees, jungle canopy, and like factors. Many times a combination of these factors dictated a blend of the three patterns.*[69]

Random Search

The Spectre accomplished route reconnaissance in high-threat areas by making right- and left-hand turns that cut the LOC at random points and at random angles (figure 27). This pattern enabled the NOD and FLIR to scan a road or waterway for considerable distance in both directions while crossing it at different angles. Since turns back to the LOC were random, crews searched for hidden storage areas and truck parks off the main area. It might take longer to cover a road or waterway in this

---

*Descriptions of the three search patterns in the next five paragraphs are based on: Pamphlet (no class), 14th SOWg, Gunship Tactics, 1 Oct 70, pp 29-32.

AC-130 RANDOM PATTERN

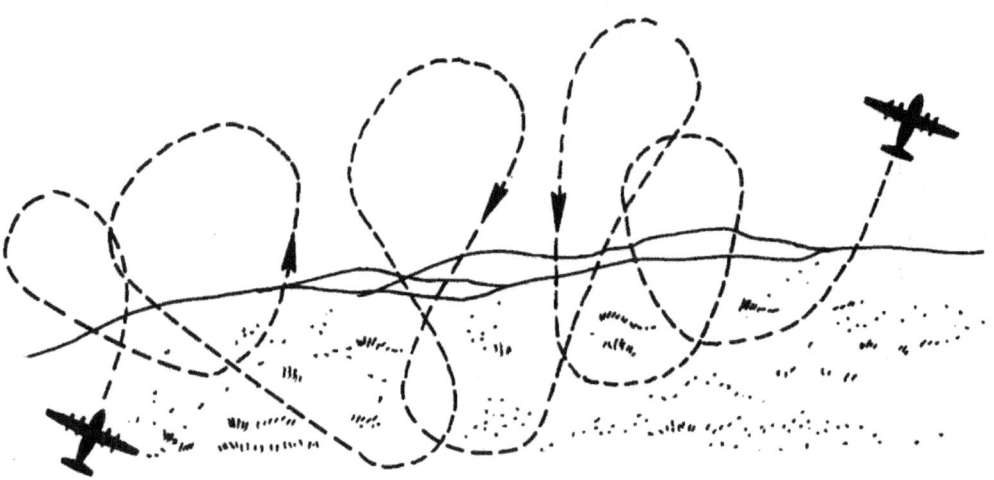

Figure 27

manner but coverage was fairly thorough. More important the time exposed to enemy tracking and firing was shortened. Once a sensor--either the NOD or FLIR--detected traffic that sensor was designated as primary. The other sensor then aligned on the primary and confirmed the target.

The gunship now began its pylon turn while firing on the target. At times the pilot deemed it best to continue on a heading for some distance before turning into the target for a fast attack (figure 24). Ordinarily this cut down exposure to ground fire and allowed the AC-130 to make a deliberate pass with only a short time in orbit.

Parallel Search

During parallel search the gunship paralleled the trail, stream, or river while the sensor operator kept one sensor forward along the artery. This freed the other sensor to scan the LOC for any traffic. Since some traffic might be visible

AC-130 ATTACK ORBIT

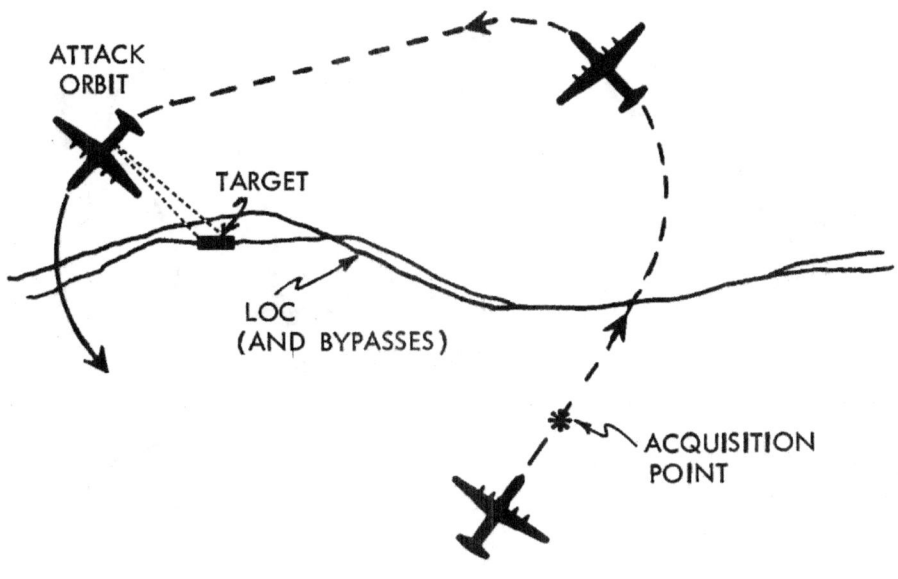

Figure 28

to one sensor and not to another, there was frequent switching between the FLIR and the NOD. Once traffic was discovered, the detecting sensor locked on the target and a normal firing pass started.

With this pattern the AC-130 could track a LOC no matter what its direction. On a snaking road the gunship tracked the middle path rather than each turn. This permitted the other sensors to probe for choice targets without violently maneuvering the aircraft. If the LOC made a definite turn toward the gunship, the pilot flew over it, executed a 270° turn and paralleled the road once more (figure 25). This method rapidly covered a road but often put the gunship on a flight path less than a mile from areas occupied by enemy AAA batteries.

AC-130 PARALLEL SEARCH PATTERN

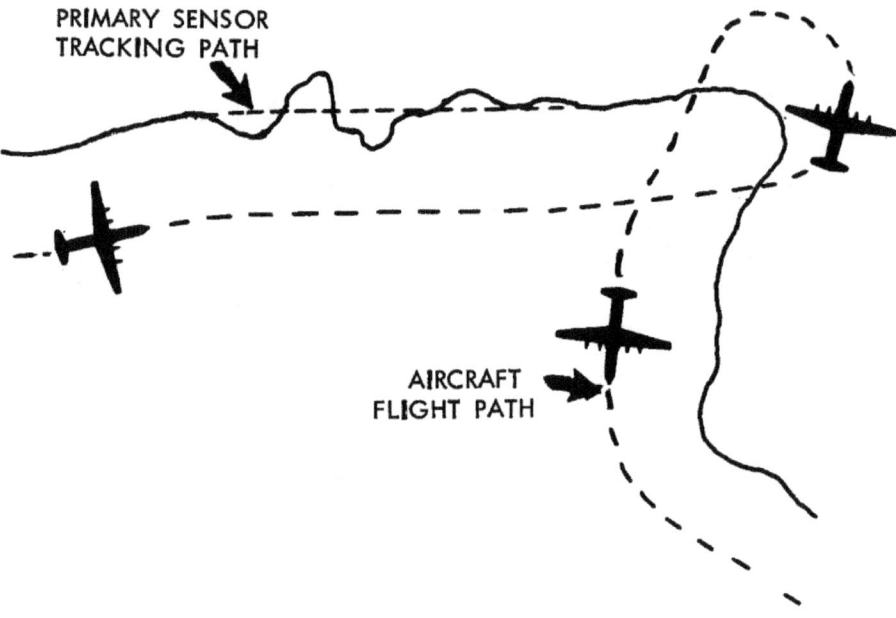

Figure 29

Spiral Search

When on spiral search, the gunship "spiraled" down the road using a combination of sensors to maintain its position in the area. Many times the NOD was designated the primary sensor to track a point on the ground. The pilot kept the AC-130 in orbit by target steering while the other sensors searched the area thoroughly in all directions. Then the NOD was moved down the LOC to a point about one-half its field of view. Next the pilot reacquired the orbit and continued the pattern (figure 26). Very often the primary sensors were switched to let all devices search an area. Although spiral search offered more complete coverage than other patterns, it exposed the gunship to any AA threat in the area.

AC-130 SPIRAL SEARCH PATTERN

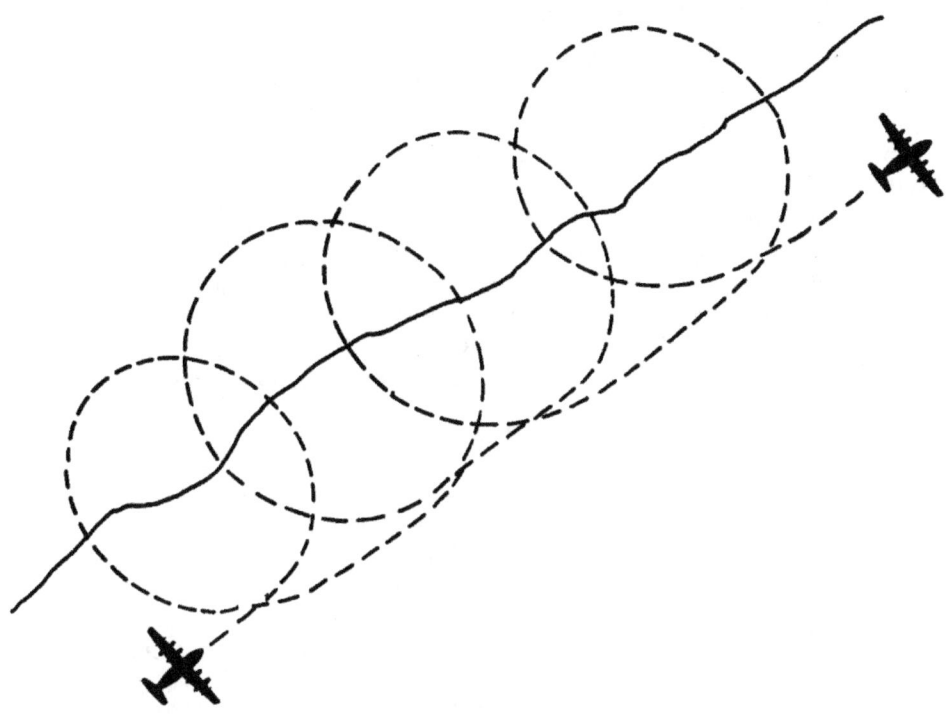

Figure 30

AC-130 Attack Procedures

If the target was a truck convoy, the AC-130 always tried to attack and destroy the first and last vehicle. This blocked the road and prevented the escape or dispersal of the rest. Once the gunship assumed an effective orbit, it was simply a matter of keeping the sensors locked on the target. The pilot made repeated orbiting passes (30° of bank) while spraying the target area with 2- to 3-second bursts of cannon fire.[70]

During the first half of 1969, the four AC-130's flew 516 sorties and destroyed or damaged 2,105 trucks--a rate of four vehicles per sortie. Nevertheless, the area ceased to be lightly defended, for the North Vietnamese had moved many AAA guns into Laos to defend the Trail complex. Flying at 5,500 feet AGL the converted transports offered enemy gunners an inviting target. In the Commando Hunt I operations (1968-1969 dry season) several gunships sustained battle damage.[71]

Inasmuch as the AC-130 Spectre was not designed to shoot it out with the enemy, its main defensive maxim was to avoid the guns whenever possible. New gunship tactics included varying approaches to the target, partial orbits, and higher operating altitudes. (The latter tactic, however, degraded sensor capabilities.) Oftentimes the Spectre orbited a safe distance away from the guns and waited for the enemy trucks to go to a lightly defended area. In addition, the crews practiced techniques to track, fire, and roll out before completing more than 90°-120° of their pylon turn. The most effective remedy for the enemy's AAA fire, however, was the introduction of an F-4 flak-suppression escort.[72]

AC-130/F-4 Flak-Suppression Tactics

The first F-4 unit to devote full time to gunship flak-suppression was the 497th Tactical Fighter Squadron (the Night Owls) stationed at Ubon AB. Selection of the 497th had distinct advantages. Its crews were experienced in night combat and the aircraft operated from the same base as the AC-130's. This arrangement enabled Phantom and Spectre crews to mission plan and brief together before takeoff.* There was the ever-present danger of air collision at night. (The Spectre flew blacked out except for formation lights and a small, shielded, red rotating beacon on top. The F-4's of the Night Owls had their bottoms painted black.) Hence it was essential that each crew know the procedures to follow should it become necessary to suppress enemy AAA fire.†[73]

Three F-4's escorted each Spectre mission and worked a target area for about 3 hours before returning to base. The fighters took off 30 minutes apart to provide one escort over the AC-130 at all times. The first fighter lifted off, refueled with a KC-135 tanker (usually at 18,000-20,000 feet), and joined the gunship as it began surveillance. When the second F-4 arrived, the first Phantom recycled back to the tanker which was completing the refueling of the third aircraft (figure 31).‡[74]

---

*This arrangement resembled that of the 56th Special Operations Wing (see p 99).

†After January 1970 the Night Owls discontinued interdiction missions and performed full-time gunship escort. [Hist (S), 7th AF, 1 Jan-30 Jun 70, I, 15.]

‡The tankers were periodically repositioned as Spectre moved along the LOC's. [End of Tour Report (S), Colonel Wendell L. Bevan, Jr., Commander, 432d TRWg, 3 Sep 68-7 Jun 69.]

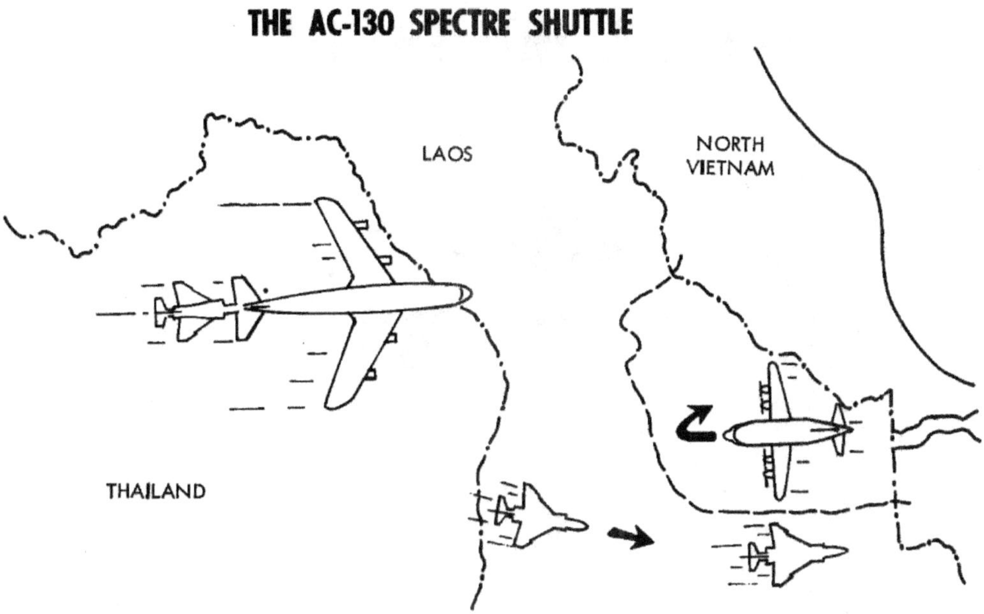

THE AC-130 SPECTRE SHUTTLE

Figure 31

    The AC-130 usually reconnoitered at 160 knots IAS and 5,000-7,000 feet AGL. The F-4 escort positioned himself in the right-rear quadrant, 2-3 miles behind and 6,000-8,000 feet above the gunship--using the latter's red rotating beacon to visually maintain position. Since the AC-130 flew a straight course, the faster F-4 escort had to fly a series of S-curves or a large elliptical orbit (figure 32) to keep the required interval. When the gunship entered its firing orbit, the fighter enlarged its orbit about the same point (figure 33). To keep its 8 or 10 o'clock position the F-4 varied the circumference of the circular pattern by introducing a steeper bank. The escort continually jockeyed to regain or retain the preferred position, but at times ended up on a heading reciprocal to the gunship's. When this occurred, the technique was to "S-off" and try to get in position.[75]

F-4 ESCORT TACTICS

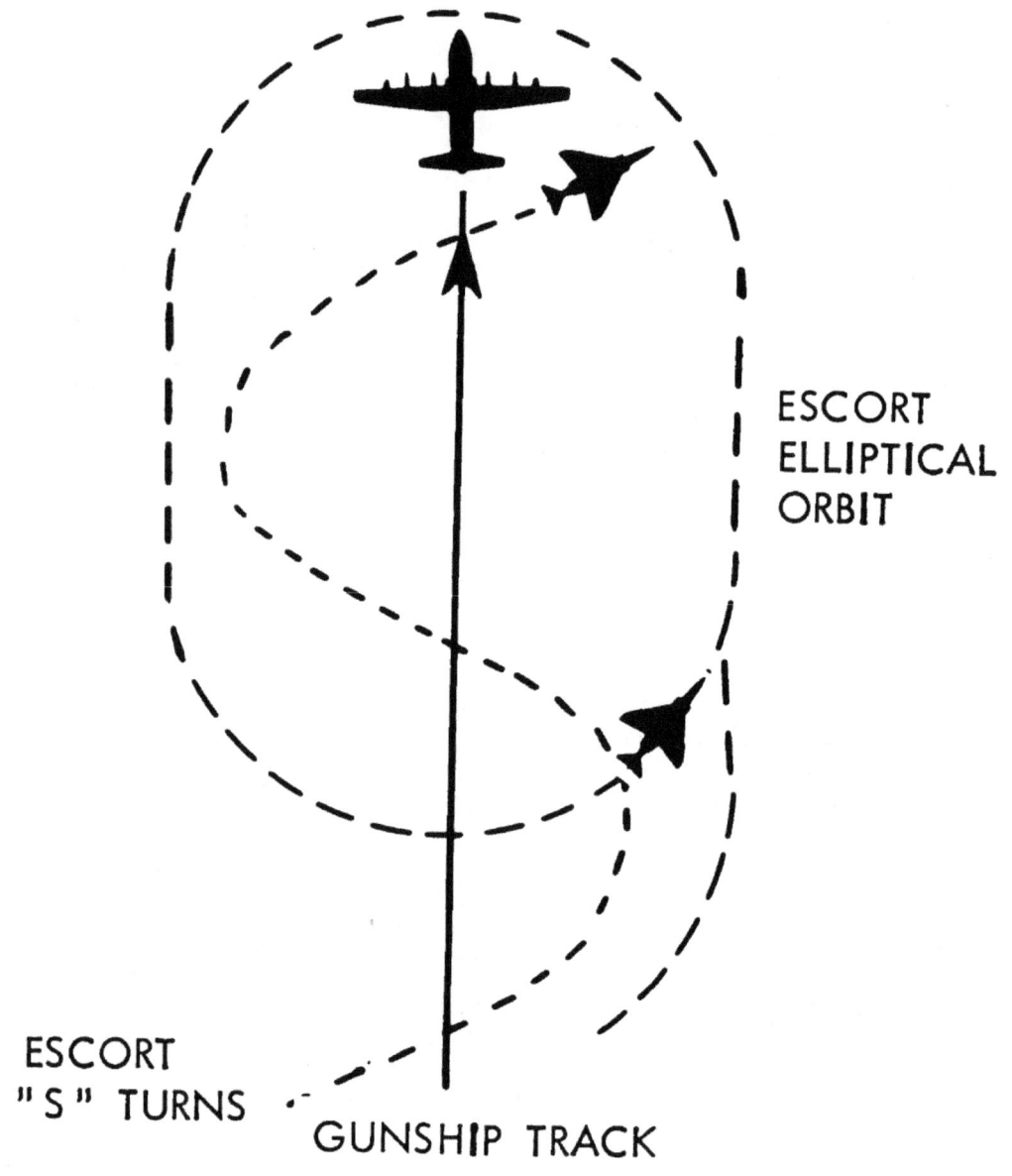

Figure 32

GUNSHIP ESCORT POSITION

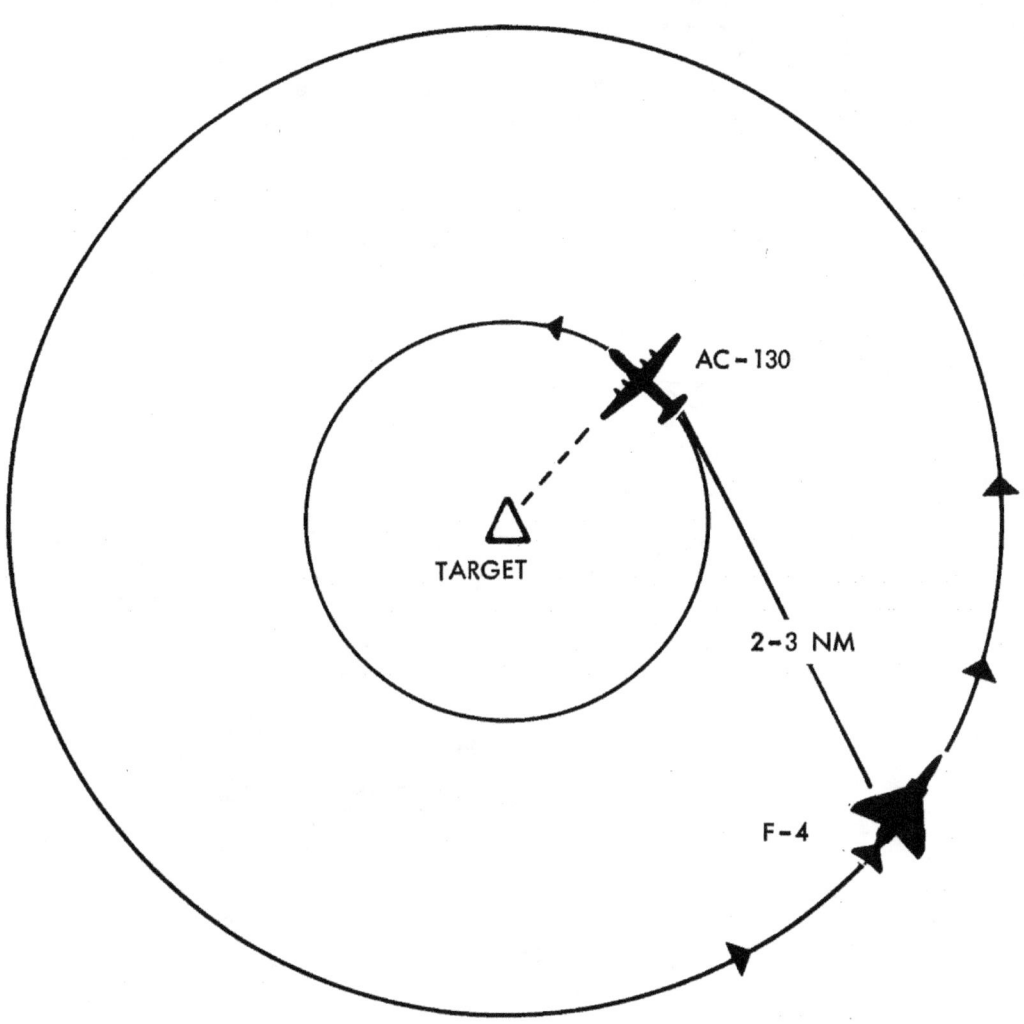

Figure 33

When enemy gunners fired (usually at the gunship's right side), the AC-130 moved off the target and informed the flak-suppression aircraft. If a strike was in order, the F-4 would be cleared in immediately (figure 30). Frequently, the gunship reentered the pylon-turn orbit to perform BDA for the escort or to continue firing at the target. Normally, the F-4 flew through and back out the gunship's altitude, dropping one CBU cannister or a 2,000-pound bomb with a fuze extender attached.* Repeat passes were made as necessary.[76]

F-4 FLAK SUPPRESSION FOR AC-130

Figure 34 (S)

---

*Normal load was three 2,000-pound bombs and eight CBU-24 or CBU-49 cannisters. [End of Tour Report (S), Col. W. L. Beven, Jr., 3 Sep 68-7 Jun 69.]

There were occasions when the gunship met only light AAA fire, and it was productive to expend ordnance on the gun sites. In these instances the AC-130 served as a FAC. It searched for targets with its sensors, dispensed flares or markers, and directed the flak-suppression F-4's on armed reconnaissance targets discovered along the LOC's.[77]

Flak-suppression tactics may well have saved the AC-130's interdiction mission in Laos. With escorts, the gunships could operate over most of the Trail complex. Exceptions included such areas as Mu Gia Pass and Tchepone that bristled with AAA batteries. In February 1969, the five AC-130's destroyed 210 trucks; in March, 292; and in April, an alltime high of 486.*[78]

It was not completely one-sided, however. The North Vietnamese responded to the AC-130's success by assigning the highest priority to shooting down a gunship. To this end they modified their tactics. One gun fired on the gunship. Then another gun opened up on the escort as he began the attack, seeking to distract him from his original target. With the escort fully committed, the gunners knew they were for a moment safe from attack. Hence, they barraged fire at either the F-4 or the gunship.[79] The gunships began taking hits and several times only outstanding flying made it possible to return the aircraft to Ubon. Finally, an AC-130 was destroyed on 24 May 1969 while attempting an emergency landing after being hit with two rounds of 37-mm fire.[80]

The enemy AAA buildup, after the Rolling Thunder campaign ended, prompted further Air Force countermeasures. Work was already under way to enhance both the gunship force's ability to survive enemy fire and its effectiveness. One result--an updated AC-130 known as the Surprise Package--was another step toward realization of a self-contained night attack aircraft. The Air Force added, for example, a new fire-control computer, improved sensors, and larger caliber guns that could inflict greater damage at longer ranges. Surprise Package entered the theater in December 1969 for test and evaluation--as the eighth and last programmed AC-130A Spectre.[81]

---

*The psychological aspects of flak-suppression cannot be overlooked. Night Owl crews, like A-1 pilots, used the 2,000-pound bomb not so much for its destructive capability but for its big bang. Also "putting something on Charlie" bolstered the confidence of gunship crews. [Intvw (S), author with Col. Carl H. Cathey, Jr., HQ USAF, (Plans) 2 Jul 71.]

The Surprise Package (Coronet Surprise)

To the three primary sensors of Spectre, the Surprise Package joined these special features: LLLTV with laser ranging, MTI radar, S-band ignition system detection, improved navigation equipment, and a digital computer fire-control system. Also included was an inertial/targeting system which could store or memorize targets of opportunity and then enable the aircraft to return to the area for an attack on the target (figure 35).[82]

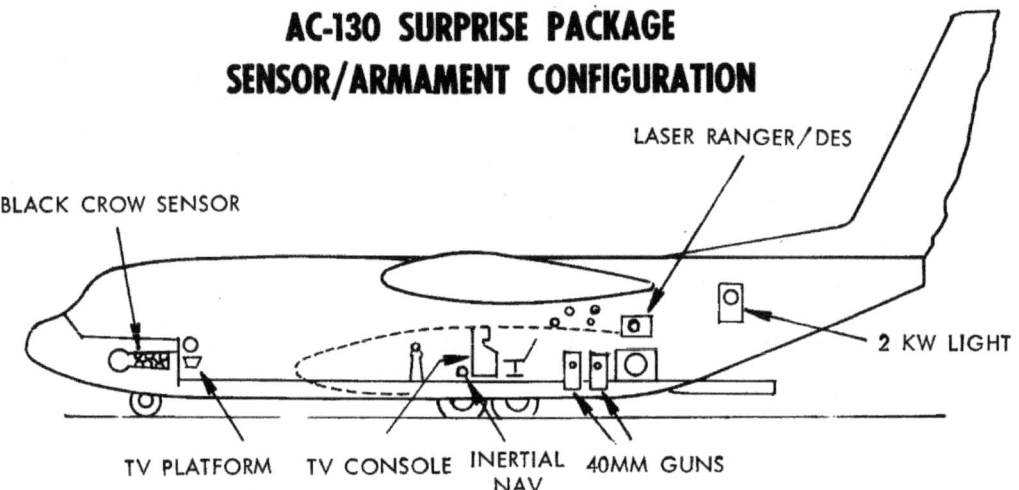

Figure 35 (S)

The Air Force developed the S-band ignition system detector (Black Crow) for the AC-123 Black Spot aircraft.* The detector identified and acquired targets by sensing electrical impulses from vehicles and other equipment using an ignition system. It also furnished the fire-control system accurate azimuth and elevation information on the targets. The Black Crow initially detected about 65 percent of all Surprise Package targets.[83]

---

*Discussed later in this chapter.

The MTI displayed the normal radar picture or only moving targets, canceling out all other video. Its alerting feature cued the operator to moving targets as he looked at the normal display. To pinpoint vehicles, a control permitted display of the customary background with the MTI. The set's variable range extended to 20 miles and it detected targets moving from 3 to 500 knots.[84]

Superiority of the Surprise Package digital computer over the Spectre's AN/AWG-13 analog computer was the really <u>significant</u> difference between the two aircraft. To control fire accurately, the digital computer continually processed information from the navigation equipment and sensors plus certain manual inputs. It accepted azimuth and angle data from up to six sensors. More important, it enabled Surprise Package to fire accurately from various airspeeds and altitude. In contrast, the AN/AWG-13 computer restricted firing to specific airspeeds and altitudes.[85]

The Surprise Package configuration replaced two of Spectre's 20-mm guns and two of its miniguns with two barrels from the U.S. Navy's Ml 40-mm antiaircraft artillery gun, commonly known as the Bofors. This weapon loaded manually using standard four-round clips, fired singly or at 120 rounds-per-minute, and had a muzzle velocity of 2,870 feet-per-second. With Bofors the aircraft could now work at altitudes up to 14,000 feet with a standoff range in excess of 2 1/2 miles.[86] Surprise Package further carried a BDA recorder to record either TV video or infrared imagery on video tape along with the accompanying audio. This information confirmed battle damage reports and served as a source for reconnaissance intelligence in the planning of other strikes.[87]

Surprise Package employed standard gunship tactics but from higher altitudes (8,000-9,000 feet AGL) and longer slant ranges (2.5-3 miles). In addition, the improved navigation system and sensor equipment provided capabilities beyond those of Spectre. The aircraft adopted two armed reconnaissance search patterns. The first entailed a rapid search of the fragged area to identify any traffic moving at the time. If targets were observed, the gunship went directly to them and attacked, utilizing the first sensor that acquired the target. If no targets were seen, the spiraling search pattern (figure 30) was flown.[88]

Understandably, the complicated Surprise Package system ran into a host of technological problems. During the evaluation the total system seldom functioned. The MTI radar, for instance, proved an unreliable detection device. The fire-control system needed precise maintenance, including tedious boresighting before each mission. On the other hand, the Black Crow demonstrated it could detect a variety of targets in any weather. In fact, if it could track accurately enough to be used as a primary sensor, it could give the gunship an all-weather capability.[89]

Despite the need for sensor improvement, Surprise Package took a high toll of enemy vehicular traffic. In the 1969-70 dry-season campaign it averaged 7.34 trucks destroyed per sortie compared with the Spectre's 4.34. In the summer of 1970, the Air Force returned the five AC-130 Spectres and the Surprise Package to the United States for modification and updating. The Spectres were configured the same as Surprise Package.[90]

The AC-119G/K

The Air Force did not have sufficient C-130's to divert more of them from airlift missions for conversion to gunships. Secretary of the Air Force Harold Brown, therefore, approved modification of the twin-boom C-119 transport (Flying Boxcar) into the gunship configuration. (At the time the C-119's were assigned to U.S. Air Force Reserve units.) In early 1968 a contract was awarded to Fairchild-Hiller for modification of the Flying Boxcar.[91]

Stateside testing of this new addition to the gunship family showed it to be a very stable gun platform. It also had the ability to remain over the target with less pilot effort than the AC-47 Spooky required. Single-engine performance was marginal, however, and its endurance only 2 1/2 hours compared to Spooky's 4 1/2 hours. Consequently, the AC-119's deployment was far down the Seventh Air Force priorities list. Nevertheless, the Air Force deployed the aircraft to South Vietnam.*[92]

---

*The author remembers attending a force-deployment conference at Headquarters, Thirteenth Air Force in September 1968. The Seventh Air Force representatives remarked that the AC-119 gunships were being forced on them. Seventh's chief objections were the gunship's marginal single-engine capability and the low manpower ceiling for South Vietnam.

The AC-119G Shadow arrived in South Vietnam in mid-December 1968, the AC-119K Stinger a year later. Shadow had four 7.62-mm miniguns for armament plus a four-tube pneumatic flare launcher (24 flares), night operating device, fire-control computer, and a lead-computer gunsight. It carried a crew of eight and possessed an endurance time of around 6 1/2 hours. Similar to Shadow, the Stinger was fitted with such additional equipment as two 20-mm guns, FLIR, beacon-tracking radar, doppler computer, RHAW, and auxiliary jet engines. Its crew numbered 10 and it could stay aloft about 5 hours.[93]

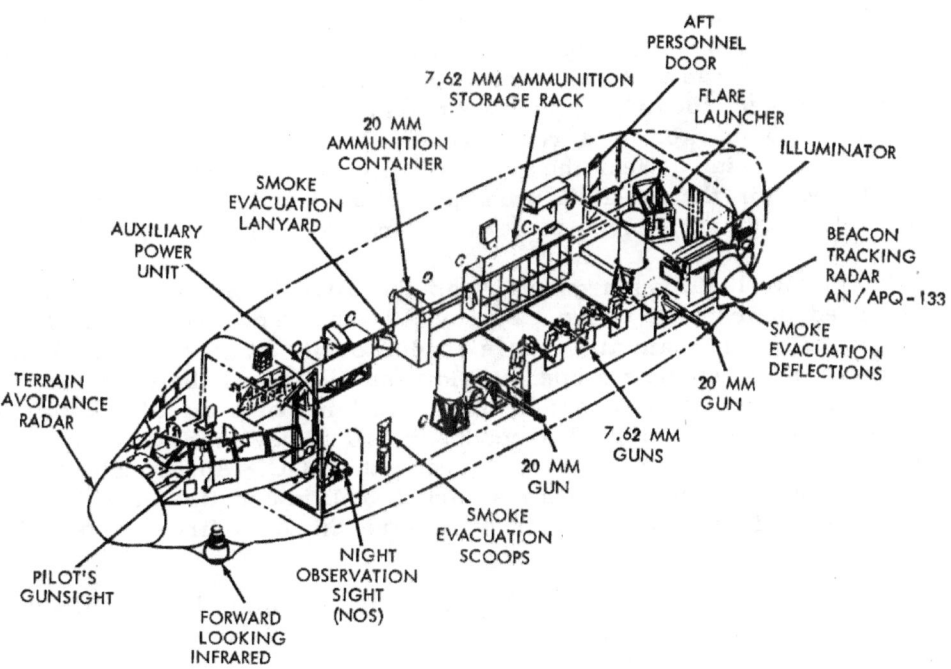

Figure 36

The AC-119's primary mission was armed reconnaissance and the Stinger devoted over 80 percent of its sorties to that end.* An operating level of 3,500 feet AGL, however, was not well-suited for Trail interdiction without an escort. Hence, the gunships confined their interdiction missions to lightly defended areas of South Vietnam. They gave top priority to defense of troops-in-contact (TIC), outposts, hamlets, and firebases--essentially the AC-47 Spooky mission.[94]

AC-119 Armed Reconnaissance

Throughout South Vietnam, Seventh Air Force designated a number of specific strike zones (shadow boxes) for AC-119G operations. Most of them were along infiltration routes, base camps, or staging areas near the Cambodian border. Intelligence, often supplied by Task Force Alpha, determined which boxes contained the most lucrative targets for the night. Shadow was then fragged into these boxes where unrestricted search was permitted. Many of these zones were in rugged mountainous terrain, so the gunship flew a TACAN radial to a prominent landmark within the box. After positively identifying the landmark, the gunship dropped a Mk-6 ground marker or a red-burning LUU-1B marker to serve as a reference point. Next the pilot descended to 3,500 feet AGL (5,000 feet for the AC-119K working in Laos) and began a random, parallel, or spiral search pattern (figures 27, 29, and 30).[95]

By 1969, such gunships as the AC-119 had modified and shortened their pylon turns. Enemy AA guns too easily tracked the aircraft if it maintained an extended orbit. It was now essential to leave an escape route open. Pilots still watched their ID 249 needle and when it showed the proper roll-in point the attack started. Immediately after firing (3-second bursts), however, Shadow or Stinger rolled out and continued across the LOC. An experienced crew could sometimes acquire a target, roll in and fire in 30° or less of turn (figure 33), and roll out before the AAA fire arrived.[96]

---

*Ammunition loads varied. On an out-country (Laos) mission, Stinger carried 8,000 rounds of 7.62-mm, 3,000 rounds of 20-mm, 12 Mk-24 flares, and 12 Mk-6 and 12 LUU-1B markers. Standard in-country load was 18,000 rounds of 7.62-mm, 1,600 rounds of 20-mm, 24 Mk-24 flares, and 6 Mk-6 and six LUU-1B markers. [Final Report (Combat King) (S), Aug 70, p 57.]

AC-119 ATTACK PROCEDURE

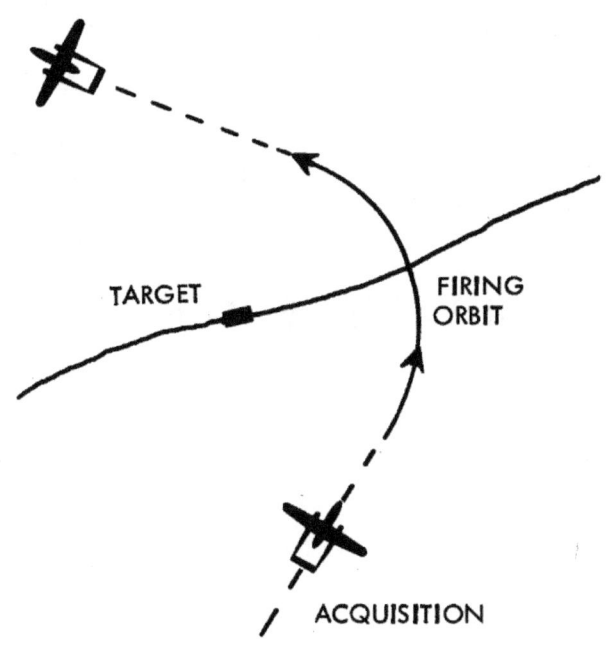

Figure 37

AC-119/A-1 Escort Operations

     Just as three F-4's had escorted each AC-130 mission, enemy AAA fire compelled Seventh Air Force to frag two A-1 Skyraiders as escort for the AC-119. The A-1 made an ideal escort because its loiter speed of 140-150 knots offered 2 1/2- 3 hours on station. Escort/flak suppression tactics likewise paralleled those of the AC-130/F-4 crews. The rendezvous point--either a set of coordinates or a TACAN fix--was within the shadow box. When the escort arrived, the AC-119 turned on its rotating beacon for no more than 5 seconds to help the A-1 pilots see the gunship. The gunship's shielded beacon and formation lights were also on and remained so during the strike phase. After joining up, the gunship crew briefed the escort on operating altitude (in relation to base), general terrain features, and the best escape and evasion area in the immediate vicinity. Before any armed reconnaissance was attempted, the crews discussed and fully understood the procedures to be followed in event the enemy began firing.[97]

After join-up, the lead A-1 flew at 7,000 feet AGL, his wingman 500-1,500 feet above him, 1 mile to the rear and offset to the right (figure 38).[98]

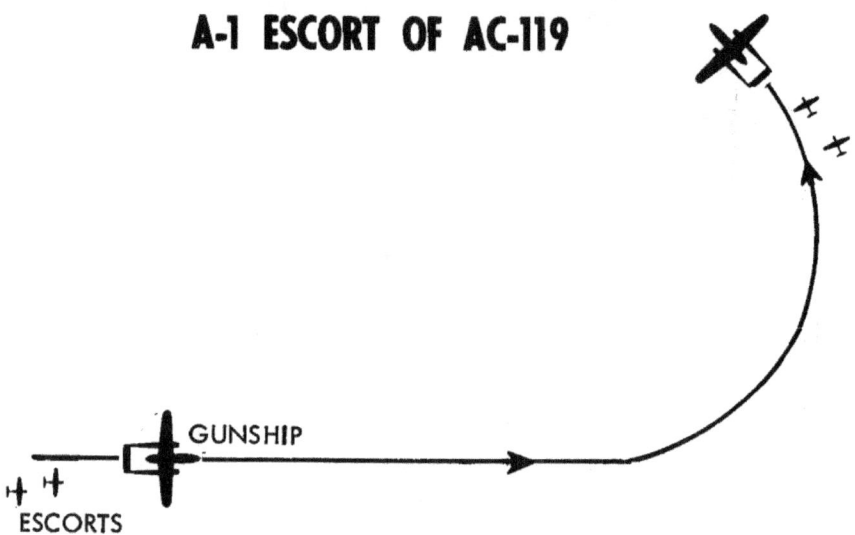

Figure 38 (U)

When AAA fire was seen, the A-1 escort called to the gunship "_____ has the guns at your (clock-code position), have you in sight, am I clear?" When the gunship replied in the affirmative, the escort started his pass. If the AAA guns lay outside the gunship's orbit, the attack began prior to receiving clearance, but the gunship had to give clearance for the pass to continue. If inside Shadow's or Stinger's orbit, the gunship needed to acknowledge it was "breaking out" or "ceasing fire" before the run-in could begin. The cardinal rule, observed by all, was that no attack on a gun site could occur without the AC-119's clearance.[99]

Commando Hunt V: The Gunship Shooting Gallery

Prestige of the AC-130/119 gunships rose to new heights during the 1970-71 dry-season campaign in Laos (Commando Hunt V). Success or failure of this third Laotian air interdiction effort was of crucial importance to both the North Vietnamese and the Air Force. The United States, for example, needed time for carrying out its Vietnamization program relatively unhampered--"to give South Vietnam a fighting chance"--as it was phrased. This left it squarely up to the Air Force (and the fighters on U.S. Navy carriers) to make certain no enemy offensive disrupted this program in the summer of 1971.[100]

General Giap's North Vietnamese forces faced difficult problems too. They not only needed to obstruct American efforts but do it without many of their Cambodian sanctuaries, particularly the ports. (These had been lost with the overthrow of the Prince Sihanouk regime on 18 March 1970). The enemy's alternate avenues were through the DMZ, across-the-beach, or over the Ho Chi Minh Trail. Of these choices only the Trail network, with an increase of vehicles and new road construction held promise.[101]

Thus, with the arrival of the 1970 wet season, the North Vietnamese departed from past practice in Steel Tiger--they did not return their engineer/construction battalions to North Vietnam. Instead, the troops remained to build and improve roads. West of Ban Bak, for instance, construction continued on a new road to bypass a system of interdiction points heavily pounded by airstrikes during Commando Hunt III. Within the panhandle in North Vietnam, road construction also picked up. Vehicles to transport supplies over the new and improved roads were plentiful. Reconnaissance photos revealed about 6,500 trucks nesting in parks in and around Hanoi and Haiphong. In short, this stepped-up wet-season activity served notice that the North Vietnamese would launch an intensive resupply effort in the dry season.[102]

Seventh Air Force countered with a plan for funneling 9,800 (70 percent) of the 14,000 available sorties into Steel Tiger against interdiction targets. The AC-130/119 force was almost entirely devoted to this operation.* If there was any question of the gunship's validity as a weapon system, Commando Hunt V clearly answered it. The AC-130's flew 1,311 sorties against trucks, racking up a record total of 14,922 vehicles struck with 12,741 destroyed or damaged. The AC-119K Stinger force also stung. In 558 sorties it attacked 3,128 vehicles, destroying or damaging 2,400. This performance of gunships as truck-killers at night was unmatched.†103

AC-123 Black Spot

The AC-123 Black Spot marked another development of the Shed Light program pointing toward the SCNA system. Not a gunship but a CBU bomber, Black Spot carried certain advanced night detection sensors. It was designed to operate in lightly defended areas at 2,500-3,000 feet AGL, with the optimum effective range of its sensors limited to 5,000 feet. The Air Force deployed two of these aircraft to Korea in August 1968 for testing of the sensor equipment against North Korean attempts to infiltrate South Korea by sea. In mid-November 1968, the aircraft were transferred to Phan Rang, South Vietnam, then finally to Ubon, Thailand, in February 1969.‡104

The Black Spot sensor system consisted of forward-looking radar with MTI plus three sensors--LLLTV, FLIR, and laser ranger. One aircraft also contained the Black

---

*Sixteen AC-119K's and 12 to 14 AC-130's were available during the 1970-71 dry-season campaign. [Commando Hunt V Report (S), May 71, pp 155, 261.]

†The 10 B-57G's were not far behind the AC-119K's in effectiveness. In over 840 sorties the Canberras attacked some 2,800 enemy vehicles, destroying or damaging 1,931. [Commando Hunt V Report (S), May 71, pp 61, 155.]

‡Black Spot was originally designated NC-123--the "N" meaning "special test." The change to "AC" came in early 1969. [Ltr (S), DCS/Plans & Ops to WRAMA, subj: Request for Change, Type Designation NC-123 Aircraft, 19 Feb 69.]

Crow vehicle ignition detector.* The radar occupied the nose radome. The LLLTV, FLIR, and laser ranger fitted in the fiberglass ball turret which was mounted in the nose undersection. Of the three sensors the FLIR was primary. An analog computer tied the systems together and provided necessary computations for target-positioning and weapon release. A specially designed, environmentally controlled compartment--located to the rear of the cockpit and forward of the munitions dispenser-- housed the operators and their display equipment.[105]

CUTAWAY OF AC-123

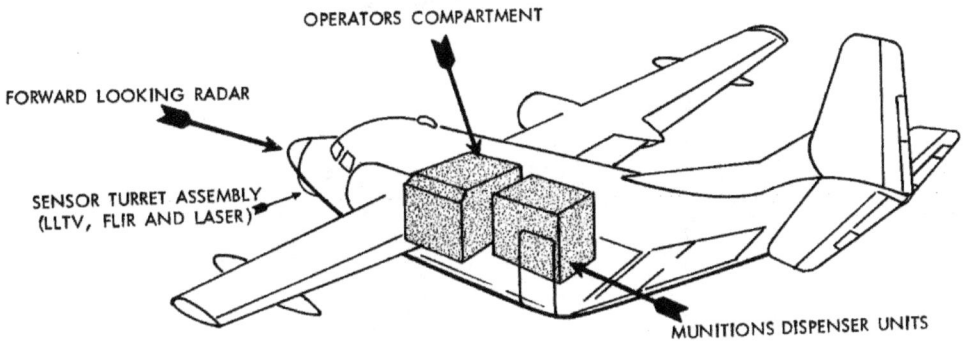

Figure 39 (S)

Black Spot utilized the SUU-24 munitions dispenser <u>assembly</u> that had been originally designed for the B-47/B-52 bomb bays. The assembly consisted of two box-frame units, one stacked on top of the other. Each unit had 12

---

*Black Crow was also installed in one C-130 Blindbat in early 1969. [7th AF (Dir/Plans) input (S) to Hist (S), 7th AF, 1 Mar-30 Jun 69.]

vertical chutes and every chute held three cube-shaped munitions canisters, for a total capacity of 72 canisters. Stacking the two units permitted six canisters to be dropped from each chute. A timer in each canister could be set for any interval from 1-90 seconds. It allowed the BLU bomblets to fall free and disperse.[106]

The BLU-3B and BLU-26 bomblets employed were antimateriel fragmentation types with 16- and 11-grain steel balls propelled radially upon detonation (figure 36).* The dispenser's 72-canister configuration could dispense 12,700 of these BLU-26 bomblets. For normal operations, however, the dispenser was loaded with 36 canisters of BLU-3B bomblets and 36 canisters of BLU-26 bomblets.[107]

BLU-3 AND BLU-26 BOMBLETS

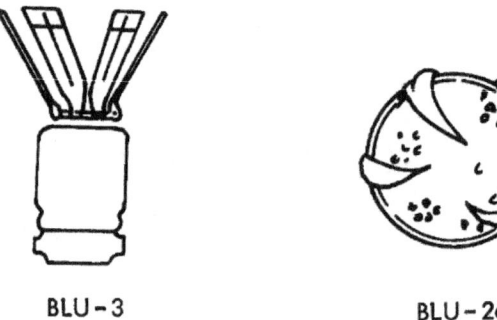

BLU-3   BLU-26

Figure 40 (C)

---

*The spinning motion imparted to the BLU-26B bomblet by flutes and edges on its circumference caused it to arm. Detonation occurred at ground impact. [Bul 3 (S), Combat Analys Div, USAF Ftr Wpns Sch, 31 Mar 66, p 8.]

AC-123 Tactics

Black Spot's search and acquisition techniques were somewhat similar to those of the gunships. The navigator directed the AC-123 on the fragged roadway at 150 knots true air speed (TAS) and 4,900 feet AGL (approximate upper limits of the weapon computer).* Navigation was conducted by doppler-fed map display corrected by radar, TACAN, and geographic-coordinate readouts from the analog computer. The navigator watched the relationship of the road to the aircraft's centerline and informed the operators of the LLLTV (primarily a cuing sensor) and the infrared sensor. When one of the sensors detected a target, the pilot centered his steering needle and the aircraft proceeded down the bomb run. The systems operator programmed the munitions panel and determined the type of weapon to be delivered and the rate of delivery. From detection of the target to bomb-release took 20-25 seconds. BDA was accomplished by photography off the infrared sensor scope or visually by the flight engineer stationed in the rear of the aircraft. At times, a second pass on the target was necessary. Black Spot then either flew a racetrack pattern to come back over the target from the same direction as the first pass, or executed a teardrop pattern in which it approached the target from the opposite direction.+108

Two Black Spot aircraft under call sign Triton flew 106 sorties during a 57-day test period (15 Nov 68-9 Jan 69). The table below shows the targets attacked and results.109

Targets	Boats	Vehicles
Sighted	103	305
Attacks	63	172
Destroyed	55	98
Damaged	24	84
Secondary Fires & Explosions	79	182
Results Not Observed	24	123

---

*In the lightly defended Mekong Delta the operating altitude was 3,500 feet AGL. [Rprt (S), Black Spot Combat Evaluation, Jan 70, p 27.]

+Loss of the doppler radar was cause for aborting the mission. [Rprt (S), Black Spot Combat Evaluation, Jan 70, p 27.]

It was particularly significant that 58 percent of the attacks on trucks were made on the first pass, and only 16 percent of such attacks required more than two passes. A different type of munitions would have enhanced Triton's effectiveness even more. Often, direct hits on trucks with fragmentation bombs had no effect whatever. Nevertheless, the aircraft's ability to detect and attack trucks had been proven, and CINCPAC extended Black Spot deployment through the Commando Hunt III campaign. By late May 1969 --the end of the Laotian dry season--Black Spot had destroyed 418 trucks and damaged 273 others.[110]

Despite its truck-killing success, Triton quickly faced the same predicament that had confronted the gunships. Too many enemy guns flanked the Ho Chi Minh Trail and upping the aircraft's operating altitude was not enough for survival. A flak-suppression escort was needed and the A-1 Hobos from the 1st Special Operations Squadron (56th SOWg) filled the role. Due to Triton's poor wing lighting, however, and the A-1's own limited visibility, the Hobos were hard-pressed to keep the aircraft in sight on these missions. A right turn by Triton made tracking virtually impossible by the A-1E's.* As a result, the escort effort did not succeed.[111]

The second deployment of Black Spot (late 1969--early 1970) witnessed improved A-1 escort tactics. This time, the night-dedicated Zorros, rather than the Hobos, flew escort. Operating in pairs, the single-seat A-1's rendezvoused with Black Spot about 150-200 miles southwest of Nakhon Phanom area with the lead A-1 maintaining a position 1,000 feet above Black Spot and his wingman flying 500-1,000 feet above him. The Zorros "played their turns" to stay above and behind the aircraft, so as to have a relatively unrestricted view of the area. When enemy AAA batteries opened up, the A-1's attacked using procedures resembling A-1 escort operations with the AC-119's (described above). The lead secured clearance from Black Spot before attacking the gun site. After he pulled off the target, the two A-1's switched positions and the wingman made his attack.[112]

---

*The E model of the A-1 had side-by-side seating.

VI. RECONNAISSANCE AND ROLLING THUNDER

U.S. Air Force reconnaissance in the Vietnam War was inaugurated in January 1961. At that time, the Air Force withdrew a camera-equipped SC-47 from operations along Korea's DMZ and deployed it to Vientiane, Laos, to support the aerial reconnaissance requests of the U.S. air attache. This aircraft flew 38 sorties before it was shot down over the Plaine des Jarres in late March 1961.[1]

During the autumn of 1961, four McDonnell RF-101 Voodoos and a photo processing cell (PPC)* were detailed temporary duty from Kadena AB, Okinawa, to Tan Son Nhut, South Vietnam. Ostensibly, their mission was to provide the Vietnamese government with photoreconnaissance of the country's flooded areas. The deployment's true nature, however, was to obtain mosaic coverage of border infiltration routes and suspected Vietcong strongholds. After flying 67 sorties, the Voodoos returned to Kadena in late November 1961.[2]

RF-101C

---

*A facility for processing, printing, and interpretation of reconnaissance sensor/intelligence products.

Meanwhile, the faster tempo of Communist activities in Laos caused the Air Force to deploy a second RF-101 reconnaissance task force (RTF). Coded Able Mable, it arrived at Don Muang AB, Thailand (near Bangkok) in November 1961--the same month Farm Gate arrived in South Vietnam. As the year closed, Able Mable had flown 130 sorties and processed over 53,000 feet of film.[3]

None of these missions were at night. The air commandos of Farm Gate (chapter II) flew the first night photo sorties. At first, all Farm Gate's B-26's operated only by day, for they lacked the necessary wiring for night and infrared photography. Then in May 1962, two of Farm Gate's B-26's were returned to Clark AB, Philippines, for this modification. When the refitting was completed, the two aircraft were sent to Don Muang and placed under the Able Mable commander's operational control. Here they performed Black Watch missions--night photo reconnaissance of Laos. Between 29 May and 29 July 1962, these two aircraft flew 50 such missions. After the Laotian ceasefire agreement was reached, the Black Watch aircraft returned to the Farm Gate operation at Bien Hoa.*[4]

In December 1962, the four RF-101's returned from Kadena to South Vietnam, boosting the total to six aircraft. Two infrared-equipped RB-57E's (nicknamed Patricia Lynn) further bolstered this force in April 1963.+ The addition was essential because the RF-101 had an unsatisfactory night capability due to inadequate navigation equipment. The inadequacy mirrored the state-of-the-art technology at the time (1957) Tactical Air Command accepted the aircraft as a replacement for the RF-84F. The RF-101 was not designed to give the navigation accuracy needed in Southeast Asia. Consequently, it could not be effectively employed at night.‡[5]

---

*While the two Farm Gate B-26's were being rewired, their serial numbers were marked on the two B-26's from Kadena that replaced them. [Capt Mark E. Smith, USAF Reconnaissance in Southeast Asia (TS), (HQ PACAF, Project CHECO), 25 Oct 66, p 7.]

+A third RB-57E arrived in December 1964 and a fourth the following month. [Smith, Reconnaissance in SEA, p 22.]

‡Modification 181--mating at RF-84F flash-cartridge pod to the KS-72 camera--was a 1964 attempt to give the Voodoo a night capability. The modification failed due to the limitations of the aircraft's navigation equipment. [Tactical Air Reconnaissance in SEA 1 Jan 65-31 Mar 68, I, xxii.]

RB-57

        The Patricia Lynn RB-57E's, with the use of photoflash cartridges, possessed a night optical capability. For 5 years following their deployment these Canberras operated with several different infrared scanners. The HRB Singer Reconofax VI, the first of these sensors, was designed for drone rather than manned aircraft use. It was hastily modified and installed in the RB-57E while research and development concentrated on newer and more sophisticated systems. A stopgap innovation at best, Reconofax malfunctioned on 48 percent of the RB-57E sorties and it eventually gave way to the RS-7. Poor engineering design, however--both in quality and convenience--caused the RS-7 to be replaced by the updated RS-10. The latter made use of a tape recorder to record IR-generated impulses, but it was not compatible with the VR-3A cockpit viewer. The RS-10 could "see" a 6-inch object at 1,000 feet; at the same altitude the VR-3A could display only a 4-foot object. This situation lasted until mid-1968 when a viewer compatible with the RS-10 was installed.[6]

        The RB-57E's shared the RF-101's lack of a sophisticated or accurate navigation capability such as the INS or mapping radar. To compensate for this shortcoming the Canberra used its IR radar as a navigational aid. This was a satisfactory substitute provided the mission was on a moonlit night. Then the pilot could keep the aircraft on course while the navigator devoted full time to locating and pinpointing targets on his B-scope. Missions on moonless nights or under overcast skies were a different story. The navigator had to split his attention--focusing chiefly on navigation rather than target detection.[7]

In light of their many problems, it is easy to see why the Patricia Lynn RB-57E's attained but marginal success. During 15 months of operation, the aircraft fulfilled only 21 of 29 requests. In summary, the night photography effort in the first 2 years of involvement in Vietnam produced little usable photography.[8]

OV-1 Mohawk

From November 1962 to May 1964, all reconnaissance operations were confined to South Vietnam. This standdown in reconnaissance sorties for Laos stemmed mainly from the Geneva Accords. When Project Yankee Team* started, however, reconnaissance missions for Laos resumed. Nonetheless, the bulk of the reconnaissance effort continued to be flown in support of the immediate tactical intelligence and operational needs of U.S. and Vietnamese field commanders. These needs centered on information regarding the enemy's strength, movement, and activity. Requests for photo support usually originated at company level, moved up the chain of command to corps headquarters, then to the Air Operations Center (AOC). After the mission was flown, the PPC processed the film (normally within 24 hours), then returned it by courier aircraft to the requesting unit. Commanders considered this procedure too slow in a war demanding

---

*Yankee Team grew out of North Vietnamese/Pathet Lao attacks against the Neutralists on the Plaine de Jarres in May 1964. The reconnaissance force consisted of RF-8's and RA-3B's from the Seventh Fleet and RF-101's from Tan Son Nhut. [Rprt (S), PACAF Phase--Report on the War in Vietnam, HQ PACAF, Jun 68.]

quick reaction to fluid battlelines and minute-to-minute changes to enemy action.*9

The U.S. Army's slow-flying OV-1 Mohawk offered just such a rapid response for field commanders. Within a few minutes, the OV-1's observer could transfer SLAR or IR scope image to film, develop and scan it, then radio possible targets to the supported unit's headquarters. Additionally, Mohawk photography could be developed by portable processing units attached to each aviation company or, in many instances, at the supported unit's headquarters. Thus the results would be in the hands of commanders within a few hours. By the end of 1966, the Army was flying 3,000 Mohawk reconnaissance sorties per month compared to 1500 for the Air Force. Unfortunately, little of this Army intelligence information found its way into Air Force channels.[10]

In 1967, the Army added a data-link terminal that enabled the Mohawks to effectively transmit their findings before landing. As the aircraft flew over the countryside, it automatically sent SLAR and IR responses to the ground terminal.+ There, a second observer viewed the imagery and recorded the data on film, just as in the aircraft cockpit. If either observer detected a target, he passed the information to all Army activities concerned. Artillery fire, for example, could be placed on targets just as soon as the data was received. Later, the films were turned over to unit intelligence sections for more detailed analysis.[11]

Although the Mohawk's "real-time response" capability was superior to equipment in the USAF inventory, it should be borne in mind that the Air Force after 1953 placed its primary emphasis on gathering of strategic intelligence. This does not mean to imply that tactical reconnaissance was neglected. On the contrary, cameras and equipment for photographing <u>conventional</u> battlefield targets had been developed and were employed in

---

*The channels a request passed through were burdensome and time-consuming. Nevertheless the routing insured that the numerous requests reached the agency most capable of honoring them and giving priority to those deserving it. [Montagliani, <u>Army Aviation in RVN</u>, pp 54-55.]

+Data link was later added to the RB-57E.

Vietnam. The RF-4C, for example, possessed an IR capability but its AAS-18 sensor operated in the 8- to 14-micron* range that could detect hot engines and not in the 3- to 5-micron range that was more capable of spotting cooking fires. Then, too, almost all requests for Air Force photos in South Vietnam involved strike BDA or Category III targets (broad-area coverage, i.e., 10x10 kilometers).†12

Nor was the Mohawk reconnaissance system faultless. In marginal weather the SLAR supplied the only usable photography, but severe conditions rendered it ineffective. IR--regardless of the military service using it--was not an all-weather sensor for the aircraft had to fly beneath cloud layers to detect emissions. Haze, mist, fog, and rain further degraded the Mohawk's system. During the dry season, the many fires from slash-and-burn farming left little chance to positively identify friend from foe. Heavier enemy small-arms fire against low-flying aircraft--especially slow-movers--made any type of reconnaissance hazardous. Finally, the want of terrain-following radar handicapped the Mohawk (as well as the RF-101 and RB-57E) in mountainous terrain.13

Problems Inherent in Night Reconnaissance

Reconnaissance crews encountered many of the problems in night operations that beset strike crews. Photo runs in Laos are a case in point. They followed a path that skimmed over the towering karst formations. Shadows cast by flares and reflected from clouds produced an environment conducive to vertigo and spatial disorientation. Pilots had to be highly skilled in reading instruments and flying by them. Moreover, reconnaissance crews encountered heavy enemy AA fire and were just as aware of potential midair collisions in crowded areas as were strike pilots.14

In addition, reconnaissance crews experienced several problems unique to their night mission. Aerial photography rarely revealed the enemy's movements under the

---

*A unit of length equal to one-thousandth of a millimeter.

†Of necessity the Air Force had to allow its aircraft a long responsive time in photographing Category III targets.

dense canopy of trees or in heavy jungle foliage. While infrared might uncover "hot spots," it could not tell if they were friendly or enemy. Heavy haze or bad weather could hamper the locating and photographing of small fleeting targets. The area's high moisture content diffused the thermal emissions of targets, further distorting the infrared picture. Also reconnaissance crews--perhaps more than strike crews--required pinpoint navigation aids to accurately position themselves prior to a photo run. With the single exception of the RF-4C, however, such equipment was notably lacking. Limitations imposed by equipment and terrain impeded identification of the target. In the darkness the crews could accurately identify few targets either visually or with forward-looking radar. Hence, photo runs often began on the coastline or with some prominent radar return, and continued with precise control of heading, airspeed, and time.[15]

The RF-4C Phantom

The RF-4C was a day/night, high-altitude, all-weather reconnaissance version of the Phantom II. Besides optical-framing and panoramic cameras, it was equipped with IR detection plus

RF-4C

side-looking and forward-looking radar sensors designed for high- and low-altitude night missions. Special features included an inflight refueling capability, inflight photographic film processing, a mapping and terrain-following radar, and the same inertial navigation system found in the fighter version.[16]

Following Secretary of Defense Robert S. McNamara's visit to Southeast Asia in 1965, the Air Force decided to deploy the RF-4C to the theatre. The first nine aircraft of the 16th Tactical Reconnaissance Squadron arrived in October 1965. One year later, 60 RF-4C's were assigned to various units throughout South Vietnam and Thailand.[17]

Night in-country reconnaissance consisted chiefly of infrared strips, infrared area coverage, and photoflash cartridge strips. Ordinarily, single RF-4C sorties performed both IR and photoflash reconnaissance, flying at 2,000 feet AGL and 360 knots IAS. Inasmuch as enemy defenses were of low order, the aircraft used 20-30 photoflash cartridges per strip. This let much longer strips be taken.*[18]

RF-4C Out-Country Operations

Probably more than any other group of flyers, the RF-4C crews arrived in Southeast Asia better prepared for the type of enemy defenses they would meet up with over North Vietnam. This preparedness derived from their tactical training that recognized the Soviet deployment of the SA-2 Guideline surface-to-air missile (SAM) throughout Eastern Europe in the early 1960's. The Soviets designed this Mach 3.5 radar-guided missile for medium-to high-altitude interception of subsonic nonmaneuverable aircraft. In July 1965 the Air Force first discovered that SAM's were being used in North Vietnam. These missiles possessed a range of around 20 miles. If not degraded by countertactics,

---

*Most times the RF-4C carried 40 photoflash cartridges. [TIA (S), Apr 69, pp 1-16.]

they could achieve an effective kill probability from 1,500 feet to well above the service ceilings of U.S. aircraft.*[19]

The SAM's compelled the Air Force to adopt low-level, high-speed reconnaissance (or strike) tactics. The technique was to pick a route with terrain that would best mask the aircraft, and to penetrate enemy territory at lowest possible altitude and high airspeed. Pilots popped up over the target just long enough to obtain photo coverage (or dispense ordnance), then dropped "on the deck" to leave the area. This doctrine governed all tactical reconnaissance training. Accordingly, the RF-4C crews arrived in Southeast Asia well versed in low-altitude, high-speed tactics suited for high-threat areas of North Vietnam. Until October 1966, most night reconnaissance covered low- to medium-threat areas of the panhandle of Laos and North Vietnam. But as Rolling Thunder gathered momentum, sorties were also fragged into the northern route packages which were more heavily defended.[20]

The principal photo system applied in North Vietnam contained the KS-72 framing camera and a M-123 photoflash cartridge of 260-million candlepower. The RF-4C's camera compartment could be configured to house a single vertical KS-72 camera (3-inch focal length) and a pair of KS-72's (6-inch focal length), arranged in a split vertical array. The intralens shutter of the camera(s) was tripped by the photoflash terrain light detector when the photoflash cartridge reached peak light intensity. Camera limitations kept most photo runs between 2,500 and 3,000 feet AGL. This allowed aircrews to change altitude vertically and confuse the tracking solution of enemy gunners.[21]

Before entering North Vietnam, the RF-4C descended to low level, often as low as 200 feet AGL over flat level terrain. Upon reaching North Vietnam, the Phantom flew an altitude of 500 feet above the highest mountain peak along the route chosen.

---

*The author found no RF-4C training syllabus dated prior to October 1967. At that time, 11 night missions (28 hours) were scheduled for both pilot and navigator. These missions, flown at 2,000 feet AGL and 360-450 knots TAS, used both photoflash and infrared. [Training Syllabus (U), USAF Tactical Reconnaissance Aircrew Training Course, RF-4C, TAC, Oct 67.]

As the aircraft approached a high-threat area, it further descended to 500 feet AGL utilizing the terrain-following mode of the FLR. If the target happened to lie in the flat delta area of Route Package VI, the RF-4C might fly as low as 250 feet and at airspeeds up to 540 knots. 22

A no show target* called for the selection of the initial point to be a positive radar return no more than 10 miles from the target. (Detailed mission planning was required to properly pinpoint such definable IP's.) In flight, the navigator directed an approach to the target by aligning the aircraft through the IP on the correct ground track to avoid any heading change at the IP. Over the target, the pilot increased aircraft altitude to 1,500-2,000 feet AGL for photo coverage (800-1,000 feet AGL for infrared). Exposure time during a cartridge run was held to five cartridges to prevent the enemy from barraging AAA fire. After the pictures were taken, the aircraft departed at minimum altitude until clear of defended areas--particularly SAM sites. 23

In August 1967, the Seventh Air Force introduced certain operational changes to RF-4C reconnaissance tactics, due to the enemy buildup in North Vietnam of radar-directed guns and SA-2 SAM's. The RF-4C began carrying two QRC 160B/ALQ-71 ECM pods for defense. The single-ship night sorties continued the same low-altitude, terrain-masking profile. This was necessary because ECM backup from EB-66's and other aircraft was not present at night. As for day sorties, they returned to altitude ranges of 5,000-10,000 feet. The night Phantoms did not adopt the constant-jamming techniques of the two-ship day sorties. Instead they turned on their pods and jammed, only when a SAM radar posed a definite threat to the aircraft. Jamming was at 10-second intervals. When the SAM radar operator turned back the scope gain to counter this jamming, the RF-4C dropped chaff, turned off the pods, and quickly descended to the "deck" using the terrain-following override mode of the FLR.+ With jamming

---

*A target not showing up on the aircraft's radar.

+The FLR presented the terrain ahead of the aircraft and permitted the pilot to fly more safely at lower altitudes, especially at night. (The override mode shifted the FLR from automatic to manual control.)

now stopped, the enemy radar operator tuned his gain back up--
only to pick up the chaff. These ECM techniques worked quite
well.[24]

For added protection to reconnaissance crews, fighter
aircraft applied flak-suppression tactics essentially the same as
those discussed in chapter IV. Briefly, an F-4D loaded with CBU
perched high above the RF-4C. If it was necessary to suppress
an enemy AAA site, the fighter coordinated his roll-in with the
first photoflash ejection from the reconnaissance aircraft. If
delivery angle and timing were correct, the F-4D released ordnance as soon as the enemy guns opened fire.[25]

Night infrared missions resembled photoflash ones
except that the pop-up altitude was 800-1,000 feet. The Air Force
relied chiefly on infrared to film the LOC's in North Vietnam that
threaded into the south because the IR film supply was greater
than that of the KS-72 photoflash system. The RF-4C--as had the
OV-1 Mohawk and the RB-57 Canberra--experienced shortcomings
with the IR sensor (AAS-18). Its top altitude for photographing
trucks, for example, was 1,500 feet--an altitude that placed the
aircraft within range of enemy AA fire. At higher levels the film
resolution suffered; above 4,500 feet the imagery lost all tactical
value. Below 1,500 feet AGL the IR picture improved, but lateral
coverage was but 3,400 feet. Moreover, the RF-4C needed to
maintain a near-level attitude to avoid image distortion. This
meant that accurate coverage of the typical winding artery of the
Ho Chi Minh Trail was hard to obtain.*[26]

Additionally, the recce Phantoms carried out night airborne alert missions. The ABCCC assigned targets that usually
brought the RF-4C to an area where he joined up with a FAC.
The latter briefed him on type of target, its location, and the
expected enemy defenses, then illuminated the target for identification. The Phantom pilot activated photoflash cartridges and sensors
as the target disappeared under his plane's nose. If no FAC was
available, the crew accomplished in-flight mission planning.

---

*The Air Force conducted experiments utilizing the RF-4C
and an argongas laser (Project Compass Count). At this writing
the laser appears to hold promise for future reconnaissance photography. It has, however, the same resolution/lateral coverage problems as IR photography. [TIA(S), Apr 69, pp 1-18.]

TYPICAL LOW-LEVEL PROFILE, RF-4C

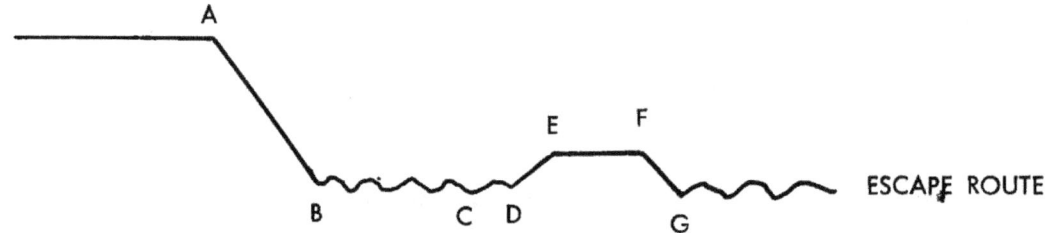

A. APPROACHING THE NORTH VIETNAM BORDER A DESCENT TO LOW LEVEL BEGAN.

B. AT LOW LEVEL THE ALTITUDE FLOWN VARIED WITH THE DEFENSIVE ENVIRONMENT. IN THE HIGHLY DEFENDED AREAS IT WOULD BE FLOWN, USING THE TERRAIN FOLLOWING OVERRIDE MODE OF THE FLR, AS LOW AS 250 FEET AGL.

C. THE IP MUST BE LOCATED WHILE AT LOW ALTITUDE FOR TIMING FOR THE PHOTO RUN.

D. ABOUT 1 NM FROM THE TARGET A RAPID CLIMB TO PHOTO ALTITUDE BEGAN.

E. LEVEL OFF AT PHOTO ALTITUDE WAS PLANNED TO COINCIDE WITH THE START POINT FOR THE PHOTO RUN.

F. AT THE END OF THE PHOTO RUN A DESCENT BACK TO MINIMUM ALTITUDE BEGAN.

G. EXIT FROM THE TARGET AREA WAS MADE AT MAXIMUM AIRSPEED AND MINIMUM ALTITUDE.

Figure 41

Besides plotting the target and photo run, the crew determined minimum enroute altitudes and airspeeds. Based on these quick calculations, the navigator directed the aircraft to the target by FLR and INS.[27]

The 432d Tactical Reconnaissance Wing teamed with Army OV-1's to identify and confirm truck traffic passing through the Tally Ho area near the DMZ. A common time-over-target (TOT) was fragged for the RF-4C and the Mohawk. The Phantom held a given point while the OV-1 used side-looking radar with MTI to locate moving trucks. Upon spotting them, the Mohawk first predicted their direction and speed before giving the RF-4C an ETA to a predetermined geographic point. The jet planned a target run-in to make good the ETA and tried to photograph the vehicles with photocartridge illumination. In 26 missions, however, just three trucks were photographed. Apparently there were too many variables to achieve anything but mediocre success. Among them were incorrect ETA estimates, changes in target speed, and the RF-4C inability to meet the ETA.*[28]

Rolling Thunder

Operation Rolling Thunder--the third separate air campaign aimed at bringing the Communists to the negotiating table--began on 2 March 1965. On that date, 104 USAF aircraft (B-57's, F-105's, F-100's, and KC-135 tankers) along with 19 VNAF A-1H's struck North Vietnamese military targets at Quong Khe and Xom Bang. This daylight mission ended the purely retaliatory strikes of Operation Flaming Dart started 1 month earlier.+

---

*To detect enemy shipping, single-ship RF-4C missions using SLAR flew at 30,000 feet AGL and 20 miles offshore along the coast of North Vietnam. [End of Tour Report (S), Col. V.N. Cabas, 19 Sep 67-3 Sep 68.]

+Flaming Dart was the direct result of the 7 February 1965 Tet attack against the airbase at Pleiku which killed seven Americans. On the same day, 49 aircraft of the Seventh Fleet bombed the staging base and barracks at Dong Hoi in reprisal. Two days later a Vietcong attack on a U.S. enlisted man's barracks at Qui Nhon (21 U.S. dead, 22 wounded) and several ambushes and assassinations with a 72-hour period triggered another heavy retaliation raid. [Jacob Van Staaveren, USAF Plans and Operations in Southeast Asia, 1965 (USAF Hist Div Liaison Ofc, Oct 1966), pp 8-9.]

Rolling Thunder continued until October 1968 with air strikes accelerating to a 2-a-day occurrence.[29]

The objective of the U.S. air campaign against North Vietnam was to cause Hanoi to cease its aggression in South Vietnam and to make continued support of the Vietcong difficult and costly. By steadily increasing military pressure against North Vietnam the United States hoped that Ho Chi Minh would see the folly of his ways. Unfortunately, the lulls in this "guaranteed response" enabled the determined enemy to adjust to any shortages and dislocations resulting from U.S. air operations.[30]

North Vietnam (63,000 square miles) is slightly smaller than the State of Washington and covered by rough mountains. West of the Red River the mountain peaks rise from 7,000-10,000 feet, elsewhere not more than 6,000 feet. The Red River Delta extending to the east resembles South Vietnam coastal areas. North Vietnam's weather is monsoonal. From May to September heavy rain drenches most of the country except for the strip of land east of the mountains. October marks the transition to the northeast monsoon. While the mountains dry out, this monsoon pours rain on the coastal and delta areas--Hanoi's annual average being 66 inches. The low ceilings and protracted low visibility of this weather inhibit air strikes over the Red River Delta.[31]

The Republic F-105 Thunderchief became synonymous with the Rolling Thunder campaign. Affectionately known as Thud or Lead Sled by its crews, the F-105 flew more sorties into heavily defended areas of North Vietnam and incurred higher losses than any other aircraft. About 43 percent of all F-105D/F's were lost in Southeast Asia combat. At the outset of the war in the North, the Air Force had available for strike operations both the F-105 and the F-100. The Thunderchief, however, excelled the Super Sabre in several ways--it had more speed and range, demonstrated marked handling superiority at top speeds, and carried twice the munitions load. Notwithstanding, the F-105's bombing system of Korean War design required field modification in Southeast Asia to better suit it to iron bombs. As was the case with the F-4 and other strike aircraft, the F-105's bombing set was not designed for the high accuracy needed for night operations. Moreover, the aircraft's cockpit lighting was marginal. Despite these shortcomings, the Air Force employed the F-105 in night operations utilizing the internal bombing radar. These missions bore the nickname Commando Nail.[32]

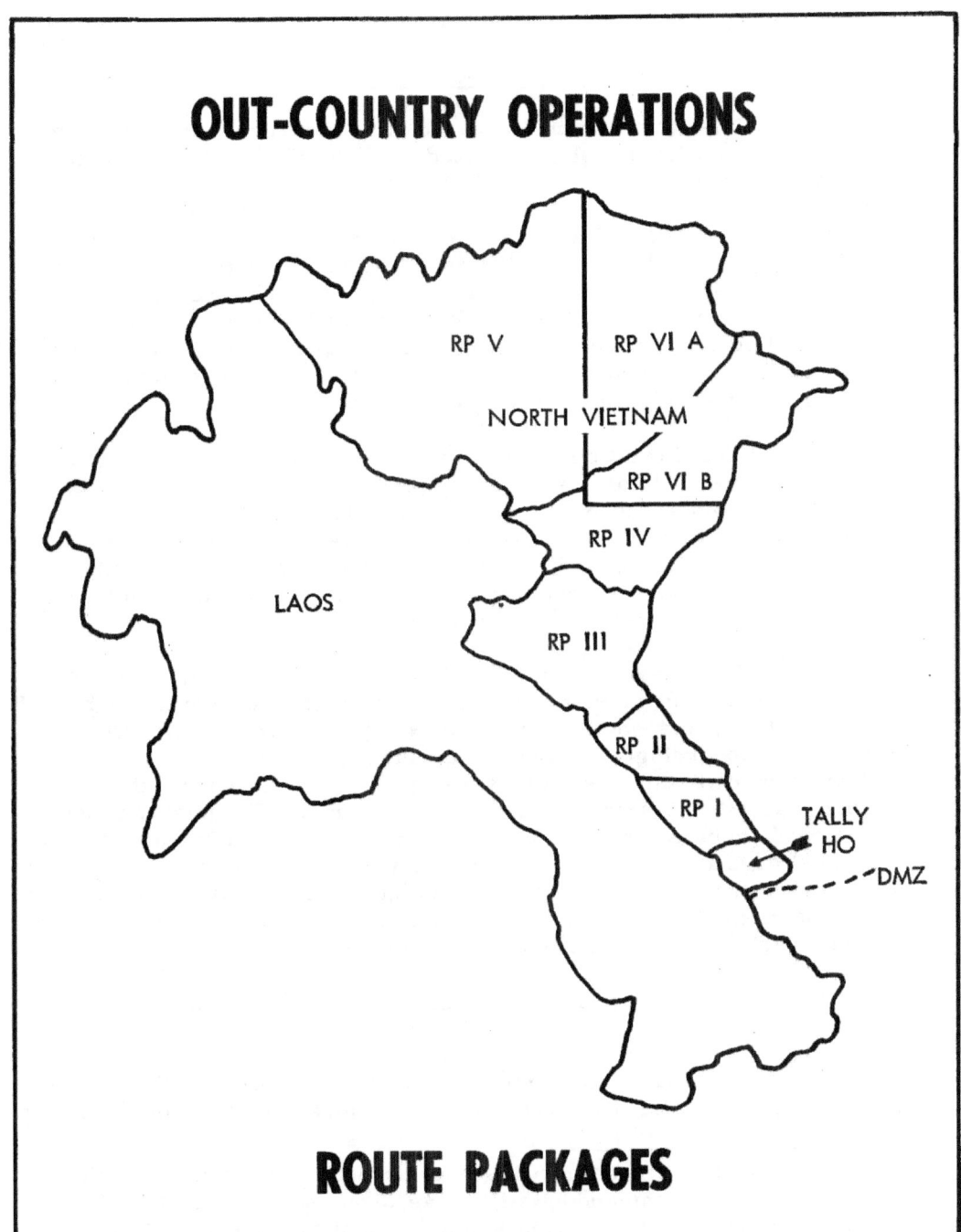

The Commando Nail F-105

The Thunderchief engaged in Commando Nail operations was the 2-seat F model, also used in Wild Weasel hunter-killer operations against enemy SAM sites. The F-105F was a basic F-105 with the fuselage extended to accommodate a duplicate cockpit to the rear of and separated from the pilot's seat. Originally a trainer, the F model's rear cockpit essentially duplicated the front seat. The aircraft likewise carried electronic radar warning receivers installed for Wild Weasel, together with B-14A radar. Local modification of the B-14A expanded the scope picture, furnished a fast sector-sweep to lengthen the radar return's duration, and added a radarscope camera.*[33]

The first Commando Nail crews (later dubbed Ryan's Raiders) reported for training in April 1967. Three months later, this group joined the 388th Tactical Fighter Wing at Korat, Thailand. The back-seaters, however, were electronic warfare officers and not qualified navigator-bombardiers (Air Force Specialty Code 1525). Thus--through no fault of their own--they were slow in mastering the F-105's radar equipment.

In the late summer of 1967, the crews went on their first night radar missions in the low-risk area of Route Package I. At that time, the southern part of North Vietnam did not have SAM's. Accordingly, it proved an ideal place for crews to conduct night orientation missions and pick up experience before venturing into high-threat areas to the north. Targets commonly assigned included truck parks and supply points within nonrefuelable flying range of Korat. The somewhat relaxed atmosphere allowed crews to choose attack headings giving the best radar presentation and permitted them to perform BDA as well. Attack altitudes on these early missions varied from 8,000-15,000 feet AGL.

Commando Nail Operations in Route Packages V and VI

Commando Nail missions began with a Seventh Air Force frag order, as did all strike/reconnaissance missions in Southeast

---

*Unless other authorities are cited, the remainder of this discussion on Commando Nail is based on Maj. Albert L. Michael, Ryan's Raiders (S) (Aerospace Studies Institute Special Report 70-24, ASI, Maxwell AFB, Ala, Jan 70.)

Asia. Received early in the morning for a mission that night, the order contained merely refueling support data, TOT, and the target's description and coordinates. The crew determined route and altitude to the target, the IP, and bombing offsets.* It was most important to plot a course that changed direction about every 5 minutes and low enough so the aircraft could take advantage of terrain features to "hide" from enemy radar. Each leg of the course was measured for precise distance and computed for the exact flying time. Every turn was precomputed for the correct bank angle to be flown. A crew not assigned to fly that night frequently would cross-check the calculations of the scheduled crew.

In addition, the F-105 crew selected and checked an average altitude for each leg of the flight. Many times they chose an altitude 500 feet below the minimum height of the ridge line considered to be between enemy radar and the aircraft. If it became necessary to plot a route down a valley toward a known enemy radar, 1,000 feet AGL was the absolute minimum planned. After the Commando Nail flight plan was approved, a coordination message was sent the 355th Tactical Fighter Wing, Takhli, Thailand. This message confirmed the TOT and gave the penetration point and final attack heading selected by the F-105 crew. The 355th passed the information to the RB-66 crew alerted to support night operations (not just Commando Nail). The RB-66 had several orbits in Laos that permitted observation of enemy radar signals and radioing of warnings to the Commando Nail crew.

Similar coordination was achieved with the Wild Weasel crew assigned to fly cover for the low-level mission. This crew would plan a high-altitude orbit outside the SAM coverage and opposite the planned bomb run heading of the Commando Nail The aim was to distract the defense during the bombing attack. (To offset this tactic, enemy radars kept operations to short periods when the Weasel was on an outbound leg of its orbit).

Commando Nail crews considered mission planning incomplete until the electronic warfare officer (EWO) had finished

---

*The initial point was used as a starting point for the bomb run to the target. Offset bobming employed a reference or aiming point other than the actual target.

studying the target area. Scant scope photography of North Vietnam or the specific target existed, so freehand predictions were used. The radar prediction officer, working with unit intelligence personnel, would draw what he believed the target would look like on radar from the altitude and heading provided him by the EWO. However, the absence of up-to-date terrain-feature charts and scope photography severely hampered the prediction officer's efforts.

After a few hours rest, a complete weather briefing, and intelligence updating, the crew prepared to take off. Commando Nail F-105's usually carried six 750-pound high-explosive frag bombs, each fuzed for impact detonation. For the internal M-61 cannon, 1,000 rounds of 20-mm ammunition were included. Furthermore, an external ECM pod nested under each wing. On some sorties two heat-seeking AIM-9 missiles replaced one of the external ECM pods.

This load put the aircraft at maximum gross weight for takeoff even before its centerline fuel tank was filled. The added fuel served as backup in case air refueling was missed. Without it a sortie to northern route packages, not afforded air refueling, would have to abort and jettison its bombs safely before the aircraft could land. Consequently, crews preferred an overweight takeoff rather than running the risk of jettisoning ordnance. Eventually, heavy gross-weight takeoffs became routine.

After takeoff, the navigator checked the radar calibration by using the known elevation of a terrain feature. This check was a must in planning to avoid certain parts of the terrain during operations. Further the navigator ran a simulated bombing problem to verify the circuitry between the radar and bombing computer.

Radar ground controllers aided the air refueling rendezvous and maneuvered the tanker and F-105 within the refueling area. The fighter's radar or visual contact controlled the final run-in heading for hookup. Refueling completed, the Commando Nail climbed and cruised at high altitude to the final checkpoint prior to descending to low level. An isolated TACAN station in northern Laos (Site 85) often supplied this final position, and its known position was used to update the aircraft's doppler radar. It was paramount that the F-105 fly low to screen itself from enemy radar. From this point on the aircraft held tightly to flight plan,

utilizing terrain-masking and frequent heading changes. At the
planned IP, the pilot accelerated to 500 knots TAS and steadied
the aircraft at 1,000 feet AGL. After ordnance release, the
F-105 jettisoned external fuel tanks, jinked to elude enemy
searchlights and ground fire, then left the area.

From 6 April to 4 October 1967, Commando Nail aircraft flew 415 low-level sorties at night in Route Packages I, V, and VIA. Much of their work was harassment and its effectiveness could never be definitely determined. The reasons were a lack of high-speed film for scoreable photography and inability of crews to accomplish BDA due to darkness or enemy defenses. After October 1967, the aircraft were utilized in the Wild Weasel configuration in the upper route packages* or continued as Commando Nail aircraft in the panhandle (Route Package I)--but at higher altitudes.

These later Commando Nail operations--lasting until the bombing halt in October 1968--were in reality a return to the orientation strikes first flown. The strikes now entailed simpler planning because low-level operations were eliminated, although pre-strike air refueling was retained. The crews could plan any attack heading that offered the best radar presentation. With the strikes conducted at 6,000-12,000 feet AGL, the pilot enjoyed complete freedom of maneuver. Moreover, in the lower route packages, crews could orbit the area to observe bomb impact. Although more secondary explosions and fires were reported, the missions were essentially harassment sorties. Chief "blame" for this lay in the aircraft's radar set; it was not designed to drop iron bombs within the tolerances needed. The F-105's circular error average (CEA) stood at 2,260 feet compared with the F-4's 1,050 feet. Clearly the Thud's bombing system had to be improved. Yet, any improvements of the F-105 for night operations would be marginal in light of the aircraft's age. Meantime, all Commando Nail activities ceased in December 1968 with the personnel absorbed into other units.34

Development of Iron Hand and Wild Weasel

The F-105F discharged the additional duty of SAM suppression because the once basic North Vietnamese defense system

---

*Numbers of route packages grow larger from southern to norther North Vietnam (see map 2).

had become complex and modern. The Air Force quickly discovered that low altitude, high-speed tactics, workable in Europe or a general war, were unsuitable for the limited war in Southeast Asia. There, with relative ease, the enemy could concentrate intense AA or small-arms fire in small areas--posing a serious threat to low-flyers. On the other hand, the SAM's would have a field day if the pilot decided to fly at higher altitudes without some type of ECM/suppression escort. This defense network's constant threat to strike aircraft and its successes challenged the Air Force to find some way to suppress it.[35]

At first, crews returned to medium altitudes and perfected evasive tactics. Then it was found that given timely warning and visual acquisition pilots could outmaneuver the SAM at altitude.* EB-66's, EC-121's, and Navy EA-3B's supplied electronic countermeasures support. In addition, the Air Force developed jamming pods for the strike force to carry under the wings. It further created a hunter/killer team of specialized aircraft for SAM suppression. These anti-SAM missions--nicknamed Wild Weasel and Iron Hand--combined electronic means of detecting and locating sites with various weapons to attack and destroy them.[36]

The two-seat F-100F pioneered in the SAM suppression role. The Air Force picked this jet tactical fighter because it was available and had an extra cockpit for the electronic warfare officer and his equipment. This freed the pilot to conduct search and target-marking as well as maneuver to evade launched SAM's. Tactics specified that the Wild Weasel ferret out the enemy radar, mark the site with a 2.75 rocket (just as a FAC would do), then lead the Iron Hand F-105's in for visual attacks. During daylight and against fixed sites this tactic worked well. The enemy quickly countered, however, by rapidly moving his missiles from one spot to another. More important, AA defenses ringed the SAM sites. Furthermore, the North Vietnamese relied more on early warning and acquisition radars for crosstell⁺ information,

─────────

*Strike crews received two types of warning--standoff (chiefly by College Eye EC-121) and onboard radar homing and warning. By 1967 virtually all strike aircraft entering high-threat areas carried RHAW equipment. [Rprt (S), Analysis of Combat Aircraft Losses in Southeast Asia, DID Report R-14D, Apr 68, IV, 54.]

⁺Crosstell--transfer of information between facilities at the same operational level.

so their Fan Song tracking radar came on the air just long enough to complete a missile firing. The Weasels soon found it harder to detect sites and their attrition rate from enemy AA fire became unacceptable.[37]

By mid-1966 the F-105F aircraft had replaced the F-100F and the AGM-45 Shrike missile had become the main ordnance for Wild Weasel aircraft. The AGM-45 was a passive, radar-homing air-to-surface missile specifically designed to destroy enemy radars. It could be fired at ranges of 10-12 miles or less by direct fire or lofted trajectory and its seeker head homed in on enemy radar emissions. On the other hand, the missile had no memory circuit and possessed limited destructive capability (only a 14-pound warhead). Moreover, it was still necessary to point the aircraft in the general direction of the emitting radar. Thus, the momentary shutdown of the Fan Song defeated the Shrike, since it depended on the radar's homing signal. Nonetheless, for a moment the Shrike effectively suppressed the SA-2 threat to the strike aircraft.[38]

F-105F Thunderchief

The enemy retaliated by extending highly redundant Fan Song radar coverage over key areas of North Vietnam. The Hanoi-Red River Valley area grew into one giant SAM and AA complex. New site construction mushroomed (including dummy sites and flak traps) and the enemy moved missile battalions from one place to another. This site proliferation prompted Iron Hand/Wild Weasel missions to switch from purely hunter/killer to escort for strike aircraft flying north. The F-105F flew most of its night missions as escort.[39]

The Seventh Air Force fragged two suppression aircraft each night. The sorties were usually in support of Commando Nail operations or any Navy, Marine, or Air Force mission--including B-52 Arc Light. Each F-105F carried two Shrike missiles, one equipped with a "shorting plug" that permitted the pilot to perform a dive delivery. When supporting a Commando Nail sortie, Weasel crews deferred mission planning until the Nail crew had selected their run-in heading. Once this was done, the Weasel flight leader could figure a TOT so as to be in position for best support of the strike aircraft. Occasionally, one Weasel might support up to four different sorties with widely-spaced TOT's. A KC-135 tanker refueled the F-105F.[40]

Ten minutes before the scheduled Commando Nail departure the F-105F flight would take off with their 650-gallon centerline tanks empty. This reduced takeoff distance, the only penalty being 2-3 minutes with a tanker. After taking 9,000-10,000 pounds of fuel from a KC-135, the flight traveled to Route Package I to troll for about 10 minutes. Inasmuch as the Commando Nail aircraft followed but a short distance behind, the F-105F's positioned themselves between the target and the threat area. The Nail aircraft radioed the Weasels their ETA to the target. After that, the ideal situation would have a Weasel flying inbound to the target at Shrike firing altitude (10,000-15,000 feet AGL) just as the fighter-bomber prepared for bomb release. This rarely happened, however. The enemy hardly ever bothered to fire SAM's at night. Perhaps he knew single-ship night sorties were only harassment or he didn't want to give his position away. Most of the AA fire at night was barrage or visually directed.[41]

If a Weasel attacked a site, it headed straight for the suspected source of the signal. When 12-14 miles from the target, the aircraft nosed up at a 30°-40° angle. Next, it fired the missile and broke to the side and down in an effort to see the impact point. In another variation, the Weasel dove directly at the target and launched the weapon from 8-10 miles out. Many times the crews could not see ground damage at night. Hence, they considered the suppression successful if the radar went off the air. This satisfied the mission requirements.[42]

In February 1968, the Air Force introduced a new air-to-ground antiradiation missile (ARM)--the AGM-78 Standard ARM. This new weapon may eventually replace the AGM-45. Like the Shrike, it has a passive-seeker guidance system. However, the Standard ARM is a much bigger weapon (220-pound warhead), possessing redundant fuxing, and a greater standoff capability (at 40,000 feet it can be launched 70-75 miles from the target). An important modification gives the AGM-78 a memory circuit to keep it on proper trajectory even if enemy radar is turned off. Nor does this new missile need to be pointed in the direction of a SAM site to be fired. Launched at any angle or direction it turns toward the target after release. This feature blunts the enemy radar crew's ability to tell from the Weasel's heading whether or not the site is under attack. Nevertheless, the aircraft at first fired the new missile boresight, so the North Vietnamese wouldn't suspect any change in tactics that signaled the introduction of a new weapon. When modified to accept the AGM-78, the F-105F becomes the F-105G.[43]

F-4 Operations in North Vietnam

F-4 bomber crews in North Vietnam generally flew two types of missions--armed route reconnaissance and attacks on point targets. On both kind of sorties the Night Owl crews flew a two-ship formation and at times a three-ship one. For armed reconnaissance missions the frag order gave two sets of coordinates and the formation operated within them. If part of the area was heavily defended with SAM's or radar-directed AA artillery, the aircraft furnishing ECM coverage needed to be on station and in radio contact with the F-4 flight. Otherwise, the latter was forbidden to enter that portion of the area. F-4 tactics were those used for armed reconnaissance in Laos.*[44]

---

*Manual (S), 8th TFWg, Night Combat Tactics, 10 Sep 66. The discussion on F-4 tactics in North Vietnam is based on this manual.

The Night Owl crews disliked flying armed reconnaissance missions in North Vietnam using flares. Not only did it lose surprise, but in heavily defended areas the enemy barraged all available flak at the flarelight. Gunners quickly learned that by fuzing shells for around 7,000-10,000 feet, the F-4's had to penetrate the barrage to drop ordnance. Being tied to the flarelight the flight could not maneuver, so it usually tried but one pass. Thus a clear moonlit night was ideal for performing armed reconnaissance.

Point Targets

Point targets encompassed bridges, storage areas, barracks, SAM sites, and airfields. Night Owl crews memorized the target and surrounding area from photos and study maps. Due to the inherent navigation problems, crews selected routes having distinct terrain features both en route and in the target area. They also took weather into account; for example, large highway bridges could be attacked on clear moonlit nights without using flares.

For point targets, the F-4 carried enough fuel to arrive over the target and return to base--plus an additional 2,500 pounds. The extra fuel allowed maximum jinking and altitude changes going to and coming from the target area. At the edge of the target zone the flight accelerated to 480 knots, the wingman flying 3-5 miles back of the leader and offset 15° to either side. The lead pickled 16 flares on the first pass, broke hard away from the target, climbed to base altitude,* and reset his switches.

After the first flare ignited, the wingman started a wide climb to base-leg altitude outside the 3 o'clock or 9 o'clock flare position. If the enemy barraged the lighted area, the wingman remained clear while acquiring and tracking the target under the flarelight. The danger here was the enemy's locking on the aircraft with radars that controlled the AA guns and the SAM's.[†] As the flarelight began to die, the wingman called his clock-code position to the lead and attacked the target, rippling all bombs on a single pass. This maneuver was followed by both F-4's jinking

---

*Base altitude was never above 7,000 feet in a SAM environment.

†Sometimes it was better to offset the flares to decoy the gunners.

Two F-4's Break Away from KC-135 Refueling Tanker

and departing the area. The lead climbed for altitude to save fuel. The wingman stayed low and 10 miles behind until he was sure there were no MIG's in the area. Then, he also climbed while scanning the entire area between him and the lead, so he could warn the latter of any MIG's appearing between them. The flight resumed formation until reaching a safe point for turning on lights and checking one another's aircraft for hung ordnance.

Three-Ship Attack on Point Target, Heavily Defended Area

Considering the 2-ship flight's vulnerability, F-4 units sometimes adopted a three-ship formation that flew at low level. These night flyers penetrated the Fansong and Firecan radar areas at altitudes under 300 feet AGL to steer clear of the intense groundfire experience during low-level daylight missions. To visually maintain ground clearance on these low-level sorties, the Night Owls relied on the surrounding light. Hence the moon phase played an important part in the fragging and mission-planning of the three-ship formation. The moon cycle needed to be between the first and third quarter for 2 hours after moonrise to 2 hours before moonset. This yielded an operational period of about 15 days a month.*45

Crews highly seasoned in night operations flew these low-level missions. The sorties were planned exactly as those for low-level reconnaissance. Crews marked off strip maps for precise distance and time. They selected dead-reckoning as the main method of navigation with radar and INS serving as backup. The GIB handled the navigation to let the pilot focus on flying the aircraft. Inasmuch as these flights called for inflight refueling, a good identifiable postrefueling checkpoint was essential for starting a time-hack.+ A TACAN bearing usually met this need.

After departing the tanker, the F-4 formation assumed proper spacing on the cruise and descent to the starting point. Aircraft radar established a trail formation with 20-second spacing between aircraft (40-second spacing if the first aircraft was a flareship). The flight passed the starting point at 100-300 feet AGL and the lead called his time-hack as an added check, since the radar was often ineffective for acquisition at low level. This was the final radio transmission until the lead called for pop-up at the target. From this point on, each aircraft did its own navigating.

The formation took full advantage of terrain-masking to keep clear of radar detection until the aircraft broke out of the mountains into the flat Red River delta. Arriving at the target area, the flight leader called for the pop-up--the top altitude being 2,500 feet to keep the time at altitude to 15 seconds or less. The flight made most bomb runs at a dive angle of 15°, 420 knots TAS, and a mean release altitude of 1,200 feet AGL. The formation repeatedly met heavy AA fire over the target but mainly behind and above the aircraft. The 20-second spacing

---

*Major Laurence F. Gardner, "Night Strike Mission in a Sophisticated Defense Environment," Tactical Analysis Bulletin (S), 67-2 (27 Mar 1967), 1-3. The remainder of this discussion on low-level F-4 tactics in North Vietnam is based on this Bulletin.

+Time which is set or "hacked" on a watch to the precise second.

between planes afforded the least time over the target and prevented enemy gunners from barraging fire on any one ship. During the entire attack phase the GIB acted as backup pilot. He continually called airspeed, altitude, and release altitude to the pilot.

Each of the three planes commonly carried 18 Mk-82 bombs and a centerline fuel tank. If the target required illumination the lead aircraft substituted two 16-flare dispensers and two CBU-2/2A cannisters for the Mk-82 bombs. The attack procedure then altered a bit. The flight leader popped up a bit sooner than for bomb delivery and leveled off at 3,000 feet AGL on a course designed to create a flareline. He released four flares at 5-second intervals--allowing only 15 seconds at 3,000 feet AGL. His CBU was loaded to permit dispensing between flare drops with no switch changes. The other two pilots offset their pop-up so the attack was across the flareline. The 40-second spacing put the second aircraft at his roll-in almost simultaneous with flare illumination. The CBU impacting about the same time as flare ignition caused added confusion in the target area. After the ordnance had been released, the flight continued at low level until out of range of the enemy defenses.

MSQ-77 Combat Skyspot

One of the more effective blind-bombing methods developed and employed by the Air Force in Southeast Asia was the MSQ-77 Combat Skyspot. In March 1966, this bomb-directing and controlling radar first arrived in South Vietnam. TAC and SAC crews, however, had used it since the early 1950's to score simulated bomb runs. Then known as the MSQ-35, its computer could be programmed with ballistics of many special weapons and various aircraft. On U.S. and European training missions the crews made simulated bomb runs against specified targets. From the aircraft's TAS, bombing altitude, and true heading at release, the radar bomb scoring (RBS) site could compute the precise simulated point of impact on the ground.[46]

(U) In the Korean War, this procedure had been reversed. The controller directed the pilot to fly a specified altitude, heading, and airspeed to the target--the coordinates of which the controller had plotted on a map at his control table. At the proper point, the crew opened the bomb-bay doors and armed the bombs. Next, the controller began his countdown to zero, at which point the bombardier released the bombs. This method relieved the aircraft crew of any actual target acquisition, but it was necessary to keep the aircraft flying fairly straight and level. After the Korean War, the B-45/B-66 crews in TAC used these reverse MSQ techniques widely.[47]

In late 1965 and early 1966 at Matagorda Island, Tex., the Air Force ran extensive tests of the reverse MSQ procedure, utilizing live ordnance. Subsequent to testing and modification it deployed the first of these MSQ sites to Bien Hoa, South Vietnam. Sites were also set up at Pleiku, Dong Ha, and Da Lat in South Vietnam and at Nakhon Phanom in Thailand.[48]

The early MSQ sites directed and controlled F-100 aircraft engaged in close support of ground forces--especially hamlet/outpost defenses. Using the reflected radar signal from objects (skin paint), the range of these early tracking radars was 45 miles. This range grew to almost 200 miles when working with aircraft equipped with X-band beacons.* By November 1966, all MSQ sites except Da Lat had been modified for the greater range.+ As kits became available in the theater, strike aircraft were likewise modified. This enhancement of beacon equipment gave blind-bombing coverage to almost 90 percent of all corps areas in South Vietnam.[49]

An isolated facility directed the ground-vectored bombing of North Vietnam. This site housed a TACAN and a TSQ-81 (a modified version of the MSQ). The equipment made a small package that could be transported by helicopter to remote locations. The site controlled bombing operations into North Vietnam (coded Commando Club) from November 1967 until early March 1968 when the enemy overran the facility. Excluding sorties in Route Package I, the TSQ-81 directly slightly over 23 percent of the 427 strike missions flown into North Vietnam during this period.[50]

---

*The beacon's coded blip showed up much larger on the MSQ site's radar scope that did a skin-paint blip. [Strike Ops in SEA...Strike Aircraft, p 294.]

+The MSQ sites at Nakhon Phanom and Dong Ha controlled aircraft in Steel Tiger and the DMZ.

Tactics of strike crews under Commando Club direction approximated those of aircrews on MSQ-directed sorties in South Vietnam. A key difference lay in the stricter control exerted by the site responsible for operations into North Vietnam. Moreover, the frag order for the one or two strike aircraft headed north at night contained detail other than target coordinates. It further set forth the true airspeed as well as heading and altitude required for a controlled-release bomb run.[51]

The standard ordnance load for Combat Skyspot aircraft varied with the type of aircraft fragged for the mission and the nature of the target. Below are listed the types of ordnance used most frequently:[52]

    M-64 (500-pound bomb)   Mk-81 (250-pound bomb)
    M-65 (1,000-pound bomb) Mk-82 (500-pound bomb)
    M-117 (750-pound bomb)

Once aerial refueling was over with, the leader of the Combat Skyspot flight radioed the MSQ site to check in and supply essential information for setting up the ground controller's computers. Number and type of aircraft were critical items in calculating the proper release point. Next the controller positioned the fighter on the desired track to the target. As the aircraft approached the release point, he radioed two warning calls--one at 1 minute and one at 30 seconds prior to "bombs away." In addition he constantly passed corrections to the pilot for maintaining the desired track over the ground.* The final 2 minutes of the bomb run became crucial because release was computed for a fixed airspeed, altitude, and heading. Any deviation meant an aborted mission. The ground controller called for the crew to hold the aircraft steady and get ready for countdown. The countdown proceeded "5, 4, 3, 2, 1,--Hack!"[53]

Necessity for almost stereotyped tactics was one drawback to Combat Skyspot missions. Holding a heading, altitude, and airspeed favored enemy gunners and posed great danger to

---

    *To cancel out a crosswind, the aircraft was vectored along a track parallel to a line through the target. The perpendicular distance between these lines was the adjustment for the crosswind effect.

aircraft in the vicinity of a SAM ring. At night the aircraft crew could more easily see the ignition flash of an enemy missile but difficulty in estimating distances made evasion difficult.* Furthermore the maps of North Vietnam and Laos fell short of the accuracy the Air Force desired for its MSQ operations. Hence if the target coordinates cranked into the thumb wheels of the MSQ computer were incorrect, the bombs would fall on some spot other than the target.[54]

In summary, the Combat Skyspot missions into North Vietnam at night proved more of a harassment to the enemy than anything else. They were marginally effective against fixed targets but offered no help at all in interdicting truck traffic.

F-111 Operations

In late February 1968 Secretary of Defense McNamara approved the deployment of six F-111 aircraft to Southeast Asia to test this newest Air Force plane in combat. The operation (coded Combat Lancer) focused on development of the F-111's night/all-weather capability. The original concept envisioned single-ship penetrations against Rolling Thunder/Steel Tiger targets that could be acquired by radar, using either direct or offset modes of attack.[55]

The F-111 promised to be a major improvement over jet strike aircraft then in the theater. Its INS permitted precise navigation to the target at altitudes below those of enemy acquisition and tracking radars. This negated to a great extent the SAM and AA threat, and the plane's high speed at low level neutralized enemy small-arms fire. The INS, coupled with high-resolution attack radar, yielded precise navigation with errors of less than 2 miles each hour without updating. Once in the target area, the F-111's radar could positively identify many more targets than was possible with former tactical fighter systems. Its terrain-following radar (TFR) and radar altimeter assured safe flight at 500 feet AGL in mountainous terrain and 200 feet AGL in nonmountainous terrain.[56]

---

*Aircraft of the 388th Tactical Fighter Wing would make a diving turn to position the enemy missile at right angles to the aircraft, then be ready to pull up or break when the missile approached to within about 7,000 feet of the aircraft. [Manual (S), Combat Tactics, 388th TFWg, 14 Sep 68.]

The Seventh Air Force normally fragged four F-111 sorties each night. Takeoff times were scattered throughout the hours of darkness--from 1830 to as late as 0400. All missions had routes that took them through at least one type of known radar-directed AA or SAM site. Terrain-masking was therefore necessary along with avoidance of level terrain insofar as possible. Random TOT's were chosen to aid in surprise. After ordnance was delivered, the F-111's varied their tactics in leaving the target area so the enemy could not predict them.[57]

Combat Lancer F-111's would depart their home base of Takhli, Thailand and climb out to 8,000-10,000 feet over Thailand until they reached the Thai-Lao border. There the aircraft descended across Laos to altitudes of 200-500 feet AGL. These low levels were maintained into North Vietnam by using the TFR. The F-111 targets included bivouac areas, truck parks, and oil-storage depots.* Once the navigator acquired the target, the pilot adjusted altitude as needed to be out of the bomb-fragmentation envelope. Ordinarily, the F-111's carried general-purpose bombs ranging in size from 750-2,000 pounds. After dropping the bombs, the crews flew at low altitude on a generally southeast heading until over the Gulf of Tonkin. There they climbed to 20,000-30,000 feet and headed west for Takhli.[58]

The F-111 Southeast Asia test and evaluation program ended after 55 combat sorties. Missions were flown without air refueling and averaged 2 hours and 45 minutes. All of the targets struck were in Route Package I. No defensive groundfire was observed on any mission below 1,000 feet. Not a single SAM was fired at any of the aircraft.[59]

The F-111's ability to penetrate enemy defenses and depart undetected held great promise for the future. The same could not be said of the aircraft's ability to destroy targets. Of the sorties <u>attacking targets</u> (71 sorties were launched) four did not drop bombs. Results of another 12 were unknown due to a lack of BDA. Seven runs were gross errors and eight were made using INS or other alternate mode. Eighteen sorties were normal (target identified in time, crosshairs placed upon it, and automatic release obtained). Thus only 25 percent of the total 71 sorties were effective. The 18 normal sorties achieved a CEP of 470 feet. This compared with the 200-foot CEP the Air Force desired for effective night/all-weather interdiction in Southeast Asia.[60]

---

*The F-111 was incapable of attacking trucks, sampans, and other moving targets.

CONCLUSIONS

Will the knowledge and experience gained in Southeast Asia air operations shape future Air Force organization, equipment and training? More important, can any of this knowledge and experience be applied to future war? A few answers are in evidence. In 1972 the Air Force is giving top priority to acquisition of the F-15 air superiority fighter, the B-1 bomber, and a new close-support attack aircraft. The F-111, despite its mediocre performance in Southeast Asia, and the gunship, are the only USAF aircraft currently possessing self-contained attack capabilities. But, whether the gunship force should be retained in the postwar inventory is a question which cannot be readily answered.

What is clear, however, is that gunships cannot survive a powerful enemy air force and a modern antiaircraft system. The original gunship evolved to meet the specific need of hamlet/outpost defense in South Vietnam. Larger and more sophisticated gunships were employed for night interdiction in Laos, where they detected and destroyed hundreds of trucks at night. Strengthened enemy defenses, however, soon forced them to fly escorted. Their utility over the plains of Europe, for example--where they would face a modern, in-depth enemy defense system--raises a question of their survivability. If, on the other hand, the Air Force continues to become involved in insurgencies, brushfire situations, or limited wars and air superiority can be maintained, the chances for gunship success appear quite good. Unfortunately, the Air Force cannot divine the nature of future wars. It can only hope to be prepared for all contingencies.

Important conclusions can be drawn from the lessons learned in Southeast Asia. One involves organization. The greatest success in night operations was achieved by night-dedicated units as opposed to day-units flying scattered night missions. The accomplishments of the 56th Special Operations Wing, the gunships, and the 8th Tactical Fighter Wing Night Owls are well documented. It would seem that night-dedicated units with aircraft manned by volunteer crews should be part of the postwar air arm. Had such units been on hand in 1965, the night interdiction campaign certainly would have achieved quicker and better results.

In Vietnam, as in Korea, U.S. air superiority by day restricted Communist forces to night movements. The enemy used the mantle of darkness to overrun rural hamlets and outposts, ambush convoys and to infiltrate men and materiel down the Ho Chi Minh Trail from North Vietnam. To impede these night operations the Air Force was compelled to improvise and adopt stopgap measures. In some instances, the addition of a relatively simple night detection device, such as the Starlight Scope, altered the tactical advantage the enemy possessed. In others, off-the-shelf avionics mated with old, reliable airframes sufficed. The various improvisations, many of them temporary "fixes," took place over a 7-year period. In the future, "leftover" weapons and on-the-shelf equipment may prove inadequate, insufficient, or ineffective. It would appear there is still a requirement for the Self-Contained Night Attack Aircraft, to detect and destroy mobile surface targets at night and during all-weather conditions.

In Southeast Asia, enemy night operations over the trail network exacted the last ounce of flexibility from U.S. air power. An action on one side triggered a reaction on the other. Swift adjustment by both sides prevented the pendulum from ever moving too far off center. Gen. Henry H. ("Hap") Arnold, Commanding General of the Army Air Forces in World War II, anticipated this in his final report to Secretary of War Robert P. Patterson in November 1945. "The basic planning, development, organization and training of the Air Force," he wrote, "must be well rounded, covering every modern means of waging war, and the techniques of employing such means must be continuously developed and kept up to date." Air Force doctrines, he also emphasized, "must be flexible at all times and entirely uninhibited by tradition."[1]

NOTES

Chapter I

1. Lawrence J. Hickey, Night Close Air Support in RVN (S) (HQ PACAF, Project CHECO, 15 Mar 67); CHECO SEA Reports, vol III, Chronology, Oct 61-Dec 63, May 64; presentation to Lt Gen D.A. Burchinal, DCS/Plans and Prgms (S), by Counterinsurgency Ops Div, Dir/Ops, DCS/Ops, subj: Air Force Role in Counterinsurgency, 1 Jun 62, pp 18-20 [hereinafter cited as Burchinal Briefing]; Jacob Van Staaveren, USAF Plans and Policies in South Vietnam (TS) (Ofc/AF Hist, Jun 1965), p 18; intvw (TS), Aerospace Studies Institute (ASI) Oral Hist Gp, with Brig Gen Benjamin H. King, Comdr, 4400th CCT Sq (1961-1962), 4 Sep 69.

2. Rprt (U), Tac Spt Eval Bd, Characteristics of Aircraft Currently Employed in COIN Operations, 1 Aug 62, pp 15-17; memo (S), Brig Gen Edward G. Lansdale, Asst to SECDEF, to SECDEF Robert S. McNamara, subj: Defense Resources for Unconventional Warfare, 12 Jul 61; Doc 7 (S) to hist (S), SAWC, 27 Apr-31 Dec 62 [hereinafter cited as SAWC History w/appropriate dates]; intvw (S), author with Maj Charles W. Brown, Hq USAF, 14 Sep 70.

3. Study (U), Ofc/AF Hist, "History of Night/All-Weather-Tactical Air Operations in World War II and Korea, 1963."

4. Ibid.; Robert F. Futrell, The United States Air Force in Korea, 1950-1953 (New York, 1961), p 258.

5. Futrell, USAF in Korea, pp 258-59.

6. Study (U), "History of Night/All-Weather Operations in World War II and Korea, 1963."

7. Hist (TS), Historical Div, PACAF, Rules of Engagement in Southeast Asia, 1957-1965, Nov 68, p iv.

8. Ibid., p iii.

9. End of Tour Report (TS), Lt Col Robert L. Gleason, Comdr, Det 2, 4400th CCT Sq (17 Nov 61-2 Mar 62), in Hist (S), SAWC, 27 Apr-31 Dec 62, Tab I.

10. Intvw (S), J. Grainger, 2d ADVON Historian, with Lt Col M. M. Doyle, Comdr, Det 2, 1st Air Commando Sq, 16 Feb 63, in Hist (S), 2d ADVON, 15 Nov 61-8 Oct 62, Doc 195.

11. Tab B, Additional Subjects, in Book of Actions in Southeast Asia, 1961-1964 (S), in USAF Archives 6-4995-52; hist (S), 34th Tac Gp, 1 Jan 64-30 Jun 64, p 58; intvws (S), author with following Farm Gate members: Lt Col (then Capt) John Pattee, 18 Sep 70, Lt Col (then Capt) Donald C. Hatch, 18 Sep 70, Lt Col (then Capt) John Piotrowski, 21 Sep 70, and Maj (then 1st Lt) James D. Carson, 17 Sep 70 [hereinafter cited as Farm Gate intvws]; intvw (TS), Brig Gen Benjamin H. King, 4 Sep 69; intvw (S), Maj Charles W. Brown, 14 Sep 70.

12. Msg (TS), PACAF to 13th AF, 142300Z Dec 61, subj: Concept of Employment of Farm Gate; Book of Actions in Southeast Asia, 1961-1964 (S); Charles H. Hildreth, USAF Counterinsurgency Doctrines and Capabilities, 1961-1962 (TS) (Ofc/AF Hist, Feb 1964), pp 12-13; intvw (TS), Brig Gen Benjamin H. King, 4 Sep 69, pp 11, 24; Farm Gate intvws.

13. King intvw (TS), 4 Sep 69, pp 50-52.

14. Ibid., pp 53-54; Brown intvw (S), 14 Sep 70.

15. Hildreth, USAF Counterinsurgency Doctrines, p 25.

16. 2d Air Div Reg 55-18 (S), Procedures for Night Close Air Support, 2 Aug 63, in CHECO SEA Reports, Doc 41, V-A.

17. Atch, C-47 Tactics [ca 1963-64], in hist (S), 34th Tac Gp, 1 Jan 64-30 Jun 64; intvw (S), author with Maj (then Capt) Roy Lynn, HQ USAF, 9 Sep 70. In 1963 Lynn served as a Farm Gate C-47 pilot.

18. See note above; 2d Air Div Reg 55-18 (S), 2 Aug 63.

19. See note 17; 2d Air Div Reg 55-18 (S), 2 Aug 63.

20. Lynn intvw (S), 9 Sep 70.

21. 2d Air Div Reg 55-18 (S), 2 Aug 63. Brig Gen Rollen Anthis, Comdr, 2d ADVON, briefed this tactic to SECDEF Robert S. McNamara in March 1962; hist (S), 2d ADVON, 15 Nov 61-8 Oct 62, p 128.

22. Lynn intvw (S), 9 Sep 70.

23. Gleason End of Tour Report (TS), 17 Nov 61-2 Mar 62; Carson intvw (S), 17 Sep 70; Pattee intvw (S), 18 Sep 70.

24. Pattee intvw (S), 18 Sep 70.

25. Presentation (S), Brig Gen Rollen Anthis, Comdr, 2d ADVON, to SECDEF McNamara at Mar 62 SECDEF conf, subj: Air Operations, in Hist (S), 2d ADVON, 15 Nov 61-8 Oct 62, Doc 203.

26. Brown intvw (S), 14 Sep 70; Farm Gate intvws.

27. See note above.

28. 2d Air Div Reg 55-18 (S), 2 Aug 63; Brown intvw (S), 14 Sep 70; Piotrowski intvw (S), 21 Sep 70.

29. Brown intvw (S), 14 Sep 70.

30. Ibid.

31. Farm Gate intvws.

32. Piotrowski intvw (S), 21 Sep 70; Brown intvw (S), 14 Sep 70.

33. Brown intvw (S), 14 Sep 70.

34. Ibid.

36. Draft paper (S), Farm Gate Tactics and Techniques, Jun 62; ltr (S), Dep Comdr for Ops, 8th TFWg, to 7th AF Dir/Analys, subj: Information for Air Staff Report, 14 Dec 68 [hereinafter cited as 8th TFWg Ltr].

Notes to pages 17-22

37. Draft paper (S), Farm Gate Tactics, Jun 62.

38. Hist (S), 34th Tac Gp, 1 Jan-8 Jul 65, p 4; Brown intvw (S), 14 Sep 70.

39. Draft paper (S), Farm Gate Tactics, Jun 62.

40. Brown intvw (S), 14 Sep 70; PACAF Tactics and Techniques Bul 15 (C), 6002d Stan/Eval Gp, 22 Jul 65, 34th Tac Gp and PACAF Tactics and Techniques; hist (S), 34th Tac Gp, 1 Jan-8 Jul 65.

41. Brown intvw (S), 14 Sep 70.

42. Hist (S), TAC, Jan-Jun 1963, p 42; Robert F. Futrell, Chronology of Significant Airpower Events in Southeast Asia, 1954-1967 (S) USAF Hist Div, ASI, Dec 67), p 16.

43. Msg (TS), CINCPAC to JCS, 090340Z Nov 62, subj: Air Augmentation in SVN; hist (S), TAC, Jul-Dec 1962, p 532.

44. Futrell, Chronology of Significant Air Events; hist (S), TAC, Jul-Dec 1962, p 532; memo (S), PFOCO (PACAF) to PFPDC (PACAF), et al., subj: Farm Gate Augmentation, 3 Jan 63.

45. Hist (S), SAWC, 1 Jan-30 Jun 63, pp 115, 150, 158, 278; HQ PACAF, In-Country and Out-Country Strike Operations in Southeast Asia, 1 Jan 65-31 Dec 69, II, Hardware Strike Aircraft (S), Oct 70, p 200 [hereinafter cited as Strike Ops in SEA... Strike Aircraft].

46. End of Tour Report (S), Maj William D. Palank, [undated], in Hist (S), SAWC, 21 Apr-31 Dec 62, Tab I.

47. Hist (S), 2d Air Div, Jan-Jun 1964, chap III, pp 26-28.

48. Ibid., p 46.

49. Ltr (U), Dir/Combat Tactics (13th AF) to Dep Comdr (13th AF), subj: Staff Visit Report, RVN (6-20 Jan 64), 24 Jan 64, in Hist (S), 13th AF, 1964, Doc II.

50. Intvw (S), J. Grainger, 2d ADVON Historian, with Lt Col M. M. Doyle, Comdr, Det 2, 1st Air Commando Gp, 16 Feb 63, in Hist, 2d ADVON, 15 Nov 61-8 Oct 62, Doc 195. David Halberstram, *The Making of a Quagmire* (New York, 1964), p 116.

Chapter II

1. Book of Actions in Southeast Asia, 1961-1964 (S), p 25; Hickey, *Night Close Air Support*, p 32; intvw (S), Lt Col Ray L. Bowers, Ofc/AF Hist, with Maj Charles West, Maxwell AFB, Ala., 5 May 70. Maj West served TDY with Mule Train from Jan-May 1962 then a PCS tour as Chief, Stan/Eval Sec (C-123), from Apr 1963-Jan 1964.

2. Intvw (S), Maj Dean Gausche, Proj Checo, with Lt Col Thomas B. Kennedy, Comdr, 315th TCGp, 4 Feb 64; intvw (S), with unnamed C-123 navigator, intvw tape 26 for study 5, ASI, 27 Sep 67.

3. See note above; End of Tour Report (S), Lt Col Harry G. Howton, Comdr, 311th Air Commando Sq, 6 Sep 65.

4. Msg AFTU-V-O-10-63A-1 (S), 2d Air Div to PACAF (PFLPL), 10 Jan 64, subj: COIN Lessons Learned, in supporting documents to Hist (S), 2d Air Div Jan-Jun 1964, IV.

5. Ibid.

6. PACAF Tactics and Techniques Bul 7 (C), 6002d Stan/Eval Gp, 25 May 65.

7. Ibid.

8. Hist (S), 2d Air Div, Jan-Jun 1964, chap II, p 9.

9. Ibid.; Fact Sheet 4 (TS), Night Operations, RVN, in Doc 5 to Warren A. Trest, *Control of Air Strikes in SEA, 1961-1966* (TS-NOFORN) (HQ PACAF, Project CHECO, 1 Mar 67).

Notes to pages 27-31

10. Kenneth Sams, First Test and Combat Use of the AC-47 (S) (HQ PACAF, Project CHECO, 8 Dec 65), pp 1-2; Kenneth Sams, Escalation of the War in Southeast Asia, July-December 1964 (S) (HQ PACAF, Project CHECO, no date), pp 53-55.

11. Ltr (U), Gen John McConnell to Gen Walter Sweeney, Comdr, TAC, (no date), quoted in Sams, First Test and Combat Use of the AC-47, p 3.

12. Ibid., p 16; hist (S), 6250th CSGp, 1 Jul-31 Dec 65, pp 16-17. Perhaps with tongue-in-cheek, the unit historian noted: "During the latter part of December 1965, the FC-47 designation changed to AC-47, denoting "attack" aircraft and to appease any possible antagonism from fighter pilots."

13. Doc 17, II, Hist (S), 6250th CSGp, 1 Jul-31 Dec 65, p 11; hist (S), 4th Air Commando Sq, 1 Jan-30 Jun 66, II, 2.

14. Ibid., p 16.

15. Hist (S), 14th Air Commando Wg, 1 Jan-30 Jun 66, p 53; hist (S), 2d Air Div, Jan-Jun 1964, chap IV, pp 13-14; Hickey, Night Close Air Support in RVN, p 25.

16. Maj Richard F. Kott, The Role of USAF Gunships in SEASIA (S) (HQ PACAF, Project CHECO, 30 Aug 69), pp 11-12; hist (S), 4th Air Commando Sq, 1 Jan-30 Jun 66, chap II, p 3.

17. PACAF Tactics and Techniques Bul 56 (C), 6002d Stan/Eval Gp, 13 Feb 67; hist (S), 4th Air Commando Sq, 1 Jan-30 Jun 66, chap II, paras 11-14.

18. Kott, The Role of USAF Gunships in SEASIA, pp 11-12; ltr (S), Dep Comdr/Ops, 14th Air Commando Wg to 7th AF (DOA), subj: Impact of Night and Weather on Air Operations in SEA, 23 Dec 68, in supporting documents to Lt Col Philip R. Harrison, Impact of Darkness and Weather on Air Operations in SEA (S) (HQ PACAF, Project CHECO, 10 Mar 69) [hereinafter cited as Ltr, 14th Air Commando Wg to 7th AF (DOA)].

19. PACAF Tactics and Techniques Bul 56 (C), 6002d Stan/Eval Gp, 13 Feb 67.

20. Ibid.

21. Ibid.

22. Sams, First Test and Combat Use of the AC-47, p 5.

23. Hist (S), 4th Air Commando Sq, 1 Jan-30 Jun 66, pp 19-20; Doc 17, II, Hist (S), 6250th CSGp, 1 Jul-31 Dec 65.

24. Doc 17, II, Hist (S), 6250th CSGp, 1 Jul-31 Dec 65.

25. Trest, Control of Air Strikes in SEA, 1961-1966, pp 68-69; Warren A. Trest and SSgt Dale E. Hammons, Air Operations from Thailand-1966 (S) (HQ PACAF, Project CHECO, 31 Oct 67), p 72.

26. Hist (S), 4th Air Commando Sq, 1 Jan-30 Jun 66, chap II, paras 11-13d.

27. Hickey, Night Close Air Support in RVN, p 10.

28. Trest and Hammons, Air Operations from Thailand-1966, p 110.

29. Ibid., p 100; Kott, The Role of USAF Gunships in SEASIA, p 15.

30. Hickey, Night Close Air Support in RVN, p 10.

31. Ltr, 14th Air Commando Wg to 7th AF (DOA).

32. Kott, The Role of USAF Gunships in SEASIA, p 15.

33. Ltr, 14th Air Commando Wg to 7th AF (DOA).

34. Hist (S), 315th Air Div, 1 Jul-31 Dec 65, I, 3-5, 10; hist 315th Air Div, 1 Jan-31 Dec 66, pp 65-66.

35. 315th Air Div OpOrd 5-68 [C-130 Blindbat], 1 Jan 68, in 7th AF DOCF File Jan-Dec 1968.

36. PACAF Tactics and Techniques Bul 7 (C), 6002d Stan/Eval Gp, 25 May 65; Tactics Manual (S), 606th SOSq, The Candlestick Forward Air Controllers Tactics Manual, 22 Mar 68 [hereinafter cited as 606th Candlestick FAC Manual].

Notes to pages 38-43

37. PACAF Tactics and Techniques Bul 10 (C), 6002d Stan/Eval Gp, 7 Jun 65; TAC Tng Reg 65-47 (U), C-130 Night Owl Procedures, Jul 1965; Trest and Hammons, Air Operations from Thailand-1966, p 110.

38. PACAF Tactics and Techniques Bul 10 (C), 6002d Stan/Eval Gp, 7 Jun 65; TAC Tng Reg 65-47 (U), C-130 Night Owl Procedures, Jul 1965.

39. Ibid.; rprt (TS), 7th AF, Commando Hunt III, May 1970, p 40.

40. PACAF Tactics and Techniques Bul 55 (C), 6002d Stan/Eval Gp, 24 Jan 67.

41. Ibid.; Trends, Indicators, and Analyses (S), DCS/Plans & Ops, Aug 68, p 2-19 [hereinafter cited as TIA with appropriate date].

42. Ibid.

43. PACAF Tactics and Techniques Bul 55 (C), 6002d Stan/Eval Gp, 24 Jan 67.

44. Ibid.

45. Ltr (S), 20th TASSq to 7th AF Dir/Tng (Tac Tng), subj: Night Tactics Employed by O-2 FAC Aircrews, [ca 1967] [hereinafter cited as Ltr (S), 20th TASSq to 7th AF Dir/Tng (Tac Tng)].

46. Futrell, Chronology of Significant Air Events, p 19; Lucien M. Biberman, Airborne Infrared Reconnaissance Capability: 1965 (S) (Institute for Defense Analysis, 1965), p B-3; Kenneth Sams, Maj John C. Pratt, C. William Thorndale, and James T. Baer, Air Support of Counterinsurgency in Laos July 1968-November 1969 (S) (HQ PACAF, Project CHECO, 10 Nov 69, p 70; Ernie S. Montagliani, Army Aviation in RVN (S) (HQ PACAF, Project CHECO, 11 Jul 70), p 54.

47. Sams, et al, Air Support of Counterinsurgency in Laos July 1968-November 1969, p 70; Montagliani, Army Aviation in RVN, pp 54-56.

48. Sams, et al, *Air Support of Counterinsurgency in Laos July 1968-November 1969*, p 71; Montagliani, *Army Aviation in RVN*, p 56; Capt Melvin F. Porter, *Tiger Hound* (TS) (HQ PACAF, Project CHECO, 6 Sep 66), p 9.

49. Hickey, *Night Close Air Support in RVN*, p 9.

50. Ltr (S), Dep Comdr for Ops, 35th TFWg, to 7th AF (DOA), subj: Night/Weather Operations, 14 Dec 68, in doc to Harrison, *Impact of Darkness and Weather on Air Operations in SEA* [hereinafter cited as 35th TFWg Ltr]; TIA, Sep 1968, p 2-22.

51. TAC Tng Reg 65-47 (U), C-130 Night Owl Procedures, Jul 1965; hist (S), 6315th Ops Gp, Jan-7Aug 1966.

52. 315th Air Div OpOrd 5-68, 1 Jan 68.

53. Hist (S), 315th Air Div, 1 Jan-30 Jun 68, p 122.

54. Hist (S), 7th AF, 1 Jan-30 Jun 70, I, 195-97.

55. The author has condensed flareship operations problems from many sources, among them: Harrison, *Impact of Darkness and Weather on Air Operations in SEA*; Herman S. Wolk, *USAF Plans and Policies, R&D for Southeast Asia, 1965-1967* (TS) (Ofc/AF Hist, Jun 1969), p 77; ltr (S), PACAF (DOCOO) to Hq USAF (AFXPD), subj: End of Tour Report (Brig Gen William D. Dunham), 8 Aug 67; Lt Col Edward M. Head, "Night Operations in Tactical Warfare," *Tactical Air Warfare Center Report*, II (March 1970), 18-23. He has also drawn on his many interviews with strike pilots and navigators.

56. Figures quoted are in study (S), DCS/R&D, Operation Shed Light, 1966, I.

57. Gen G.J.M. Chaussin, "Lessons of the War in Indochina," *Interavia*, VII (1952), 670-75.

58. Wolk, *R&D for Southeast Asia, 1965-1967*, pp 59-60; George T. Fouse and Lt Col Lorean A. Anderson, *Displays for Night Operations, Highlights* (S) (AF Avionics Lab, AFSC, Wright-Patterson AFB, Ohio, 1968), I, 2; hist (S), TAC, Jul-Dec 1967, pp 267-69.

59. Wolk, *R&D for Southeast Asia, 1965-1967*, pp 60-61.

Chapter III

1. Study (S), Dir/Ops, 7th AF, no subj, Dec 65.

2. Testimony of former Ambassador to Laos William Sullivan, 20-22 Oct 69, in Hearings before Senate Subcommittee of the Committee on Foreign Relations, 91st Cong, 1st sess, United States Security Agreements and Commitments Abroad--Kingdom of Laos Hearings, p 376. Ambassador Sullivan served in Vientiane from Nov 1964 to Apr 1969. At the time of the Senate Hearings he was Deputy Assistant Secretary of State for Far East Asian Affairs [Hereinafter cited as Sullivan Testimony, Senate Hearings].

3. L. E. Paterson, Evolution of the Rules of Engagement for Southeast Asia (TS) (HQ PACAF, Project CHECO, 30 Sep 66), pp 34-35.

4. C.G. Reinhardt and E.H. Sharkey, Air Interdiction in Southeast Asia (S) (Rand Corporation, 1969), pp 10-11.

5. Ibid., p 12.

6. Ibid., p 12.

7. Rprt of Joint Technical Coordinating Group (JTCG/ME) for Munitions Effectiveness (S), 1967.

8. Capt Melvin F. Porter, Night Interdiction in Southeast Asia (TS) (HQ PACAF, Project CHECO, 9 Sep 66), p 22.

9. Maj Louis Seig, Impact of Geography on Air Operations in SEA (S) (HQ PACAF, Project CHECO, 11 Jun 70), p 12.

10. Ibid., pp 16-19.

11. 7th AF Handbook DPLP-70-0097 (S), Southeast Asia Interdiction, 1 Apr 1970, pp 4-5 [hereinafter cited as 7th AF Handbook--SEA Interdiction].

12. Ibid., pp 61, 69-70.

13. Jacob Van Staaveren, USAF Plans and Policies in South Vietnam and Laos, 1964 (TS) (Ofc/AF Hist, Dec 1965), pp 73-74.

14. Ibid., pp 73-79; Sullivan Testimony, Senate Hearings, pp 476, 481.

15. Van Staaveren, USAF Plans and Policies in South Vietnam and Laos, 1964, p 72.

16. Sullivan Testimony, Senate Hearings, pp 399, 517.

17. Ibid., p 399.

18. Ibid., pp 468, 485, 488.

19. Msg (TS), JCS to CINCPAC, 092258Z Jan 65, subj: Barrel Roll.

20. Msg (TS), COMUSMACV to CINCPAC, 050950Z Feb 65, subj: Barrel Roll; intvw (S), author with Lt Col (then Capt) Donald C. Hatch, Hq USAF, 18 Sep 70. Colonel Hatch served with Farm Gate from October 1962-March 1963 and on a second SEA tour with 56th SOWg as an A-26 pilot.

21. Paterson, Evolution of the Rules of Engagement for Southeast Asia, pp 38-39; Van Staaveren, USAF Plans and Policies in South Vietnam and Laos, 1964, pp 25, 54-58.

22. Porter, Night Interdiction in Southeast Asia, pp 14-15; Scientific Advisory Group Working Paper 16-67 (S), Evaluation of Laos Interdiction Program.

23. Study (S), Rand RM-5760, Infiltration of Personnel from North Vietnam 1959-1967, Oct 68, in TIA, Dec 1968, p 2-10.

24. Capt Melvin F. Porter, Interdiction in SEA, 1965-1966 (TS) (HQ PACAF, Project CHECO, 25 May 67), p 47.

25. Msg (TS) CINCPACAF to CINCPAC, 280004Z Mar 65 [retransmittal of msg (TS) Carrier Task Force 77 to CINCPACFLT, 271848Z Mar 65, subj: Udorn Conference]; msg (S), PACAF to 13th AF and 2d Air Div, 260412Z Jan 65 [retransmittal of msg (S), CINCPAC to JCS, 211959Z Jan 65, subj: Night Interdiction Strikes by U.S. Air in Laos].

Notes to pages 60-65

26. Typewritten excerpts (TS), PACAF Commanders Report, Feb 1965.

27. End of Tour Report (S), Maj Leslie R. Leavoy, 10 Sep 66. Major Leavoy was Comdr, 416th TFSq from Nov 1965-Sep 1966 and later of the 308th TFSq and 90th TFSq. Leavoy commanded the 416th when it deployed from Cannon AFB, N.M.

28. Hist (S), TAC, Jul-Dec 1966, pp 563-570.

29. A-1E Pilot Syllabus (U), TAC, Jun 1967.

30. Typewritten copy of intvw (S), Lt James M. McClaugherty, Ofc/Hist, Hurlburt Field, Fla., with Lt Col Ernest R. McCready, 21 Apr 71.

31. Ibid.

32. Hist (S), TAC, Jul-Dec 1966, p 563.

33. Hist (S), TAC, Jan-Jun 1967, pp 474, 485; ltr (S), Dep Comdr for Ops, 35th TFWg, to 7th AF (DOA), subj: Information for Air Staff Report, 17 Dec 68, in doc to Harrison, Impact of Darkness and Weather on Air Operations in SEA; intvw (S), author with Maj Dennis P. Sharon, Hq USAF, 17 Jul 70. Major Sharon spent 3 years at Davis-Monthan AFB as an F-4 instructor pilot and 1 year in SEA as an RF-4C pilot in the 432d TRWg. During this period he flew over 180 combat missions, including 86 over North Vietnam. Sharon noted that the F-4 syllabus was not changed until 1967 when more data from SEA became available, for example, the need for additional night training.

34. MSgt Robert T. Helmka and TSgt Beverly Hale, USAF Operations from Thailand, 1964-1965 (TS) (HQ PACAF, Project CHECO, 10 Aug 66), p 60.

35. Porter, Tiger Hound, p 18.

36. Porter, Night Interdiction in Southeast Asia, p 27.

37. Porter, Interdiction in SEA, 1965-1966, p 42.

38. Ibid., p 43.

39. Porter, Night Interdiction in Southeast Asia, p 28.

40. Porter, Tiger Hound, p 31; working paper (S), Scientific Advisory Group, Evaluation of Laos Interdiction [undated], p 29.

41. Maj A. W. Thompson, Strike Control and Reconnaissance (SCAR) in SEA (S) (HQ PACAF, Project CHECO, 22 Jan 69), pp 30-31; MR (S), [originator unknown], subj: Tiger Hound Historical Report, 1 Jan-30 Jun 66, in Trest, Control of Air Strikes in SEA, 1961-1966, Doc 8.

42. Thompson, Strike Control and Reconnaissance (SCAR) in SEA, p 15.

43. Futrell, USAF in Korea, pp 83, 99, 101.

44. Thompson, Strike Control and Reconnaissance (SCAR) in SEA, p 3.

45. Trest, Control of Air Strikes in SEA, 1961-1966, p 64.

46. Tng manual (U), 4410th CCT Sq, The Airborne Forward Air Controller, 8 Feb 67, pp 4-6.

47. Ibid., p 6.

48. Ibid., p 7; intvw (S), author with Capt David Shields, 524th TFSq, Cannon AFB, N.M., 10 Jan 72. From May 1967-May 1968 Captain Shields served as FAC, logging over 70 night sorties in the O-1 and O-2 aircraft.

49. Capt Melvin F. Porter, Control of Airstrikes, January 1967-December 1968 (S) (HQ PACAF, Project CHECO, 30 Jun 69), p 35.

50. Hist (S), 504th TASGp, 1 Jan-31 Mar 67, p 20; tng manual (U), 4410th CCT Sq, The Airborne Forward Air Controller, 8 Feb 67, p 9; Shields intvw (S), 10 Jan 72.

51. Porter, Control of Airstrikes, January 1967-December 1968, pp 35, 57.

52. Tng manual (U), 4410th CCT Sq, The Airborne Forward Air Controller 8 Feb 67, pp 11-13.

Notes to pages 72-76

53. Seig, *Impact of Geography on Air Operations in SEA*, p 29.

54. Trest, *Control of Air Strikes in SEA, 1961-1966*, p 75.

55. Porter, *Control of Airstrikes, January 1967-December 1968*, pp 35-36.

56. *Ibid*.

57. Interrogation rprt 6028 1001 68 (C), Def Intel Analys, 11 Mar 68; interrogation rprt 6026 1425 67 (C), Def Intel Analys, 23 Apr 67.

58. Interrogation rprt 6027 4928 68 (C), Def Intel Analys, 27 Mar 68.

59. Hist (S), 504th TASGp, 1 Jan-31 Mar 67, p 39.

60. Capt Edward Vallentiny, *USAF Operations from Thailand, 1 January 1967-1 July 1968* (S) (HQ PACAF, Project CHECO, 20 Nov 68), p 68; pamphlet (U), Night Vision Lab, Ft Belvoir, Va., New Dimensions in Night Vision.

61. Hist (S), 504th TASGp, 1 Apr-30 Jun 67, p 81.

62. End of Tour Report (S), Col Charles E. Simpson, Dep Dir/7th AF TACC, 30 Apr 66, in Trest, *Control of Airstrikes in SEA, 1961-1966*, Doc 31; End of Tour Report (S), Capt Robert N. Havard, [unit unknown], 28 Mar 67, in Doc T-25 to Thompson, *Strike Control and Reconnaissance (SCAR) in SEA*; stf study (S), TAWC, Aircraft for SEA Operations--Evaluations B--Forward Air Controllers.

63. Thompson, *Strike Control and Reconnaissance (SCAR) in SEA*, pp 32-33.

64. Ltr (S), 20th TASSq to 7th AF Dir/Tng (Tac Tng); tactics manual (S) 23d TASSq, Nail Tactics, 1968; Tactics Manual 55-3 (U), 504th TASGp, Forward Air Controller Tactics Manual, 1 Mar 70, p 14-2; intvw (S), author with Maj Richard Starner, HQ AFSC, 8 Mar 71. From February-September 1969 Major Starner served in SEA as an O-2 navigator/FAC/starlight scope operator, logging over 70 night sorties in the O-2 aircraft.

65. Tactics manual (S), 23d TASSq, Nail Tactics, 1968; Tactics Manual 55-3 (U), 504th TASGp, Forward Air Controller Tactics Manual, 1 Mar 70; Starner intvw (S), 8 Mar 71.

66. Ltr (S), 20th TASSq to 7th AF Dir/Tng (Tac Tng); Starner intvw (S), 8 Mar 71.

67. Tactics manual (S), 23d TASSq, Nail Tactics, 1968; Tactics Manual 55-3 (U), 504th TASGp, Forward Air Controller Tactics Manual, 1 Mar 70.

68. Starner intvw (S), 8 Mar 71; ltr (S), 20th TASSq to 7th AF Dir/Tng (Tac Tng).

69. 23d TASSq Nail Tactics and Tactical Doctrine (S), 355th TFWg, 1 Jun 69, p 48.

70. Condensed from Ibid.; ltr (S), 20th TASSq to 7th AF Dir/Tng (Tac Tng); Tactics Manual 55-3 (U), 504th TASGp, Forward Air Controller Tactics Manual, 1 Mar 70; Starner intvw (S), 8 Mar 71; tactical doctrine (S), 8th TFWg, Dec 1967; rprt (S), 56th Air Commando Wg (DCOO) to CINCPACAF (DPLP), 56th ACW Weekly Activities Report, 1 Feb 67 [1 Feb 68].

71. Ibid.

72. Ibid.

73. Tactics Manual 55-3 (U), 504th TASGp, Forward Air Controller Tactics Manual, 1 Mar 70; Starner intvw (S), 8 Mar 71.

74. Manual (S), 23d TASSq, FAC Night Operations, 1 Sep 68.

75. Starner intvw (S), 8 Mar 71; rprt (TS), 7th AF, Commando Hunt III, May 1970, p 88.

76. Ibid.; End of Tour Report (S), Col Frank L. Gailer, Jr., Cmdr, 35th TFWg, Aug 1969.

77. Tactics Manual 55-3 (U), 504th TASGp, Forward Air Controller Tactics Manual, 1 Mar 70; Starner intvw (S), 8 Mar 71; HQ PACAF, In-Country and Out-Country Strike Operations in Southeast Asia, 1 Jan 65-31 Dec 69, II, Hardware Munitions (S), Oct 70, pp 11-12, 18 [hereinafter cited as Strike Ops in SEA...Strike Munitions.

78. Starner intvw (S), 8 Mar 71; Strike Ops in SEA...Strike Aircraft, pp 20, 120.

79. Starner intvw (S), 8 Mar 71.

80. Hist (S), 315th Air Div, 1 Jul-31 Dec 65, pp 42, 58.

81. 606th Candlestick FAC Manual.

82. Ibid.; intvw (S), author with Maj Charles A. Beckwith, JSIPS, 1 Mar 71. From April 1969-April 1970 Major Beckwith was a C-123 navigator/starlight scope operator/FAC in the 606th SOSq, flying over 190 night sorties that destroyed 90-plus trucks.

83. Ltr (S), 60th Air Commando Sq to Dep Comdr, 7th/13th AF, subj: Capability of C-123 Aircraft to Drop Flares for T-28 Aircraft, 2 Feb 67, in Doc 23 to Warren A. Trest, Lucky Tiger Combat Operations (TS) (HQ PACAF, Project CHECO, 15 Jun 67); msg (S), 7th AF Dir/Ops to 7th/13th AF, 19?223Z Feb 67 [actual DTG unknown], subj: Flare A/C Support, Trest, Lucky Tiger Combat Operations, Doc 24.

84. 606th Candlestick FAC Manual; Beckwith intvw (S), 1 Mar 71; ltr (S), Comdr, 606th SOSq, 56th SOWg, to 56th SOWg (DCO), subj: Information for Air Staff Report, 11 Dec 68, see doc in Harrison, Impact of Darkness and Weather on Air Operations in SEA [hereinafter cited as 56th SOWg Ltr].

85. 606th Candlestick FAC Manual.

86. Ibid.; Beckwith intvw (S), 1 Mar 71.

87. Beckwith intvw (S), 1 Mar 71; Technical Report ASD-TR-67-17 (S), AFSC, Low Altitude Recce/Strike Techniques, Problems, Dec 67, p 24.

88. 606th Candlestick FAC Manual; Beckwith intvw (S), 1 Mar 71.

89. 606th Candlestick FAC Manual.

90. Ibid.; Beckwith intvw (S), 1 Mar 71.

91. Ibid.

92. Ibid.

93. Ibid.

94. Lee Bonetti, et al, *The War in Vietnam, July-December 1967* (S) (HQ PACAF, Project CHECO, 29 Nov 68), p 19; ltr (S), Actg Dep Comdr/Ops, 37th TFWg to 7th AF (DOA), subj: Night/Weather Operations, 14 Dec 68, in doc to Harrison, *Impact of Darkness and Weather on Air Operations in SEA* [hereinafter cited as 37th TFWg Ltr]; memo (S), 7th AF (TACC, Weapons Force Plans) to 7th AF (Plans), subj: Misty FAC Operational Requirement, 15 Mar 68; Lt Col John Schlight, *Jet Forward Air Controllers in SEA* (S) (HQ PACAF, Project CHECO, 15 Oct 69), p 16.

95. Schlight, *Jet Foward Air Controllers in SEASIA*, p 16.

96. Microfilm copy of rprt (S), 37th TFWg, Commando Sabre Operations [ca Aug 1968].

97. Ibid.

98. Ltr (S), 37th TFWg (Dep Comdr/Ops) to 7th AF (Dir/Ops, Combat Tactics) subj: Commando Sabre Night Operations [ca Oct 1968].

99. Ibid.

100. Ltr (S), 90th TFSq to 7th AF TACC, subj: Inflight Evaluation of the PVS-3 Starlight Scope [undated]; ltr (S), Comdr, 37th TFWg to 7th AF (Tac Tng), subj: Starlight Scope Evalution [no date].

101. Ltr (S), 37th TFWg (Dep Cmdr/Ops) to 7th AF (Dir/Ops, Combat Tactics) subj: Commando Sabre Night Operations [ca Oct 1968].

102. Capt Joseph V. Potter, *OV-10 Operations in SEASIA* (S) (HQ PACAF, Project CHECO, 15 Sep 69), pp 1-4; final rprt (C), TAC, OV-10 Aircraft Introduction, Evaluation and Assistance Program in Southeast Asia, Nov 1968, pp 4,11 [hereinafter cited as TAC OV-10 Final Report.]

103. Potter, *OV-10 Operations in SEASIA*, pp 12-13, TAC OV 10 Final Report, pp 4, 11.

104. TAC OV-10 Final Report, pp 57, 64, 74.

105. Ibid., p 64, figs A-23 and A-24.

106. Ibid., p 17; msg (S), Gen Jones, 7th AF, to Gen Hardin, PACAF, 151130Z Feb 69; End of Tour Reports (S), Col Thomas G. Monroe, Jr., Dir/Rqmts, DCS/Plans, 7th AF (11 Jun 69-11 Jun 70), pp 117-18.

107. Monroe End of Tour Report (S) (11 Jun 69-11 Jun 70), pp 123-24.

Chapter IV

1. Hist (S), 34th Tac Gp, 1 Jan-30 Jun 64.

2. Hist (S), SAWC, 1 Jan-30 Jun 64, p 101.

3. Ibid., p 73; hist (S), TAC, 1 Jan-30 Jun 63, pp 417-18.

4. Hist (S), TAC, Jan-Jun 1967, pp 540-41.

5. Ltr (S), Dir/Ops, 7th AF, to CINCPACAF (Dir/Ops), subj: Concept of Operations, A-26 Aircraft, 4 Jun 66, in Trest, Lucky Tiger Combat Operations, Doc 6. Doc 14 to this Trest study contains a first-hand account by an A-26 crew using these tactics.

6. Ibid.

7. Intl rprt (S) [originator unknown], Results of A-26 Air Strikes, 15 Nov 66, in Trest, Lucky Tiger Combat Operations, Doc 13.

8. Study (S), DCS/Ops, PACAF, Effectiveness of USAF Truck Killing Operations in SEA (September 1967 through August 1968), 1 Feb 69, p 22; Sullivan Testimony, Senate Hearings, p 485; Beckwith intvw (S), 1 Mar 71; intvw (S), author with Lt Col Mark Richards, HQ USAF/OASD (PA), 16 Mar 71, Colonel Richards served with the 609th SoSq, 56th SOWg.

9. Richards intvw (S), 16 Mar 71.

10. Ibid.

11. Ibid.

12. Ibid.; tech rprt, AFSC, Low Altitude Recce/Strike Techniques, [undated], p 19.

13. Richards intvw (S), 16 Mar 71.

14. Richards intvw (S), 16 Mar 71; intvw (S), author with Maj Kenneth E. LaFave, HQ USAF, 12 Mar 71. From January-December 1968 Maj LaFave was an A-26 pilot in the 609th SOSq, 56th SOWg, flying over 125 night missions.

15. Atch (S), 609th SOSq, [ca Dec 1968], Inputs for Air Staff Report, to ltr (S), 56th SOWg (DCO) to 7th AF (DOA), subj: Information for Air Staff Report, 13 Dec 68 [hereinafter cited as 609th SOSq Atch]; Manual 55-26 (C), 56th CSGp, A-26 Operational Procedures and Techniques, 18 Dec 68, in Doc II to hist (S), 56th SOWg, Oct-Dec 1968 [hereinafter cited as A-26 Tactics Manual]; La Fave intvw (S), 12 Mar 71.

16. A-26 Tactics Manual.

17. La Fave intvw (S), 12 Mar 71.

18. Richards intvw (S), 16 Mar 71; La Fave intvw (S), 12 Mar 71.

19. Ibid.

20. Richards intvw (S), 16 Mar 71.

21. La Fave intvw (S), 12 Mar 71; hist (S), 56th Air Commando Wg, 1 Jan-30 Mar 68, p 18; Xerox ltr (U), Maj John Simons to unknown AF officer, 3 May 1967. Major Simons served as an A-26 pilot in SEA from Dec 1966-Sep 1967.

22. Richards intvw (S), 16 Mar 71.

23. Ibid.

24. Ibid.; End of Tour Report (S), Col Edwin J. White, Comdr, 56th SOWg, 5 Oct 69, pp 11-61.

25. Rprt of Joint Technical Coordinating Group (JTCG/ME) for Munitions Effectiveness (S), 1967.

26. Richards intvw (S), 16 Mar 71; White End of Tour Report (S), 5 Oct 69.

27. Hist (S), 56th SOWg, Oct-Dec 1969, I, 156.

28. Ibid.

29. Ibid., p 163.

Notes to pages 107-113

30. Ltr (S), 606th Air Commando Sq to 13th AF, subj: Proposal to Improve USAF Operations in SEA, 4 Jan 67, in Doc 16 to Trest, Lucky Tiger Combat Operations; intvw (S), author with Maj Charles Brown, Hq USAF, 9 Apr 71 [hereinafter cited as Brown intvw 2 (S), 9 Apr 71 (the author first interviewed Maj Brown on 14 Sep 70--see footnote 2, chap I)]. Maj Brown flew over 75 missions from Oct 1967-May 1968 as a T-28 pilot in the 56th SOWg.

31. Ibid.

32. Msg (S), 634th TUOC to 7th AF, 241600Z Jan 67, subj: Daily Operations Wrap-up Report for 24 Jan 67, in Doc 18 to Trest, Lucky Tiger Combat Operations.

33. Brown intvw 2 (S), 9 Apr 71.

34. Ibid. Unless otherwise noted, the rest of the T-28 section is based on Brown intvw 2 (S), 9 Apr 71.

35. Trest, Lucky Tiger Combat Operations, pp 39-40.

36. Strike Ops in SEA...Strike Aircraft, app I, p 202; hist (S), 56th Air Commando Wg, 1 Oct-31 Dec 67, p 13; chronology in hist (S), 56th Air Commando Wg, 1 Jan-31 Mar 68; rprt (S), 56th Air Commando Wg (DCOO) to CINCPACAF (DPLP), 56 ACW Weekly Activities Report, 23 Jun 68; Brown intvw 2 (S), 9 Apr 71.

37. William Green, The World's Fighting Planes (New York, 1964), pp 140-43.

38. Hist (S), TAC, Jan-Jun 1963 p 63; hist (S), 56th SOWg, 1 Jul-30 Sep 68, I, 23; SEAsia Notes.

39. Hist (S), 56th SOWg, Jan-Mar 1969, I, 34.

40. Hist (S), 56th SOWg, Oct-Dec 1970, I, 95-96; intvw (S), author with Lt Col Herman J. Methfessel, JCS (C-C), 26 Apr 71, 56th SOWg. Colonel Methfessel was Operations Officer of 22d SOSq.

41. Hist (S), 56th SOWg, Oct-Dec 1970, I, 98.

42. Methfessel intvw (S), 26 Apr 71.

43. Ibid.

44. Hist (S), 56th SOWg, Jan-Mar 1969, I, 37.

45. Methfessel intvw (S), 26 Apr 71.

46. Hist (S), 56th SOWg, Oct-Dec 1969, I, 117.

47. Ibid.

48. Comdr's comments, in hist (S), 56th SOWg, Apr-Jun 1970, II app VA; hist (S), 56th SOWg, Jul-Sep 1970, pp 46, 52; hist (S), 56th SOWg, Oct-Dec 1970, I, 36.

49. Rprt (S), SAWC, Low-Light-Level Television (Tropic Moon I), 1967, p iii; TIA, Sep 1968, p 2-11.

50. TIA, Sep 1968, pp 2-11, 2-12.

51. Ibid., pp 2-12, 2-13.

52. Ibid.

53. Rprt (S), SAWC, Low-Light-Level Television (Tropic Moon I), 1967, p 1.

54. Msg (S), CINCPACAF (Dir/Plans) to 7th AF (Dir/Plans), 090316Z Dec 67, subj: Tropic Moon I Project; unsigned working paper (S), 7th AF, subj: Tropic Moon--Concept of Operations, 10 May 68; intvw (S), author with Maj Gerald C. Schwankl, Hq AFSC, 6 May 71. From January-December 1968 Major Schwankl flew over 135 LLLTV missions as a Tropic Moon I pilot.

55. Schwankl intvw (S), 6 May 71.

56. Ibid.; TIA, Sep 1968, p 2-15. Secondary areas included routes 91 and 914.

57. Ibid.

58. Ibid.

59. Schwankl intvw (S), 6 May 71; ltr (S), Comdr, 7th AF, to Comdr, AFSC, no subj, 14 Mar 68.

60. Schwankl intvw (S), 6 May 71.

61. Ibid.; msg (S), CINCPACAF (DPL) to CINCPAC, 290239Z May 68, subj: Tropic Moon I.

62. Schwankl intvw (S), 6 May 71; unsigned summary (S), 7th AF (DPL), Tropic Moon I Comparison Laos/SVN Operations [no date].

63. Ibid.

64. Ibid.

65. TIA, Sep 1968, p 2-17; msg (S), 7th AF (DPLR) to 13th AF (DO/DM/DPL), 150232Z Oct 68, subj: Tropic Moon I Phaseout. There were 1,285 trucks sighted in Laos [unsigned summary (S), 7th AF (DPL), [ca late 1968], Tropic Moon I Comparison Laos/SVN Operations (no date)].

Chapter V

1. Green, The World's Fighting Planes, pp 90, 182; hist (S), 34th Tac Gp, 1 Jan-8 Jul 65.

2. Green, The World's Fighting Planes, pp 182-83.

3. Hist (S), 34th Tac Gp, 1 Jan-8 Jul 65; WRAMA Aircraft Weapon Systems in SEA, 1 Jan 65-31 Mar 68 (S), Doc 15 in Warner Robins Air Materiel Area Southeast Asia Document Collection III.

4. Intvw (S), author with Col James J. Gearhart, Hq USAF, 18 May 71. Colonel Gearhart flew more than 260 combat missions in the B-57 during Jun-1967-Jan 1969, while serving as Asst Ops Off and Flt Ldr in both the 13th and 8th Tac Bomb Sqs.

5. Gearhart intvw (S), 18 May 71.

6. Ibid.; Gailer End of Tour Report (S), Aug 1969; End of Tour Report (S), Lt Col Kenneth S. Smith, Comdr, 8th Tac Bomb Sq (Nov 1968-May 1969).

7. Gearhart intvw (S), 18 May 71; ltr (S), Comdr, 35th TFWg to Maj Gen Gordon F. Blood, DCS/Operations, 7th AF, subj: Mission Requirements for B-57 Aircraft, 5 Jan 69.

8. Gearhart intvw (S), 18 May 71; End of Tour Reports (S), Smith (Nov 1968-May 1969) and Gailer, Aug 1969.

9. Gailer End of Tour Report (S), Aug 1969.

10. Ibid.; Gearhart intvw (S), 18 May 71.

11. End of Tour Reports (S), Smith (Nov 1968-May 1969), Gailer, Aug 1969.

12. Ibid.

13. Hist (S), TAC, Jul-Dec 1967, p 273; Test Order 68-10, TAC Pave Moon, Aug 1968.

14. Ibid.; unsigned working paper (S), 7th AF, subj: Tropic Moon--Concept of Operations, 10 May 68.

15. Memo (S), 7th AF (DPLR) to 7th AF (Comdr), subj: Tropic Moon IIA, 3 Jan 68.

16. Ltr (S), Comdr, 7th AF, to Comdr, AFSC, [no subj], 14 Mar 68; memo (S), 7th AF (DPLR) to 7th AF (Comdr), subj: Tropic Moon II, 13 Mar 68; trip rprt (S) 7th AF (DPLR), Trip Report--Tropic Moon LLLTV, 10 May 68.

17. Wolk, R&D for Southeast Asia, 1965-1967, p 64; Herman S. Wolk, USAF Plans and Policies, R&D for Southeast Asia, 1968 (TS) (Ofc/AF Hist, Jul 1970), p 41; msg (S), HQ USAF (DCS/R&D) to AFSC, AFLC, et al, 171941Z Oct 68.

18. Wolk, R&D for Southeast Asia, 1968, p 41; rprt (S), USAF Scientific Advisory Board, Report of USAF Scientific Advisory Board on Infiltration Interdiction, 1968, III, 56.

19. TIA, Apr 1970, p 1-4; rprt (S), TAWC, Final Report B-57G SEA Combat Evaluation, Mar 1971, p 6.

20. TIA, Apr 1970, p 1-4; Fouse and Anderson, Displays for Night Operations, Highlights, p 9.

21. Rprt (S), TAWC, Final Report B-57G SEA Combat Evaluation, Mar 1971, p 8.

22. Ibid., p 14; hist (S), 8th TFWg, 1 Jul-30 Sep 70, III; MR (S), [originator unknown], subj: Chief of Staff Visit to Southeast Asia 2-12 November 1970, 16 Nov 70.

23. 7th AF Handbook--SEA Interdiction, p 23.

24. Ibid., p 23; 8th TFWg Ltr (S), 14 Dec 68.

25. Strike Ops in SEA...Strike Aircraft, pp 64-65, 73, 97-98, 103; Sharon intvw (S), 17 Jul 70.

26. Manual (S), 8th TFWg, Night Combat Tactics, 10 Sep 66, in End of Tour Report (S), Col George W. Wilson, Comdr, 8th TFWg (Dec 1965-Nov 1966) [hereinafter cited as 8th TFWg Night Combat Tactics].

27. Manual (S), 433d TFWq, Night Owl Tactics, Jun 1966 [hereinafter cited as 433d TFSq Night Owl Tactics]; manual (S), 2d ed, 8th TFWg, Tactical Doctrine, Dec 1967, pp 265-66 [hereinafter cited as 8th TFWg Tactical Doctrine, 2d ed]; Wilson End of Tour Report (S), (Dec 1965-Nov 1966).

28. End of Tour Report (S), Col Wendell L. Bevan, Comdr, 432d TRWg (3 Sep 68-7 Jun 69), p 3-28.

29. 8th TFWg Ltr (S), 14 Dec 68; 8th TFWg Night Combat Tactics.

30. 8th TFWg Night Combat Tactics; 433d TFSq Night Owl Tactics; manual (S), 366th TFWg, Tactics Manual, 10 Dec 67, p 38.

31. 8th TFWg Night Combat Tactics, manual (S), 366th TFWg, Tactics Manual, 10 Dec 67; Sharon intvw (S), 17 Jul 70; End of Tour Report (S), Col Allen P. Rankin, Comdr, 366th TFWg [undated].

32. 8th TFWg Tactical Doctrine, 2d ed, p 270.

33. Sharon intvw (S), 17 Jul 70.

34. Study (S), Aircrew Composition for F-4 and F-111 Aircraft [originator and date not given].

35. <u>Strike Ops in SEA...Strike Aircraft</u>, p 97; intvw (S), author with Col Carl H. Cathey, Jr., Hq USAF, 21 Jul 71. From late May 1968 to early February 1969 Colonel Cathey was Ops Officer of the Igloo White--dedicated 25th TFSq at Ubon, Thailand. From Feb-Jun 1969 he commanded the 497th TFSq Night Owls at Ubon, flying more than 150 combat missions including 45 over North Vietnam.

36. <u>Ibid</u>.

37. End of Tour Report (S), Col Charles E. Pattillo, Comdr, 8th TFWg (5 Jul 68-8 May 69), p 5.

38. 8th TFWg Night Combat Tactics.

39. <u>Ibid</u>.; manual (S), 8th TFWg, Mission Employment Tactics, 8 Aug 69 [hereinafter cited as 8th TFWg Mission Employment Tactics].

40. Pattillo End of Tour Report (S), (5 Jul 68-8 May 69).

41. <u>Ibid.</u>; Ltr (S), Dep Comdr/Ops, 366th TFWg, to 7th AF (DOA), subj: Project CHECO, "The Impact of Darkness and Weather on Air Operations in SEA, " 18 Dec 68, doc in Harrison, <u>Impact of Darkness and Weather on Air Operations in SEA</u> [hereinafter cited as 366th TFWg Ltr].

42. <u>Ibid</u>.

43. 433d TFSq Night Owl Tactics.

44. Cathey intvw (S), 21 Jul 71; <u>Strike Ops in SEA...Strike Munitions</u>, pp 21-22, 29, 32, 34-35.

45. 8th TFWg Mission Employment Tactics.

46. Sharon intvw (S), 17 Jul 70.

47. <u>Ibid</u>.

48. <u>Strike Ops in SEA...Strike Aircraft</u>, pp 81-82.

Notes to pages 145-150

49. Wolk, R&D for Southeast Asia, 1965-1967, p 70; study summary (S), DCS/R&D, USAF, Operation Shed Light, 1966, I, IC-33; End of Tour Report (S), Col Lewis M. Jamison, Asst Dep Ch/Ops, 8th TFWg (12 Mar 69-6 Jul 69), and Ch, Ftr Div, Dep Ch/Ops, 7th AF (7 Jul- 4 Oct 69); hist (S), 7th AF, 1 Jul-31 Dec 68, I, part 2, 428.

50. Strike Ops in SEA...Strike Aircraft, p 82.

51. Ibid.; Jamison End of Tour Report (S), (12 Mar 69-4 Oct 69); End of Tour Report (S), Col Walter P. Paluch, Jr., Dep Ch/Ops, 366th TFW (12 Apr 69-3 Apr 70).

52. Paluch End of Tour Report (S), (12 Apr 69-3 Apr 70); End of Tour Report (S), Col Donald N. Stanfield, Comdr, 8th TFWg (6 May 68- 6 May 70) in Doc 45 to hist (S), 8th TFWg, 1 Apr-30 Jun 70, II, 28-29.

53. End of Tour Reports (S), Col Stanfield, (6 May 68-6 May 70), Col Jamison (12 Mar 69-4 Oct 69), p 6; Strike Ops in SEA.... Strike Aircraft, p 82.

54. Wolk, R&D for Southeast Asia, 1965-1967, p 65.

55. Hist (S), 8th TFWg, 1 Jan-30 Jun 70, I, part 2, 283; TIA, Jan 1970, p 1-6.

56. Rprt (TS), 7th AF, Commando Hunt III, May 1970, pp 134-35.

57. TIA, Jan 1970, p 1-6.

58. Rprt (TS), 7th AF, Commando Hunt III, May 1970, p 185; hist (S), 8th TFWg, Jan-Mar 1969, p 37; ASI, Special Report 69-3 (S), Air Operations in Southeast Asia, August 1967- January 1969, Jul 1969, p 28. This report contains extracts from the End of Tour Report, Maj Gen Gordon F. Blood, DCS/Ops, 7th AF.

59. Sensor and gunship weaponry information condensed from rprt (TS), 7th AF, Commando Hunt III, May 1970, pp 184-85; hist (S), 8th TFWg, Jan-Mar 1969, pp 37-39; 7th AF OpOrd 543-69 (S), Gunship II (AC-130), Aug 1968, p B-1; Col James McGuire, Development of All-Weather and Night Truck Kill Capability (S), ASI, 1970, p 13.

60. See note above.

61. See note 59.

62. See note 59.

63. Rprt (TS), 7th AF, Commando Hunt III, May 1970, p 184.

64. 7th AF OpOrd 543-69 (S), Gunship II (AC-130), Aug 1968, p B-1; hist (S), 8th TFWg, Jan-Mar 1969, p 39.

65. Kott, The Role of USAF Gunships in SEASIA, p 27.

66. Strike Ops in SEA...Strike Aircraft, pp 223-24; msg (S), 14th CSGp to PACAF (Dir/Personnel), 050502Z Jul 68, subj: Personnel TDY; hist (S), 14th SOWg, 1 Jul-30Sep 68, pp 12-13; msg (S), 14th SOWg (Comdr) to 7th AF (DO), 070947Z Sep 68, subj: AC-130 Aircraft Transfer; msg (S), 7th AF to CINCPACAF, 120220Z Sep 68, subj: Gunship II Prototype Replacement.

67. Kott, The Role of USAF Gunships in SEASIA, p 27.

68. Pamphlet (no class), 14th SOWg, Gunship Tactics, 1 Oct 70, p 29.

69. Ibid., p 27; Description of the three search patterns in the next five paragraphs are based on this citation, pp 29-32.

70. Hist (S), 8th TFWg, Jan-Mar 1969, p 40.

71. Ibid., p 50; Strike Ops in SEA...Strike Aircraft, p 224; msg (S), 14th Air Commando Wg to 7th AF (DPLR), 221009Z Jul 68, subj: Gunship II.

72. Pattillo End of Tour Report (S), 5 Jul 68-8 May 69), p 53; Kott, The Role of USAF Gunships in SEASIA, p 30; hist (S), 8th TFWg, Jan-Mar 1969, p 50; End of Tour Report (S), Col Walter D. Druen, Jr., Dep Ch/Ops, 8th TFWg (21 Aug 69-8 Jun 70).

73. Cathey intvw (S), 21 Jul 71.

Notes to pages 158-166

74. Kott, The Role of USAF Gunships in SEASIA, pp 40-41; Beven End of Tour Report (S), (3 Sep 68-7 Jun 69); 8th TFWg Mission Employment Tactics.

75. Beven End of Tour Report (S), (3 Sep 68-7 Jun 69); Cathey intvw (S), 21 Jul 71.

76. See note above; hist (S), 8th TFWg, Jan-Mar 1969, p 51.

77. Hist (S), 8th TFWg, Jan-Mar 1969, p 51.

78. Pattillo End of Tour Report (S), (5 Jul 68-8 May 69).

79. Druen End of Tour Report (S), (21 Aug 69-8 Jun 70).

80. Kott, The Role of USAF Gunships in SEASIA, p 33.

81. Ibid., p 51.

82. Rprt (TS), 7th AF Commando Hunt III, May 1970, pp 182-183; rprt (S), TAWC, Final Report Combat Introduction/Evaluation (Coronet Surprise), Aug 1970, pp 1-2.

83. See note above.

84. Hist (S), 8th TFW, Jul-Sep 1970, I, 28-29.

85. Ibid., p 184.

86. Ibid., p 187; hist (S), 8th TFWg, Jul-Sep 1970, I, 31.

87. Hist (S), 8th TFWg, Jul-Sep 1969, p 24.

88. Rprt (S), TAWC, Final Report Combat Introduction/Evaluation (Coronet Surprise), Aug 1970, pp 4-7.

89. Ibid., p 31; Strike Ops in SEA...Strike Aircraft, p 227.

90. Strike Ops in SEA...Strike Aircraft, p 227; TIA, Dec 1970, p 1-4.

91. Wolk, R&D for Southeast Asia, 1965-1967, pp 67-68.

92. Ltr (C), 1st Combat Applications Gp (DOA) [addressee not shown], subj: Combat Hornet Operational Test and Evaluation, Jun 1968; msg (S), CSAF (AFXOP, AFSME) to TAC (DOSW, DORQ, et al), 102213Z Jul 68, subj: AC-119 Operational Test.

93. Kott, The Role of USAF Gunships in SEASIA, pp 20-21; rprt (S), USAF Sp Ops Force, TAC, Final Report Combat Introduction/ Evaluation AC-119K Gunship (Combat King), Aug 1970, p 42.

94. Hist (S), 14th SOWg, 1 Apr-30 Jun 69, p 2.

95. Ibid.

96. Pamphlet (no class), 14th SOWg, Gunship Tactics, 1 Oct 70, p 40.

97. AC-119/A-1 escort tactics condensed from Ibid., pp 45-49.

98. Ibid.

99. Ibid.

100. Rprt (S), 7th AF, Commando Hunt V Report, May 1971, pp 1-5.

101. Ibid.

102. Ibid.

103. Ibid., p 61.

104. Kott, The Role of USAF Gunships in SEASIA, p 83; Wolk, R&D for Southeast Asia, 1968; Fouse and Anderson, Displays for Night Operations, Highlights, I, 6.

105. Kott, The Role of USAF Gunships in SEASIA, pp 83-84; TIA, Feb 1969, p 2-24; rprt (S), USAF Spec Ops Cen, Black Spot (NC-123) Combat Evaluation, Jan 1970, p 1.

106. TIA, Feb 1969, p 2-26; rprt (TS), 7th AF, Commando Hunt III, May 1970; atch (S), Out-Country "Black Spot" Employment, to staff summary sheet (S), 7th AF (DOCT) to 7th AF (DO), Out-Country Black Spot Employment, 25 Nov 68.

107. Ibid.

108. TIA, Feb 1969, p 2-27; rprt (S), USAF Spec Ops Cen, Black Spot (NC-123) Combat Evaluation, Jan 1970, pp 13, 22, 35; hist (S), 8th TFWg, Oct-Dec 1969, I, 35-36.

109. Rprt (S), USAF Spec Ops Cen, Black Spot (NC-123) Combat Evaluation, Jan 1970, p 23.

110. Ibid., p 30; hist (S), 7th AF, 1 Jan-30 Jun 69, I, part 1, 34.

111. Hist (S), 56th SOWg, Jan-Mar 1969, I, 24.

112. Ibid., p 62.

Chapter VI

1. Capt Mark E. Smith, USAF Reconnaissance in Southeast Asia (TS) (HQ PACAF, Project CHECO, 25 Oct 66), p 1.

2. Ibid., pp 2-3.

3. Ibid., pp 3-6.

4. Ibid., p 7; Summary of Actions, General Wheeler's Party, Jan 1963, sec I, Tab D.

5. Smith, USAF Reconnaissance in Southeast Asia, pp 8-9, 19, 22; Harrison, Impact of Darkness and Weather on Air Operations in SEA, p 19; HQS TAC, Tactical Air Reconnaissance in SEA, 1 January 1965-31 March 1968 (TS), Nov 1969, I.

6. Ibid., 2-59, 2-60; HQS TAC, Tactical Air Reconnaissance in SEA, 1 April 1968-31 December 1969 (TS), Sep 1970, I, 4-56.

7. HQS TAC, Tactical Air Reconnaissance in SEA, 1 April 1968-31 December 1968 (TS), Sep 1970, I.

8. Aerospace Studies Institute, Evaluation of Airpower in Southeast Asia, 1954-1964 (S), 1970, II, 8-31, 8-32.

9. Hist (S), 2d Air Div, Jan-Jun 1964, pp 112-13.

10. Montagliani, Army Aviation in RVN, pp 54-55. Aerospace Studies Institute, Evaluation of Airpower in Southeast Asia, 1954-1964 (S), 1970, II, 8-57.

11. Montagliani, Army Aviation in RVN, p 57.

12. HQS TAC, Tactical Air Reconnaissance in SEA, 1 April 1968-31 December 1969 (TS), Sep 1970, I, 1-99; typed transcript of intvw (S), with Col Adrian M. Burrows (Vice Comdr, TARC), Lt Col Thomas Killion (Dir/Tac Testing, TARC), and Maj Darrel E. Freeland (Dep Comdr/Concepts, Requirements, Doctrine, TARC), [undated].

13. Montagliani, Army Aviation in RVN, pp 54-55; 7th AF DPLG File, Dec 1967-Oct 1968.

14. Condensed from Aerospace Studies Institute, Evaluation of Airpower in Southeast Asia, 1954-1964 (S), 1970, II, 8-27; HQS TAC, Tactical Air Reconnaissance in SEA, 1 January 1965-31 March 1968 (TS), Nov 1969, I, 1-84, 1-85; ltr (U) Maj Gen Rollin H. Anthis, Comdr, 2d ADVON, to Gen Jacob E. Smart, CINCPACAF, [no subj], 25 Nov 63, quoted in Hist (S), 2d Air Div, Jan-Jun 1964, pp 113-114.

15. Ibid.

16. Smith, USAF Reconnaissance in Southeast Asia, p 77; HQS TAC, Tactical Air Reconnaissance in SEA, 1 January 1965-31 March 1968 (TS), Nov 1969, I, 2-32.

17. Smith, USAF Reconnaissance in Southeast Asia, p 43.

18. HQS TAC, Tactical Air Reconnaissance in SEA, 1 January 1965-31 March 1968 (TS), Nov 1969, I, 1-148.

19. Smith, USAF Reconnaissance in Southeast Asia, p 27; PACAF Tactics and Techniques Bul 32 (revised) (C), 6002 Stan/ Eval Gp, 28 Dec 65 and 10 Jun 66.

20. Smith, USAF Reconnaissance in Southeast Asia, p 27; End of Tour Report (S), Col R. W. Shick, 432d TRWg (18 Sep 66-18 Sep 67) p 16.

21. Tactics and techniques taken from: Shick End of Tour Report (S), (18 Sep 66-18 Sep 67); Bevan End of Tour Report (S), (3 Sep 68-7 Jun 69); and Major Joseph Stapleton, *The RF-4C and Night Reconnaissance in North Vietnam* (S) Aerospace Studies Institute Special Report 71-27, ASI, Maxwell AFB, Ala., Feb 1971), pp 13, 17.

22. *Ibid.*

23. *Ibid.*

24. Lee Bonetti, *et al, The War in Vietnam, July-December 1967,* p 34.

25. HQS TAC, *Tactical Air Reconnaissance in SEA, 1 April 1968-31 December 1969* (TS), Sep 1970, I, 1-48.

26. Stapleton, *The RF-4C and Night Reconnaissance in North Vietnam,* pp 5-6; TIA, Apr 1969, p 1-16.

27. End of Tour Report (S), Col Victor N. Cabas, Comdr, 432d TRWg, (19 Sep 67-3 Sep 68), pp 39-40.

28. End of Tour Report (TS), Maj Gen Gordon F. Blood, DCS/Ops 7th AF, (Aug 67-Jan 69), p E-47.

29. Jacob Van Staaveren, *USAF Plans and Operations in Southeast Asia* (TS) (Ofc/AF Hist, Oct 1966) p 13.

30. Study (TS), Night Song Study Gp, JCS, An Examination of US Air Operations Against the NVN Air Defense System, Mar 1967, pp B-1, B-7 [hereinafter cited as Night Song Study].

31. *Ibid.,* pp B-8, B-9.

32. *Strike Ops in SEA...Strike Aircraft,* pp 32-37; memo (TS), SAF to SECDEF, subj: Night Operations in Southeast Asia, 28 Sep 66.

33. Maj Albert L. Michael, *Ryan's Raiders* (S) Aerospace Studies Institute Special Report 70-24, ASI, Maxwell AFB, Ala., Jan 70), p 16. Unless other authorities are cited, the remainder of the discussion of Commando Nail is based on this citation.

34. Ibid., pp 22-29; rprt (S), 7th AF (Dir/Combat Tactics) to TAC, CINCPACAF, subj: TACLO (7AF) Activity Report 19 (1-15 October 1968), 15 Oct 68; hist (S), 7th AF, 1 Jul-31 Dec 68, I part 2, 388.

35. Stf study (S), 7th AF (Dir/Ops) ECM Employment Concepts, 18 Apr 68; Col Gordon E. Danforth, Iron Hand/Wild Weasel (S) (Aerospace Studies Institute Report 70-12, ASI, Maxwell AFB, Ala., Jan 70), pp 3-4.

36. See note above.

37. See note 35.

38. TIA, Sep 1967, p 2-5; TIA, Jul 1970, p 1-4; Danforth, Iron Hand/Wild Weasel, pp 8-11; ltr (S), 7th AF (Dir/Ops) to PACAF (Dir/Ops), subj: EW Lessons Learned in SEA/Ref CINCPACAF Msg dtd 130053Z Jan 68, 31 Jan 68.

39. Danforth, Iron Hand/Wild Weasel, pp 10, 13.

40. Rprt (S), 7th AF (Dir/Combat Tactics) to TAC, CINCPACAF, subj: TACLO (7AF) Activity Report 12 (16-30 Jun 1968, 30 Jun 68.

41. Ibid.

42. Ibid.; TIA, Sep 1967, p 2-6.

43. Melvin F. Porter, Second Generation Weaponry in SEA (S) (HQ PACAF, Project CHECO, 10 Sep 70), pp 62-63; TIA, Jul 1970, p 1-4.

44. 8th TFWg Night Combat Tactics. Rest of this discussion on F-4 tactics is based on this source.

45. Ibid.; Maj Laurence F. Gardner, "Night Strike Mission in a Sophisticated Defense Environment," Tactical Analysis Bulletin (S), 67-2 (27 March 1967), 1-3. The remainder of the discussion on low-level F-4 tactics in North Vietnam is based on this source.

46. Wolk, R&D for Southeast Asia, 1965-1967, p 57; also author's personal experience based on 5 years with SAC as a B-52 navigator (AFSC 1525B).

Notes to pages 204-209   243

47. Futrell, USAF in Korea, p 329.

48. Wolk, R&D for Southeast Asia, 1965-1967, p 58.

49. Trest, Control of Air Strikes in SEA, 1961-1966, p 39; OPlan 439-67, 7th AF, Combat Skyspot, Mar 1967, p B-1.

50. Capt Edward Vallentiny, The Fall of Site 85 (TS), (Hq PACAF, Project CHECO, 9 Aug 68), pp viii, 2.

51. Rprt (S), 7th AF (Dir/Combat Tactics) to TAC, CINCPACAF, subj: TACLO (7AF) Activity Report 13 (1-15 July 1968), 15 Jul 68 [hereinafter cited as 7th AF TACLO Rprt 13].

52. Hickey, Night Close Air Support, pp 20-21.

53. 7th AF TACLO Rprt 13; PACAF Tactics and Techniques Bul 57 (U), 6002d Stan/Eval Gp, 27 Feb 67.

54. 8th TFWg Ltr; manual (S), 388th TFWg, Combat Tactics, 14 Sep 68; Melvin F. Porter, Control of Airstrikes, January 1967-December 1968 (S) (HQ PACAF, Project CHECO, 30 Jun 69), pp 11-12.

55. Rprt (S), USAF Tac Ftr Weapons Cen, TAC, Final Report Combat Lancer, May 1969, p B-1; TIA, May 1968, p 2-13.

56. TIA, May 1968, pp 2-13, 2-14.

57. Rprt (S), USAF Tac Ftr Weapons Cen, TAC, Final Report Combat Lancer, May 1969, pp A-2, B-18.

58. Ibid., p B-18.

59. Ibid., p A-2.

60. Memo (S), Asst SECDEF/Sys & Analys, to Dep SECDEF, subj: Relative Capabilities of the A-7D and F-111D, 5 Sep 68.

CONCLUSION

1. Gen H.H. Arnold, Third Report of the Commanding General of the Army Air Forces to the Secretary of War, 12 November 1945 (Baltimore, 1945), p 63.

GLOSSARY OF TERMS AND ABBREVIATIONS

A-1 — Single-engine (reciprocating) strike aircraft developed by Douglas Aircraft at the close of World War II; categorized as a slow mover, the aircraft had several missions in SEA with both the USAF and VNAF.

A-26 — Strike aircraft of the 56th SOWg, Nakhon Phanom RTAFB, operating in Laos; call sign Nimrod

AAS-18 — (S) Infrared sensor used by the RF-4C aircraft; it operated in the 3-5 micron range that could detect hot engines

AC-47 — The C-47 transport converted into a gunship by adding the General Electric SUU-11A minigun; the AC-47 had several nicknames: Puff the Magic Dragon, Dragon Ship, and Spooky

AGM-45 — A passive, radar-homing, air-to-surface missile designed to destroy enemy radars; nicknamed Shrike

AGM-78 — The AGM-78 Standard ARM; this air-to-ground anti-radiation missile gradually replaced the AGM-45 Shrike missile; like the Shrike the AGM-78 had a passive-seeker guidance system

AIM-9 — A heat-seeking missile

AN/AVG-3 — Improved USAF version of the starlight scope

AN/AWG-13 — Analog computer used on the AC-130 gunship; it tied sensors and ordnance together

ARN-92 Loran D — A set designed for precise navigation with predicted accuracy of 600 feet after about 250 miles of travel; the set included a computer, map display, and instrument display coupler

AA — antiaircraft

AAA — antiaircraft artillery

ABCCC — airborne battlefield command and control center

Able Mable   (S) A reconnaissance task force of RF-101 aircraft that flew the original Yankee Team missions in Laos, commencing in November 1961

actg	acting
acty	activity
ADF	automatic direction finder
ADVON	advanced echelon
AF	Air Force
AFB	Air Force base
AFEO	Air Force Eyes Only
AFSC	Air Force Systems Command
AFSME	Dir/Maintenance Engineering, DCS/Systems & Logistics, USAF
AFXDC	DCS/Plans & Operations, USAF
AFXOP	Dir/Operations, DCS/Plans & Operations, USAF
AFXOSO	Special Operations Division, Dep Dir/Strike Forces, Dir/Operations, DCS/Plans & Operations, USAF
AGL	above ground level
air commando	An Air Force member engaged in counterinsurgency operations
ALO	air liaison officer
Ambassador Sullivan's Air Force	Informal reference to the 56th SOWg, Nakhon Phanom, Thailand; only Ambassador to Laos William H. Sullivan could approve targets in Laos; since the 56th struck approved targets, hence the term
Ambassador's War, The	The war in Laos; Ambassador William H. Sullivan was Ambassador to Laos and approved all targets in Laos, hence the term
AmEmb	American Embassy
analys	analysis
AOC	air operations center
app	appendix
ARM	antiradiation missile
ARVN	Army of Republic of Vietnam
ASD	Aeronautical Systems Division
ASI	Aerospace Studies Institute
ASOC	air support operations center
asst	assistant
atch	attachment

B-57	Strike aircraft developed by the Martin Company for night intruder missions; nicknamed Canberra
BLU	Bomb Live Unit; applies to various ordnance, e.g., the bomblets dropped from dispensers and special purpose bombs
BLU-3B, BLU-26 bomblets	Used by the C-123 Black Spot aircraft, these bomblets were 16- and 11-grain steel balls propelled radially upon detonation at ground impact
BLU-27	800-pound napalm cannisters
Barrel Roll	(S) Interdiction and close air support operations in eastern Laos (beginning 14 Dec 64), later reduced to the area of northern Laos (3 Apr 65); the operations were under 2d Air Div and later, 7th AF control; most recently, Barrel Roll refers to strikes against personnel and equipment from North Vietnam
basket	The area in which the F-4 aircraft drops the bomb during Pave Way bombing
bd	board
BDA	bomb damage assessment
Big Eagle	B-26K night armed reconnaissance begun in 1966
Bird Dog	The 0-1 aircraft
Black Crow	(S) An ignition system detection sensor used on AC-130 and AC-123 Black Spot aircraft
Black Spot	(S) Converted C-123 transport (AC-123) equipped with FLR, LLLTV, forward-looking IR detector, laser ranger, advanced navigation system, weapon release computer, and weapon dispensers (CBU's)
Black Watch	RB-26 night reconnaissance of Laos, begun in 1962
Blindbat	Nickname of C-130 FAC/flareship aircraft operating in Southern Laos; eventually Blindbat became the nickname for all C-130 flare missions [see Lamplighter]
boresight line	An optical reference line used in harmonizing guns, rockets, and other weapon launchers
break right/ break left	Signal from the crew over the interphone to the pilot; it meant he should take violent evasive action

Brig Gen	Brigadier General
Bronco	Nickname of OV-10 aircraft.
B-scope	Radar display in which the signal appears as a bright spot, with bearing as the horizontal coordinate and range as the vertical coordinate
bul	bulletin
C-119	Twin-boom transport nicknamed Flying Boxcar; modified into AC-119 Shadow and Stinger gunships
C-123	Fairchild Provider transport used in airlift and as a FAC/flareship; call sign Candlestick used in latter mission
C-130	Multiengine transport developed for the Air Force by Lockheed; nicknamed Hercules
CBU-2	Fragmentation-cluster bomb; upon ground impact it expels 250 16-grain steel spheres into the air
C	Confidential
ca (circa)	about
Canberra	The B-57 strike aircraft
Candlestick	(S) The call sign for the C-123 FAC/flare aircraft in Laos
Capt	Captain
Category III targets	Targets for broad-area reconnaissance coverage, i.e., 10x10 kilometers
CBU	cluster bomb unit
CCT	combat crew training
CCT/RTU	combat crew training/replacement training unit
CEA	circular error average
cen	center
CEP	circular error probable
ch	chief
chaff	Radar confusion reflectors consisting of thin, narrow, metallic strips of various lengths and frequency responses, used to reflect echoes for confusion purposes

Christmas Tree	A SEA operational term referring to normal (non-combat) external lighting of an aircraft
CINCPAC	Commander in Chief, Pacific Command
CINCPACAF	Commander in Chief, Pacific Air Forces
CINCPACFLT	Commander in Chief, Pacific Fleet
class	classification
clean configuration or clean aircraft	An aircraft without extra fuel tanks, ordnance, and other external stores
clock-code position	Position of a target in relation to an aircraft or ship; dead-ahead position is considered 12 o'clock
Col	Colonel
College Eye	(S) Airborne EC-121D aircraft, staging out of Korat RTAFB, Thailand; the College Eye task forces furnished airborne navigational assistance and/or border warnings by use of IFF and SIF, and gave MIG warnings to friendly aircraft
Combat Lancer	(S) F-111 combat operational testing in Southrast Asia
Combat Skyspot	(S) MSQ-77 and SST-181 controlled bombing; MSQ-77 controlled bombing missions in Steel Tiger, Route Package I, and South Vietnam
comdr	commander
Commando Bolt	(S) Task Force Alpha-controlled airstrikes on moving trucks in a specified area, using sensor activations
Commando Hunt I, III, V	(S) Air interdiction campaigns directed against the flow of supplies from North Vietnam to Vietcong and North Vietnam forces in South Vietnam and Cambodia; these campaigns in southern Laos (Steel Tiger area of operations) bore numerical designations that changed with the semiannual monsoonal shift; the three northeast-monsoon, or dry-season campaigns, took place in 1968/1969, 1969/1970, and 1970/1971, and covered roughly the period from October through April

Commando Nail	Night and all-weather bombing operations conducted by aircraft equipped with airborne radar bombing systems
Commando Sabre	(S-NOFORN) Operations begun in June 1967 to demonstrate the feasibility of using jet aircraft in the FAC/SCAR role; the F-100 aircraft was used in lieu of O-1 and O-2 aircraft, the latter being too vulnerable in high-threat areas
Compass Count	(S) The 1968 operational test of the AN/AVD-2 laser reconnaissance system; a laser mounted in RF-4 aircraft swept the ground for filming
COMUSMACV	Commander, United States Military Assistance Command, Vietnam
cookoff	Ammunition firing as a result of being allowed to rest in the chamber of an overheated weapon
coupler	Arrangement of induction coils or capacitors so placed with reference to each other that an electromagnetic or electrostatic coupling exists between their circuits
Covey	(S) Call sign of O-2 and OV-10 FAC's of the 20th TASq operating in North and South Vietnam and Laos
CRC	control and reporting center
Cricket	(S) Operations in Laos of O-1E and AC-47 FAC aircraft and the C-130 ABCCC; also applied to a small geographical area in the southern panhandle of Laos
crosstell	Transfer of information between facilities at the same operational level
CSAF	Chief of Staff, United States Air Force
CSD	Combined Studies Division operated by U.S. State Department; it included U.S. Army Special Forces and Farm Gate personnel
CSGp	combat support group

Daisy Cutter	(S) Mk-82 (500-pound HE) or Mk-84 (2,000-pound HE) bombs with fuze extenders; designed to explode at the surface to kill personnel and to damage materiel
DASC	direct air support center
data link	A communications link suitable for transmission of data
DCS	Deputy Chief of Staff
dead reckoning	Finding one's position by means of a compass and calculations based on speed, time elapsed, effect of wind, and direction from a known position
dep	deputy
det	detachment
dir	director
div	division
dive toss	A weapon delivery maneuver in which the aircraft dives to a predetermined altitude and point in space, pulls up, and releases the weapon in such a way that it is tossed onto the target
DMZ	demilitarized zone
DO	DCS/Operations, 7th Air Force
DOA	Dir/Tactical Analysis, DCS/Operations, 7th Air Force
doc	document
DOCT	Tiger Hound/Tally Ho Division, Dir/Combat Operations, DCS/Operations, 7th Air Force
doghouse	A structure in the C-123 aircraft located just ahead of the prone starlight scope operator; the starlight scope hung on a traverse rod within the doghouse and pointed out the emergency bailout hatch; the doghouse also cut off any stray light that enemy gunners on the ground might detect
doppler radar	A radar system that differentiates between fixed and moving targets by detecting the apparent change in frequency of the reflected wave due to motion of the target or observer
DOR	Dir/Reconnaissance and Electronic Warfare, DCS/Operations, Tactical Air Command

DORQ	Dir/Requirements, DCS/Operations, Tactical Air Command
DOS	Dir/Special Operations, DCS/Operations, Tactical Air Command
DOSW	Dir/Special Air Warfare, DCS/Operations, Tactical Air Command
DPLP	Dir/Plans and Programs, DCS/Operations, Pacific Air Forces
DPLR	Dir/Requirements, DCS/Operations, 7th Air Force
dtd	dated
DTG	date-time group
ECM	electronic countermeasures
ETA	estimated time of arrival
et al (et alii)	and others
eval	evaluation
EW	electronic warfare
EWO	electronic warfare officer
eyeball reconnaissance	Reconnaissance by sight rather than by radar and sensors
F-4	Strike aircraft nicknamed Phantom
F-100	Strike aircraft nicknamed Super Sabre
F-105	Strike aircraft nicknamed Thunderchief; played key role in Rolling Thunder Campaign
1st Air Commando Squadron	Activated in June 1963, it absorbed Farm Gate personnel and equipment
1st Air Commando Wing	Successor to the 4400th Combat Crew Training Squadron, Eglin AFB, Fla.
FAC	forward air controller
Fan Song	(S) Nickname of enemy ground radars used for guidance of hostile SA-2 surface-to-air missiles

Farm Gate	Detachment of USAF air commandos from the Special Air Warfare Center at Eglin AFB, Fla.., which entered South Vietnam in November 1961 at President Diem's request; its twofold mission was training and combat operations
FCI	flight control indicator
fig	figure
fire arrow	Could be made of many materials; metal gas cans filled with gasoline-soaked sand were often used; ignited it was easy to see at night; hamlet defenders relayed to flare/strike aircraft the enemy's position with reference to the fire arrow
Fire Can	Code name of North Vietnam fire-control ground radars for direction of hostile AA fire; a single Fire Can normally controlled from six to eight guns of 57-mm or larger caliber
1st Lt	First Lieutenant
flak	Bursting shells fired from AA guns
flak-suppression fire	Fire used to suppress AA fire immediately prior to and during an air attack on enemy positions
Flaming Dart	Retaliatory strikes against North Vietnam in early 1965; it was superseded by Rolling Thunder in March 1965
flare	To drop flares
FLIR	forward-looking infrared radar
FLR	forward-looking radar
Flying Boxcar	Nickname of the C-119 twin-boom transport
FM	frequency modulation
FOB	forward operating base
frag	To issue a fragmentary field order covering details of a single mission, i.e., what is required, where, and when; a frag order, usually issued on a day-to-day basis, is an abbreviated form of an operations order
FSO	fire support officer (U.S. Army)
Funny Bomb	A 500- or 750-pound incendiary bomb cluster (M-31/32 and M-35/36 munitions); called Tokyo Fire Bomb in World War II

GIB	guy-in-back; the pilot navigator/observer in the rear seat of the F-4 aircraft
Gooney Bird	Nickname of the C-47 aircraft
GP	general purpose
gp	group
ground return	Reflection from the terrain as displayed and/or recorded as an image
HRB Singer Reconofax VI	First of several infrared scanners installed in the RB-57E aircraft; it was replaced by the RS-7 scanner which in turn was replaced by the RS-10
hack-watch	A watch that can be hacked (stopped) and set to within a second, i.e., the second hand can be synchronized with the minute hand
hard 180	An extremely tight 180° turn
HE	high-explosive (iron bomb)
hertz	Unit of frequency equal to 1 Hertz (a Hertz is a unit of frequency equal to one cycle per second)
high-drag bomb	Slower-falling bomb retarded by fins or parachute
hip-pocket targets	Targets that forward air controllers kept in reserve and attacked when the opportunity presented itself
hist	history
Hobo	Call sign of the 1st Air Commando Sq/SOSq A-1 aircraft operating in South Vietnam and Laos
hole nav	Navigator on the C-123 Candlestick FAC/flareship who operated the starlight scope
Horsefly	L-5 aircraft used for liaison in World War II
hq	headquarters

IAS	indicated airspeed, i.e., airspeed read from the face of the indicator in the aircraft's cockpit
<u>Ibid.</u>	in the same place
ICBM	intercontinental ballistic missile
ICC	International Control Commission
IFF	Identification, friend, or foe; a method for determining the friendly or unfriendly character of aircraft and ships by other aircraft or ships, and by ground forces using electronic detection equipment and associated IFF units
Igloo White	A surveillance system consisting of hand-implanted and air-delivered sensors, relay aircraft, and an infiltration surveillance center; Igloo White was formerly Muscle Shoals
illuminator	A laser-equipped F-4 or C-130 Blindbat aircraft working with an F-4 bomber using Pave Way bombs
inboard	In a position closer or closest to the longitudinal axis of an aircraft
in-country	That part of the Southeast Asia conflict located within South Vietnam
INS	inertial navigation system
intvw	interview
IP	initial point--a well-defined point, easily distinguished visually and/or electronically, used as a starting point for the bomb run to the target
iron bomb	A high-explosive bomb
Iron Hand	(S) Suppression flights by the F-105F aircraft against SAM sites and radar-controlled AA artillery
JAOC	Joint air operations center
JATO	jet-assisted takeoff
JCS	Joint Chiefs of Staff
jinking	An aircraft maneuver in which a series of rapid turn reversals and abrupt changes of roll and/or pitch attitude at random intervals prevents an enemy gunner from tracking the aircraft

JOC	joint operations center
JSIPS	Joint Continental Defense Systems Integration Planning Staff
JTCG	Joint Technical Coordinating Group
Jungle Jim	Nickname for USAF-developed counterinsurgency unit formed in early 1961 and stationed at Eglin AFB, Florida
KC-135	Tanker aircraft used for air refueling
KS-72 framing camera	This camera and a M-123 photoflash cartridge of 260-million candlepower was the principal photo system used for photo coverage of North Vietnam
karst	A limestone region marked by sinks and interspersed with abrupt ridges, irregular protuberant rocks, caverns, and underground streams
KCAS	knots, calibrated airspeed
KIAS	knots, indicated airspeed
knot	A speed of 1 nautical mile an hour (a nautical mile equals 6,076.115 feet or 1,852 meters)
L-5	Aircraft used for liaison in World War II; nicknamed Horsefly
LAU-62	A manually loaded and operated flare launcher, consisting of 14 semicircular tubes, used on the C-130 Blindbat; tests found the LAU-62 unsatisfactory so crews dropped flares and markers by hand
LUU-1B	Red-burning marker (a modified Mk-24 flare)
LUU-5	Green-burning marker (a modified Mk-24 flare)
lab	laboratory
Lamplighter	Nickname of C-130 aircraft operating in Northern Laos; eventually Blindbat became the nickname for all C-130 flare missions

laser	Light amplification by stimulated emission of radiation; laser light is most often invisible and infrared; it differs from ordinary light in that its individual light rays are all the same wave length and all are in step; hence its energy is not dissipated as the beam spreads out--thus permitting an intense concentration of light energy
Lead Sled	Nickname for the F-105 Thunderchief; the nickname Thud was also used for the F-105
LF	low frequency
Lid	A blind-bombing site located at Nakhon Phanom, Thailand
LIMA Site	Aircraft landing sites (dirt strips) in Laos used as resupply points for anti-Communist guerrillas
LIMDIS	Limited Distribution
LLLTV	low-light-level television
LOC	line of communication
loran	Long-range electronic navigation system that uses the time divergence of pulse-type transmissions from two or more fixed stations; also called long-range navigation
loran C	Extremely accurate long-range system of navigation similar to loran, giving accuracy within a few hundred feet for up to 1,000 miles out to sea
loran D	Tactical loran system that uses the coordinate converter of low-frequency loran C and can operate independently of ground facilities and without radiating radio-frequency (RF) energy that could reveal the aircraft's location
LOS	line-of-sight, i.e., the line between the target and the aiming reference
lower route packages	The southern route packages in North Vietnam (see map 2)
Lt Col	Lieutenant Colonel

M-31/32 and M-35/36	A 500- or 750-pound incendiary bomb cluster (Funny Bomb)

M-47	White-phosphorous bomb
M-61	Cannon used on Commando Nail F-105 aircraft which carried 1,000 rounds of 20-mm ammunition for it
M-64	500-pound general-purpose bomb
M-65	1,000-pound general-purpose bomb
M-117	750-pound general-purpose bomb
Mk-6	White flare marker/marker log used to mark ground targets
Mk-8	U.S. Navy pyrotechnic flare
Mk-24	Parachute flare that could also be rigged as a ground target marker; dropped at 5- or 10-second intervals the Mk-24 illuminated an area 1/2-mile across for 3 minutes
Mk-36 Destructor mines	A high-drag (slower-falling) version of the 500-pound GP-bomb; it detonated when any metallic object entered its magnetic field; used on land as well as waterways in SEA
Mk-81	250-pound general-purpose bomb
Mk-82	500-pound general-purpose bomb
MSQ-77	MSQ radar bomb-scoring equipment modified for radar guidance of bombers (see Combat Skyspot)
MAAC-V	Military Advisory Assistance Command-Vietnam
MAAG-V	Military Assistance Advisory Group-Vietnam
Madam Nhu Cocktail	Addition of charcoal to other napalm ingredients in the canister; named after Vietnamese President Diem's strong-willed anti-American sister-in-law
Maj	Major
marker/ marker log	A flare dropped from an aircraft to mark targets on the ground
memo	memorandum
micron	Unit of length equal to one-thousandth of a millimeter
MIG	Term applied to Soviet-built jet fighters used by North Vietnam; it included the MIG-15 (of Korean War vintage), the MIG-17, MIG-19 and the MIG-21 all-weather jet fighter
mil	1/6400 of 360°

Misty	Call sign for F-100F FAC's flying out of Phu Cat and Tuy Hoa air bases, Republic of Vietnam
Mk	ordnance designation
mm	millimeter(s)
Mohawk	OV-1 aircraft
Mosquito	T-6 aircraft used in the Korean War
mph	miles-per-hour
MR	memorandum for record
MSQ	mobile search special
MTI	moving target indicator
Mule Train	C-123 aircraft deployed to Southeast Asia on temporary duty; original mission of the three Mule Train squadrons was to furnish supplemental airlift support for the Vietnamese armed forces; however, as the Vietcong intensified night attacks against the hamlets, the Air Force pressed C-123's into duty as flareships
Nail	Call sign of OV-2 and OV-10 FAC's of 23d TASq
nape	napalm
Nimrod	Call sign for A-26 aircraft of the 56th SOWg, Nakhon Phanom RTAFB, operating in Laos
NOD	Night observation device; an image intensifier using reflected light from the stars or moonlight to identify targets
NOFORN	Special Handling Required Not Releasable to Foreign Nationals
NOS	night observation sight
no-show target	A target not showing up on the aircraft's radar
NSC	National Security Council
NVN	North Vietnam
O-2	FAC aircraft; Civilian Nickname, Skymaster
OV-1A	photo reconnaissance version of the OV-1 Spud

OV-1B	Model of the OV-1 Spud carrying side-looking airborne radar and moving target indicator
OV-1C	Model of the OV-1 Spud carrying infrared sensors
OV-10	FAC aircraft nicknamed Bronco
OASD	Office of the Assistant Secretary of Defense
ofc	office
offset bombing	Any bombing procedure that employs a reference or aiming point other than the actual target
omnirange (omni)	Radio aid to air navigation which creates an infinite number of paths in space through 360 degrees azimuth
OPlan	Operations Plan
OpOrd	Operations Order
ops	operations
outboard	In a position closer or closest to either of the wing tips of an aircraft
out-country	That part of Southeast Asia conflict outside South Vietnam, i.e., Laos and North Vietnam
P-61	World War II night fighter aircraft nicknamed Black Widow
p	page
PA	Public Affairs
PACAF	Pacific Air Forces
para	paragraph
paradrop	Delivery by parachute of personnel or cargo from an aircraft in flight
Patricia Lynn	(S) RB-57E infrared reconnaissance aircraft
Pave Way	(S) The F-4 aircraft using various guidance devices: Pave Way I....laser Pave Way II... electro-optical Pave Way III ... infrared
PCS	permanent change of station

perch	An airborne position assumed by a fighter/bomber aircraft in preparation for or anticipation of an air-to-ground strike maneuver; the term was usually associated with fighter-escorted strike or FAC missions
Phantom	Nickname of F-4 strike aircraft
photo processing cell	A facility, generally mobile, equipped for the processing, printing, and interpretation of reconnaissance sensor products and other production normally related to the reconnaissance intelligence function
pickle	To release a bomb or expend ordnance by depressing a button (pickle)
pipper	The center or bead of the minigun's ring gunsight
play time	(S) The length of time an aircraft may remain in the control point orbit before reaching that fuel state which will just permit return to base with ordnance
plug	To hit the first and last truck of an enemy convoy to prevent any escaping or pulling off the road
$\pm$	plus or minus
pop-up maneuver	A maneuver used by tactical aircraft when transitioning from the low-level approach phase of an attack mission to an altitude and point from which the target can be identified and attacked
pp	pages
PPC	photo processing cell
prgms	programs
proj	project
QRC 160B/ ALQ-71	ECM pods; the RF-4C carried two of them for defense

RF-101	Nicknamed Voodoo, this aircraft is a single-place, tactical, photo reconnaissance aircraft for support of both ground and air forces
Ranch Hand	UC-123 defoliation, herbicide operations
R&D	Research and Development
RBS	radar bomb scoring
real time	The absence of delay, except for the time required for the transmission by electromagnetic energy, between the occurrence of an event or the transmission of data, and the knowledge of the event or reception of the data at some other location
recce	Reconnaissance, to reconnoiter
recce area	armed reconnaissance area
recip	reciprocating engine aircraft
Red Haze	Passive detector on the OV-1 aircraft that emitted no radar pulses but produced detailed imagery by sensing temperature variations in the terrain and objects on the ground; infrared surveillance photography
ref	reference
reference altitude	Altitude assigned to a mission for control and separation of aircraft in the target area
reg	regulation
reticle	A system of lines, dots, crosshairs, or wires, in the focus of an optical instrument
RF	radio frequency
RHAW	radar homing and warning
RLAF	Royal Loatian Air Force
RLG	Royal Laotian Government
ROE	rules of engagement
Rolling Thunder	Nickname assigned to airstrikes against selected targets and lines of communication in North Vietnam (Mar 1965-Oct 1968)

route packages	(S) Numbered areas (I, II, III, IV, V, VIA, VIB) in North Vietnam, designated by CINCPAC to facilitate assignment of interdiction responsibilities to CINCPACAF, COMSEVENTHFLT, and COMUSMACV, and for other operational purposes, e.g., Rolling Thunder (see map 2)
RP	Route Package
rprt	report
rqmts	requirements
RTAFB	Royal Thai Air Force base
RTF	reconnaissance task force
RVN	Republic of Vietnam
SA-2	Guideline surface-to-air missile; this Mach 3.5 radar-guided missile is for medium- to high-altitude interception of subsonic nonmaneuverable aircraft; its range is around 20 miles
2d ADVON	2d Advanced Echelon
SUU-11A	Minigun used on the AC-47 gunship
SUU-24	Munitions dispenser originally designed for the B-47/B-52 bomb bays; it was used on the AC-123 Black Spot
SUU-25/A	This flare dispenser is a modified LAU-10 "Zuni" rocket launcher; it carries eight Mk-24 flares, two in each of its four tubes
S	Secret
SAM	surface-to-air missile
SAC	Strategic Air Command
SAR	search and rescue
SAWC	Special Air Warfare Center
SCAR	strike control and reconnaissance
SCNA	self-contained night attack
scope strobbing	Repeated intense flashes of light of short duration
scramble	To take off as quickly as possible (usually followed by course and altitude instructions)

SEA	Southeast Asia
SEAOR	Southeast Asia Operational Requirement
sec	section
SECDEF	Secretary of Defense
self-FAC	To be one's own forward air controller
Shadow	Call sign of AC-119G gunship
shadow boxes	A number of specific strike zones designated throughout South Vietnam for AC-119 operations
Shed Light	The overall USAF program to improve night attack/interdiction capability
short rounds	Inadvertent or accidental delivery of ordnance, sometimes resulting in death or injury to friendly forces or noncombatants
Shrike	Nickname of AGM-45 missile; a passive radar-homing air-to-surface missile designed to destroy enemy radars
SIF/IFF	selective identification feature/identification, friend or foe
single-ship	To fly singly
skin paint	A radar indication caused by the reflected radar signal from an object
Skyraider	A-1 strike aircraft
SLAR	side-looking airborne radar
slow movers	Relatively slow-moving strike aircraft (e.g., the A-1, A-26, B-57, AC-119, AC-130) as opposed to the fast movers (e.g., the F-4, F-105)
soft ordnance	Ordnance suitable for use against soft or unprotected targets; napalm and cluster bomb units were typical soft ordnance
SOSq	Special Operations Squadron
SOWg	Special Operations Wing
spec	special
Spectre	Call sign of AC-130 gunship

spin-arm	An older method of arming bombs; a spinning propeller in the bomb's nose armed it during descent, to explode according to its fuzing.
Spooky	Call sign of AC-47 gunship
spt	support
Spud	Call sign of the OV-1 Mohawk aircraft
sq	squadron
stan/eval	standardization and evaluation
starlight scope	An image intensifier using reflected light from the stars or moonlight to identify targets
Steel Tiger	(S) The geographic area in Southern Laos designated by 7th AF to facilitate planning and operations; the term also referred to strikes in Southern Laos against personnel and equipment from North Vietnam
stf	staff
Stinger	Call sign of AC-119K gunship
STOL	short takeoff and landing
Super Sabre	F-100 strike aircraft
SVN	South Vietnam
Sweet Sue	RB-26C aircraft (beginning in 1964)
switchback	A zigzag road in a mountainous region
sys	systems
T-28	Strike aircraft nicknamed Zorro
TAC	Tactical Air Command
tac	tactical
TACAN	A tactical air navigation system consisting of short-range UHF radio stations; in the form of a readout on the instrument panel the pilot continuously receives accurate distance and bearing information from the particular station tuned
TACC	tactical air control center
TACLO	Tactical Air Command liaison officer
TACS	tactical air control system

Tally Ho	An intensified interdiction campaign in southern Route Package I using O-2 FAC's in the western mountains and F-100F's in the eastern lowlands
TARC	tactical air reconnaissance center
target acquisition	Detection, identification, and location of a target in sufficient detail to permit the effective employment of weapons
TAS	true airspeed
TASGp	Tactical Air Support Group
Task Force Alpha (TFA)	(S) A filter point for sensor information received under the Igloo White/Commando Hunt concept; it was organized in 1967 under the command of 7th AF at Tan Son Nhut AB, and deployed to Nakhon Phanom AB, Thailand
TASSq	Tactical Air Support Squadron
TAWg	Tactical Airlift Wing
TCGp	Tactical Control Group
TDY	temporary duty
TFR	terrain-following radar; this radar provides a display of terrain ahead of a low-flying aircraft to permit manual control, or signals for automatic control, to maintain constant altitude above the ground
TFSq	Tactical Fighter Squadron
TFWg	Tactical Fighter Wing
Thud	Nickname for the F-105 Thunderchief; the F-105 also had the nickname Lead Sled
Thunderchief	F-105 strike aircraft; played prominent role in Rolling Thunder campaign
TIA	Trends, Indicators, and Analyses
TIC	troops-in-contact
Tiger/Tiger Hound	(S) Southern Steel Tiger south of 17° north latitude, for FAC employment (1965-1968)

timberline	The upper limit of tree growth in mountains or high latitudes
time-hack	Time which is set or "hacked" on a watch to the precise second
tng	training
TOT	time-over-target
Trail	Ho Chin Minh Trail
Triton	Call sign for the AC-123 aircraft with a self-contained night attack system
Tropic Moon I	Night-strike A-1E aircraft using LLLTV and CBU or napalm munitions (1968)
Tropic Moon II	Westinghouse LLLTV in the B-57 (1968)
Tropic Moon III	Follow-on B-57 program for night attacks in high-threat areas, forerunner to the B-57G
TRWg	Tactical Reconnaissance Wing
TS	Top Secret
TUOC	tactical unit operations center
UC-123B/K	Aircraft used for the Ranch Hand defoliation and herbicide operations; the K model was jet-augmented
U	Unclassified
UHF	ultra high frequency
upper route packages	The northern route packages in North Vietnam (see map 2)
USAF	United States Air Force
VHF	very high frequency
VC	Vietnamese Communists
VNAF	Vietnamese Air Force
vol	volume
Voodoo	Nickname of the F-101 aircraft
VOR	VHF omnirange

VT	variably timed
wet fuel tanks	Unprotected fuel tanks in contrast to those which are foamed-filled and explosion-proof
wg	wing
Wild Weasel	(S) Nickname applied to specially configured multiplace aircraft and specially trained aircrews, used to ferret out and destroy enemy-controlled SAM radar.
Wild Weasel III	(S) The F-105F aircraft, specially equipped to perform anti-SAM hunter-killer operations
Wild Weasel V	(S) The evaluation of the operational capability of the radar homing and warning system in the F-4C/D aircraft
Willy Peter/ Willy Pete	White phosphorous munitions; plasticized white phosphorous was used as a marking rocket or bomb by FAC's who directed airstrikes
Willy Peter marking rocket (2.75 inch)	A white phosphorous rocket of short life, often used with flare illumination
winchester	out of ordnance
WRCS	weapon release computer set
xenon	A heavy colorless inert gaseous element used in specialized electric lamps
Yankee Team	USAF tactical air reconnaissance missions flown in Laos using RF-101 aircraft
Yellowbird	Call sign of B-57 aircraft
Z	Zulu Time (Greenwich Mean Time)
zero-time aircraft	An aircraft that has not logged any flying time
Zorro	Call sign of T-28 and A-1 aircraft assigned to the 56th SOWg

DISTRIBUTION

HQ USAF

1. SAFOS
2. SAFUS
3. SAFFM
4. SAFRD
5. SAFIL
6. SAFMR
7. SAFGC
8. SAFLL
9. SAFOI
10. SAFOII
11. SAFAAR
12. AFCC
13. AFCV
14. AFCVA
15. AFCCN
16. AFCVS
17. AFIGPP
18. AFJA
19. AFIN
20. AFPR
21. AFPRCCT
22. AFPRCX
23. AFPRP
24. AFPRPT
25. AFRD
26. AFRDG
27. AFRDP
28. AFRDQ
29. AFRDR
30. AFSA
31. AFSAMI
32. AFLG
33. AFLGM
34. AFLGF
35. AFLGS
36. AFXOD
37. AFXOO
38. AFXOOG
39. AFXOOS
40. AFXOOSL
41. AFXOOSO
42. AFXOOSW
43. AFXOOT
44. AFXOOTR
45. AFXOOTW
46. AFXOOW
47. AFXOV
48. AFXOX
49. AFXOXF
50. AFXOXFT
51. AFXOXJ
52. AFXOXX
53. AFXOXXEP
54. NGB

TAC SUBORDINATE COMMANDS

78. USAF Tactical Fighter Weapons Center
79. USAF Tactical Air Warfare Center
80. USAF Air-Ground Operations Center
81. USAF Special Operations Force

OTHER

82-83. 3825/HOA
84. CHECO (DOAC)
85-100. AF/CHO (Stock)

MAJOR COMMANDS

55-56. AFLC
57-58. AFSC
59-61. ATC
62-63. MAC
64-68. PACAF
69-70. SAC
71-75. TAC
76. USAFSS
77. AULD